A View Of Genesis

FROM THE RUMBLE SEAT
OF A TWO-HUMPED CAMEL

First in a series

BY

PHINEHAS PHIGTREE*

STEEL
PUBLISHING PARTNERS

*Don't try finding this author in any local phone book!

*A View of Genesis
from the Rumble Seat of a Two-Humped Camel*

Copyright 2000
All rights reserved
by Steel Publishing Partners and
the Nelcon Group

First Printing April 2000

1 2 3 4 5 6 7 8 9 10

2005 2004 2003 2001 2000

Artwork by Adam Elfstrand
Cover design by Shawn O'Mara
Editing/Layout by Rhonda J. Elfstrand
Published and Printed in the United States of America

Library of Congress Card Number:
00-101377
ISBN 0-9650287-3-9

All scripture quotations are taken from the
New International Version, Zondervan Publishers,
unless otherwise noted.

For bulk purchases or more information on this series,
please phone your request to
1-877-740-0375
or visit Phinehas on the web at www.phinehas.com

STEEL PUBLISHING PARTNERS, PO BOX 25, LIBRARY, PA 15129
elfstrandenterprises@netzero.net

DEDICATIONS

To my sons, Mike, Steve, Phil, Joel, Nate, and Jeremy, because I love them;

To Nancy, because she believes in me (yes, I love her, too);

To Dick S., because he made me finish this and provided all sorts of help in countless ways;

To Chuck and Kit, my spiritual gurus, because they advised and encouraged and read and edited and told me when I was *really* out to lunch;

To Tunch and Craig and Jon and Walt and my brother Al and the other guys, because they enhance my life by their walk with Jesus, and who provided great examples for the book;

To Rhonda, because she put it all together with able assistance from Mark and Adam;

To Sue C. and Ed L., because they are enthusiastic supporters and helped in many ways;

To my Dad;

and to the Spirit of God, Who gratuitously wrote my name in the Book of Life, and without Whom I could never have written anything.

Foreword

This is a book you shouldn't miss! Its title, *A View of Genesis from the Rumble Seat of a Two-Humped Camel,* tells you immediately that it is not a conventional Bible commentary. But the title alone doesn't describe the exciting journey Phinehas Phigtree has planned for you in these pages.

Phinehas Phigtree is, of course, not the author's real name. However, as you read his book, you will learn a good bit about him from the descriptive language and the illustrations he uses. He is obviously an individual of wide personal experience, a keen observer of human events, and an outstanding communicator. Since I have known him for many years, I can add that he is a devoted husband, father and grandfather, church elder, and long-time serious Bible scholar.

Many of you were introduced to the people of Genesis — Adam and Eve, Noah, Abraham, Sarah, Jacob, and Joseph — in Sunday School, or through children's picture books. Now Phinehas Phigtree invites you to take a fresh and more mature look at these individuals and their problems through this compilation of almost 200 sparkling commentaries.

The author originally wrote them as individual messages of encouragement for a son who lived and worked in another city. Now he shares them with us. Don't expect him to plod through Genesis verse by verse as many Bible expositors do. While his commentaries cover the entire book, his method is to canter through this segment of history on his fictional camel, stopping at key points in the narrative to observe and comment.

Phinehas describes the familiar events of Genesis in contemporary language with imagination and humor, and these descriptions are in themselves well worth the price of the book. But his goal is not simply to retell Bible incidents. Each commentary is designed to focus the readers' attention on an important spiritual truth. The truths are inherent in the narrative, but Phinehas uses modern illustrations to illuminate and enhance them. He then applies them concisely and effectively to the situations we face in today's world.

A View of Genesis

If you go through this volume one message at time in your morning devotions, as my wife and I do, you will carry away with you a worthwhile thought to ponder during each day. I heartily recommend this book for that purpose. But in whatever way you choose to read it, I am certain you will find it informative, stimulating, and challenging.

Dr. Charles Coleman, Bowie, Maryland

Introduction

I used to think that I'd like to write a book someday. A book that someone other than my mother would actually read. I started to write once in my early school years about a pirate who had a wooden leg, in which was hidden a cosmic ray gun that worked only on Tuesdays. When the good guys found out his secret, they sailed their boats on the other days. So the pirate's buddies made him walk the plank because they didn't get any more loot. Fortunately, school officials in those days didn't send a kid off to a shrink for things like eating cream cheese on hotdogs instead of catsup, or writing bizarre stories. Otherwise, my father would have had to float a bond issue to pay for my treatments.

Later in my school life, I wrote a couple of poems to a hoped-for girlfriend, and like my pirate friend, I ended up walking the plank. So I put my writing career on the back burner. The way-back burner. In fact, the stove wasn't even in the neighborhood. And about the only thing I wrote after that was when I snuck a few entries on my wife's grocery list (like artichokes and jumbo black olives and chocolate chip cookies) when she wasn't looking.

Well, a couple of years ago, God snuck something on my list when I wasn't looking. One of my sons was interested in getting back into the Scripture, and God volunteered me to help. I knew that a study guide from Somnambulate Seminary wasn't going to hold his attention, so I started sending a "morning Bible fax" to him at his office. A fax with a little fun, as well as a little food for thought. Soon, several other people in his firm asked to join in the fun and, before you could say "Phinehas Phigtree," a book on Genesis was born. Accidentally. Unintentionally. Without premeditation.

Except that nothing with God is unintentional or accidental. The life experiences He has given me to prepare me for writing this book. The invitation to share a relationship with Himself that He has granted me solely by His grace, so that I might share that relationship with others. The people He has put in my life to enable me to make this book a reality. And the conviction that God is not some stodgy old Cosmic Killjoy who answers only to "Thee" and "Thou," but Who created a sense of humor in us because He likes to laugh a little bit, too.

So grab hold of the other camel hump, and hang on for the ride through Genesis. I hope that instead of rattling your brain, the trip tickles your funny bone and reaches your heart. Because your heart is the real destination God has in mind.

And don't worry about the pirate. His buddies didn't take off his wooden leg before they made him walk the plank, and he blew up the boat with his cosmic ray gun after he hit the water. They forgot that it was Tuesday. Then he floated off in an empty barrel to an island paradise, where he lived happily ever after.

Phinehas Phigtree

Genesis 1:1

"In the beginning God created the heavens and the earth." (Gen. 1:1)

God created the heavens and the earth. In His creation we have all that we need in order to survive and prosper. Because He created it all, He is the owner of it all, and all creation, including ourselves, is under His power and subject to His will. Jesus, being God, was able to command the winds and the waves to obey His will. God was able to command the great fish to be in a specific place at a specific time to swallow Jonah and bring him to dry ground. He made the sun stop so that Joshua was able to win the battle.

The amazing thing, however, is that God did not just command us, a part of His creation, to be righteous. He allowed mankind to choose his own way. And when we went the wrong way, He provided a sacrifice, His Son, to bring us back to Himself. Although He spoke the worlds into being as a function of His creative power, He expressed Himself to us in love through the gift of His Son.

How do I respond to such love, expressed in the environment of such power? By returning His love in the only way I can — acknowledging Him as my Owner, seeking His will as my Master, communicating with Him as my Friend, worshipping Him as my Maker. In this way He will express Himself through me, and His love and power will ever be in my mind and available for any circumstance which arises.

Genesis 1:2-5

"Now the earth was formless and empty, ... and the Spirit of God was hovering over the waters. And God said, 'Let there be light,' and there was light." (verses 1:2-3)

Sometimes our lives are formless and empty. There is little joy, little pleasure, nothing to take us out of the seeming futility of our existence. The sun will rise tomorrow, but so what? Just another day at the "salt mine." What Tennessee Ernie Ford sang about, "Sixteen tons, and whaddya get? Another day older and deeper in debt."

But even in this condition, the Spirit of God is hovering over the situation, waiting for the proper time to bring light into our existence. And when He says, "Let there be light," there will be light. Not necessarily like that which blinded Paul on the road to Damascus, but it may be in the Scripture verse we learned many years ago back in Sunday School; the thought of a friend; the encouraging word of a fellow-Christian; a sudden recollection of a pleasant memory; somebody who comes along to help shoulder the cross or bear the burden which is presently wearing us down; progress in solving a weighty problem. Or it might be just thinking about the blessings which Jesus, the Light of the world, has brought to us over the years.

The Spirit of God wants us to live in those blessings. We are children of God, adopted into His family, destined for heaven, objects of His love, recipients of His mercies and benefits. All these things and myriads more are the lights in our skies, which dispel the darkness as we dwell more and more upon them. If we're in the tunnel and ask God for the light, His hovering Spirit will provide it in one way or another.

And that light at the end of the tunnel won't be another locomotive coming through in the opposite direction.

Genesis 1:5-31

"And there was evening, and there was morning – the first day." (vs. 5, 8, 13 etc.)

I suppose that we might envision God, after that first day when He separated the light from the darkness, wiping His brow, sort of collapsing on His throne and saying to Himself with a sense of satisfaction, "Wow! That was a tough day! I'll get up in the morning and drag myself out to continue this creation business. Separating the light and darkness was a biggie, but what a monster job getting the earth out of the seas is going to be! And how am I ever going to create a giraffe? Anyhow, the thing I'm most worried about is this man business I have to do on Friday!"

No, God could have done it all in an instant, no sweat. For Someone for Whom time is not a factor, why should He have even bothered with the six days of creation? Maybe it was to show us that each day has its own function, its own task, its own concerns. Perhaps it was to show us that there is so much that we can do in a day, and tomorrow will take care of itself. Or it could have been that He wants us to learn to look back on what has been accomplished during the day with satisfaction ("...and God saw that it was good," vs. 10, 12, etc.) without lying awake at night thinking about the burdens we have to bear and the tasks we have to do tomorrow.

Matthew in his Gospel tells us that God knows all about our days and nights, our todays and tomorrows. He who created the lilies of the field and the birds of the air and provides for them all is aware of what is going on in our lives and what the needs of the future are, physically, materially, emotionally and spiritually. Maybe things don't always turn out like we would want, but that is because we usually are operating according to our own agenda, not His. But Matthew tells us that if we buy into God's plan, we'll have enough in our lives to dwell in the comfort zone. "Seek first His kingdom..., all these things will be given to you..., do not worry about tomorrow..., each day has enough trouble of its own." (Matthew 6:33-34). God really didn't need all that time for the creation, and He doesn't need us to worry about next Friday. Trust. Work according to His agenda. Relax. Enjoy.

And he did a pretty good job with the giraffe, too. How else could the giraffe get to the leaves at the top of the trees, if he didn't have that funny neck?

Genesis 1:26-31

"So God created man in His own image, in the image of God He created him; male and female He created them ... God saw all that He had made, and it was very good..." (1:27, 31)

Everything that God created was made perfectly. All was in order, everything in its right place and perfectly suited to its environment. His crowning achievement was the creation of man in His own image. "His own image." That doesn't mean that we look like God, for God is a Spirit. That doesn't mean that we have the capacity to be God, for He is omniscient, omnipotent, and omnipresent. Nor does that mean that we will evolve into gods, as some teach. What it means is that Adam and Eve had the same character as God; complete, righteous, sinless, created in truth and holiness. Because mankind was created in this way, they had the ability to communicate and interact with God on His level.

As we all know, mankind fell prey to the tempting of the devil, that old serpent, and our ability to operate in the "image of God" mode was lost. Righteousness was replaced with sin. Direct communication with God was out; a blood sacrifice for access to Him was in. Management of the Eden facility in comfort and peace was over; pulling weeds and thorns with toil and sweat to grow a few veggies became the new regime.

However, we're thankful to say, God didn't deep-six the whole idea of fellowship with man in His image, and made arrangements to bring it all back. It took the life of His Son Jesus to do it, but He made it work. Paul tells us in Ephesians 4:20-24 that He took the old self, and replaced it with the new self, "created to be like God in true righteousness and holiness." In His image. We can communicate with Him again, on His level. We can read and understand about Him now, because He has given us the capacity to do so. We can experience His love because He has made us spiritually alive to receive it. We are, as Paul tells us, a new creation. Man messed up the image thing once, but the new creation through Jesus is positionally incorruptible. We still sin big time, but God the Father sees us through God the Son, totally justified.

Think about it. In His image. Righteous and holy before God. He has made us again spiritually. And He doesn't make any junk.

Genesis 2:2

"By the seventh day God finished the work He had been doing; so on the seventh day He rested …"

God is into completing things. He started the creation, He completed it. Then He rested. Not because He was tired or couldn't think of anything else to do, but because He was finished and the work was perfect. There are a lot of action verbs up to this point — "created," "moved," "said," "separated," "called," "made," "gathered," "placed," "blessed," etc. Our God is an active God.

Some people want to make Him out as a Cosmic Killjoy or a Celestial Beancounter Who is marking down the times we mess up and weighing those instances against the times we're doing the right thing (whatever that is), and then whacking us over the head with His ugly stick when things get too far out of balance. But He is not a "Gotcha" God. He is active. He is creative. Yes, He does from time to time discipline those who are His children (and not all are, as the Scripture plainly points out), but His discipline is always constructive, never the get-even, you've-embarrassed-me kind. He does things right, until the finished product can be given the Heavenly-Harmony tag.

There are a couple of God's action verbs we haven't mentioned, and a product which isn't yet finished. The action verbs are "loved" and "gave." God so loved the world, that He gave His only-begotten Son, that whoever believes in Him shall not perish but will have eternal life (John 3:16). And the unfinished product is us. As Paul tells us in Romans 8:29, God is in the process of conforming us into the image of Christ. He won't rest, He won't stop that activity until we are with Him in Heaven.

Until then, He just keeps on loving, and giving, and loving, and giving, and loving, and giving …

Genesis 2:5

"And there was no man to work the ground."

Here was God and the world and all He had made at the end of the fifth day. Everything was just right, everything was exactly as it should have been. But there was something missing as far as God was concerned, and that was somebody to tend what He had planted, someone to care for the various parts of His creation. So He created man.

How can this be? Couldn't God have done this himself? Couldn't He have created plants and flowers and animals and vegetables that just tend themselves? No doubt about it. After all, there weren't any weeds in this creation to this point and a mist from the earth provided moisture, so the corn didn't need hoeing and the petunias didn't need watering. The sheep wouldn't wander off, so there was no need to build fences. Even so, God wanted man to be on the scene to not only be His gardener, but also, I suspect, to enjoy the surroundings and communicate with God Himself.

And that's the way it is today. God doesn't need any help. He can make things happen, even to the extent of calming the waves, moving a mountain or, if some of the supermarket tabloid predictions can be believed, making beachfront property just west of Phoenix. Most of His work, however, is somewhat mundane, just spreading His grace, love and kindness around, and taking care of the daily tasks (other than those performed through His natural laws) which are so necessary for the functioning of His universe and His people. He can do all that, too, but He wants men and women, you and me, to do it. Lend a helping hand. Offer a bit of bread or cool water. Put an arm around a sorrowing friend. Squeeze a lonely child. Spread a little joy, a little laughter, a little hope. Tell somebody about Jesus. And the interesting thing is that in all these little jobs it is really His Spirit working through us. He really does the work but uses us to get it accomplished. Why? Who knows? It's like all those "begats" in Matthew 1. It took Him a few people, but He got where He wanted to go. He always does.

Even more puzzling — He promises us a reward for being available. Not eternal life, because that's purely by grace, through faith in Jesus' work. Not money, or health, a soft job or a cushy life. But the knowledge of His presence. The sense of His love. The experience of His power. And the pleasure of communicating with God so that we can enjoy our surroundings, too.

"The Lord God ... breathed into his nostrils the breath of life; and the man became a living being."

Genesis 2:7

"The Lord God ... breathed into his nostrils the breath of life; and the man became a living being."

I have a Greek friend from Johnstown, Pennsylvania, whose grandmother makes the finest baklava this side of Athens. It is so good that her daughters-in-law, as well as various other people, have tried to get the recipe out of her. She will give it out, but it seems that there is always something missing so that the baklava never tastes like Grandma's. She is very jealous of the product she has created.

Almost everybody is to some extent possessive over what they have created. Check the U.S. Patent office. Or better yet, check the court docket for infringement suits. People have rights that need to be protected. God has rights, too, although they're hard to locate given the present status of the separation of church and state issue. His rights are twofold — creative, as verse 7 sets forth, and redemptive, as Peter tells us, "... it was not with perishable things such as silver and gold that you were redeemed ... but with the precious blood of Christ." (I Peter 1:18-19) So regardless of the desire of some to captain their own ships, in reality we are all chattels of the Almighty, some owned only by virtue of creation but still owned, and others, who have bowed the knee to Jesus, by redemption as well.

Just as those who own patents carefully keep track of their property, God is also interested in His. Jesus said that not a hair of our heads falls to the ground except the Father knows it (Matthew 10:29-30). (I guess He's been very busy with some of us who are getting thin on top.) He told us that God even keeps track of the sparrows, and that we are of infinitely greater value than many sparrows. Even though we might not particularly enjoy some of the circumstances and situations which enter our lives, God is never up there saying, "Drat! I just hate it when that happens!" He is always in control of His property. Sooner or later He will make it work. It works a lot easier when we are moving along with His agenda.

After all, it's not only His property. It is His breath, His life. And to perfect His property rights, He paid dearly by investing His Son.

Genesis 2:8-17

"You are free to eat from any tree in the garden; but you must not eat from the tree of the knowledge of good and evil." (2:16-17)

God had planted a garden, which undoubtedly would have taken first prize in the annual Better Homes and Gardens contest. Everything for sustenance, health and happiness was there. The works. Flowering trees, fruit trees, ornamental trees, whatever. Not only that, but the tree of life was there, too. Eat and live. Enjoy the surroundings. There was only one responsibility — tend the garden (verse 15). It's hard to imagine what there was to do to accomplish that; there were no weeds to pull, and the grass wouldn't have required mowing. Death hadn't arrived on the scene, so there would be no pruning of dead branches. Whatever it was, Adam wouldn't have worked up a sweat doing it, since even that wasn't around until he got pitched out of Eden.

There is a principle here, however, which is that when God gives us a privilege, we also have a responsibility. That responsibility is in two parts: (1) we are to utilize and care for what God has given us, and (2) we are to follow the instructions. Too many of us consider God to be little more than a combination fire extinguisher and genie-in-a-bottle. God, it's your responsibility to make sure that I get to heaven, and that I am very comfortable during the process of getting there. Sorry. That's not the program. In reality, he has given us a "garden" (not as pristine as Eden — but that's not His fault) which we are to cultivate and maintain. In that garden is all we need not just to survive, but to prosper — His definition of prosperity, not ours. Think about it. He gives us talents, intelligence, opportunity, family, friends, contacts, resources, ad infinitum ... and He expects us to utilize what He has given us. That's our responsibility, even though He helps us to fulfill it. The second part is that we are to follow the instructions. There are certain things in our environment which we are not supposed to touch, certain methodologies of accomplishing things which are not proper in God's scheme of things; it doesn't take a lot of imagination to figure out what those items are. Touching those things, adopting those methods, are deadly as far as achieving true prosperity — God's prosperity — goes. Interestingly enough, He also gives us the capacity to just say no, if we're willing to follow His agenda.

Adam found out the hard way. He accepted the responsibility, but didn't follow the instructions. Bummer.

A View of Genesis

Genesis 2:18-25

"The Lord God said, 'It is not good for the man to be alone. I will make a helper suitable for him.'" (2:18)

When I was in high school there was a popular song titled, "Doin' What Comes Naturally." One of its lines went something like this: "You don't hafta know how to read or write, To sit with your honey in the pale moon light. You don't hafta come from a great big town, To go pickin' berries in an evenin' gown. That comes naturally."

Lots of things in life are just natural. Like peanut butter and jelly. Spring and baseball. Man and woman. Love and marriage. But we have taken God's natural order of things and made changes, additions, substitutions which we legitimize by giving them fancy names. Homosexuality, which is unnatural and degrading according to Romans 1:26-27, is "an alternative life style." Abortion, which is the destruction of a person formed by, known to, and loved by God (numerous Scriptural references), is "gender selection" or some other euphemism conjured up by our politically correct society. Adultery is condoned by the concept of enlightened "open marriage." Lying is a legitimate "negotiating tactic." On and on, ad infinitum, ad nauseam.

God made Adam, and then He made Eve to fulfill, to complement the man. Without consulting Dr. Ruth, they immediately knew all about love and sex and marriage and family. It was natural. No shame. No guilt. No frustration. And Jesus reiterated the whole plan (Matthew 19:3-9) to the Pharisees, adding that disharmony in the home, and divorce, was man's invention, not God's.

The demands and expectations of the world have disrupted God's natural order of things. With our unnatural pursuit of material success, we have turned day into night and night into day and weekends into workdays and Sunday into soccer day. Because there isn't any time, instead of good old home made lumpy mashed potatoes with butter, salt and pepper, (or gravy au jus) we have instant mashed potatoes that even ketchup can't redeem. Since Mom has to do the laundry at night because she's at work all day, and Dad is out of town on some big deal (or vice versa), the kids get their values instilled by Roseanne and NYPD Blue, Beavis and Butthead and MTV.

Family love is natural. Praying together and playing together and staying together is natural. God made man for woman and woman for man and both of them for the family. Anything else, regardless of its enlightened name and status, is unnatural and a fraud.

"Now the serpent was more crafty than any of the wild animals the Lord God had made." (3:1)

"Now the serpent was more crafty than any of the wild animals the Lord God had made." (3:1)

Relationships are one of the most important influences in our lives. When in Rome, we do as the Romans, and oftentimes become like the Romans. Did you ever listen to someone who has been around a batch of Georgians for a period of time? Weal shut mah mouf! The only thing that can cure a Brooklyn accent!

As Genesis 3 opens, we find Eve hanging out with the serpent. No doubt it was all an innocent thing as far as she was concerned, because adultery and lust and dishonesty and pride were not yet known to the human species. She had no apparent reason to be on her guard. At least at the beginning of the conversation she didn't. No doubt she should have cleared the area when the serpent started to question God, what He had said, and what His motives were in putting the tree in the middle of the garden off limits. Unfortunately, she didn't do that, and as a result the mother of all the living (vs. 20) became the mother of all sorrows. Hanging out with the wrong crowd. In my boyhood, it would have been akin to lounging around at the pool room.

Then Adam joined the sorry crowd. He took a bite of the infamous apple (or whatever it was) and qualified for the same booby prize. Only he knew better. He had been in communication with God from the beginning and knew the difference. So it happened. Mankind and the whole creation was messed up. Adam got the thorns and thistles, Eve got her husband for a boss, and the serpent got to eat dust. And they all got the gate. But what was even worse, man lost his communion with God. The perfect relationships, man to God, husband to wife, man to the creation were all kaput.

A lot has been said about the results of bad relationships. A little leaven spoils the whole lump. One rotten apple destroys the whole barrel. Dead flies make the ointment stink. "He's a good boy who got in with the wrong crowd." It's obvious when someone has those kinds of associations. Some influences, however, aren't so immediately noticeable. A person who is in good communication with God will lose it if his or her buddies don't share the same views. Sooner or later his life will show it, but even before that, the joy of living with and talking to Jesus will disappear. The ember that finds its way out of the glowing coals will lose its warmth and its ability to give comfort and cheer to those around it.

The Bible never tells us to avoid those who don't love Jesus (within limitations), but it does tell us to cultivate relationships with those who do. That way, when the group eats an apple, the whole creation won't get terminal indigestion.

"... The woman who You put here with me, she gave me some fruit from the tree, and I ate it ... The serpent deceived me, and I ate." (12-13)

All parents become familiar with a little gremlin named "Notme" who runs amok in the house. "Who put dog food in the dishwasher?" "Notme." "Who put the whole roll of toilet paper in the toilet bowl?" "Notme." The gremlin is ubiquitous, and is responsible for everything bad that happens.

Flip Wilson wasn't original with the expression, "The devil made me do it." If Eve were around today, she would have sued him for copyright infringement. Adam was even worse. It's your fault, God. You gave me this woman and she messed up the whole world to kingdom come. (Fifteen minutes earlier, she had been the cat's meow.)

Isn't pinning-the-deed-on-the-donkey universal? The dog ate my home-work. My wife bought this orange polka-dot tie to wear with this green suit. If I would have known my re-election committee was doing that, I would NEVER have allowed it to happen. No sirree. Not me. (Oops! There's that gremlin again!)

If the road to hell is paved with Good Intentions, the bus that travels it the fastest is Good Inventions. We can invent better excuses than the most eloquent politician. We can cast blame farther and faster and better than the most accomplished fly fisherman with the best rod on the market. The only trouble is that our best attempts at doing this are almost always unsuccessful. With God, they are 100% ineffective. Better that we 'fess up and make the most of what might be a sticky situation. People can generally stomach anything except baloney. God handles it even better; He forgives and forgets.

Sometimes, if we really want to get to the root of the problem, the best place to look is in the mirror.

Genesis 3:21

"The Lord God made garments of skin for Adam and his wife and clothed them."

There they were, running around Eden, naked as a jaybird. The world's original streakers. Ashamed. Hiding from God. Trying to cover up with fig leaves since there wasn't any Fruit-of-the-Loom. Hopeless situation. But God came calling. They weren't looking for Him, but He was looking for them (as if He didn't know where they were!) This passage and its context tell us a lot about God, how He made things work for A & E, and gives us some insight as to how He moves to solve our problems as well.

This passage shows us that God is just. He won't tolerate sin. He didn't say to our original mother and father, "Well, guys, I know you were curious about that tree, and I can understand that. Everybody boots it once in a while, so I'll overlook your little foible this time — but don't let it happen again!" Nope. Disobedience to God is sin. No exemptions. One strike and you're out. 99 and 44/100% pure doesn't make it. His justice required action. He won't just overlook our disobedience, either. Not even once.

This passage also shows us that He is merciful, and doesn't turn His back on sinners. He had every right to tell Adam and Eve to hit the road without even a pair of socks. But He had compassion. He made them both a set of threads. Not to keep out the cold, but to cover their visible shame. David said (Psalm 32:1), "How blessed is he whose transgression is forgiven, whose sin is covered." Adam and Eve were blessed by God. He met their immediate need. He is also sensitive to our needs.

But it wasn't just a cover-up job. It cost a lot. God took one of the innocent animals He had created and sacrificed it for A & E's sake. That's where the Divine Tailor got His materials. They couldn't help themselves, and God knew it. So He took the animal, shed its blood, covered Adam and Eve's sin with the result, and restored their relationship with Him.

That's what happened on Calvary. We were running around, spiritually naked, hiding from God. Like A & E, we weren't looking for Him, but He was looking for us. He saw our need, and Jesus, totally innocent and totally righteous, gave His life so that we could be spiritually clothed and have our relationship with God restored. His justice and mercy met at the cross. Like Adam and Eve, sometimes we have to live with the physical consequences of our sin, but the channels of communication and fellowship with God are open through Christ. He wants to hear from us. Dial 1-800-Help-Me-Lord! It's a toll-free number.

"So Cain went out from the Lord's presence and lived in the land of Nod, east of Eden." (4:16)

Cain was the first child to be born on the planet. It didn't take him long to demonstrate that he had the human attitude — "I'm my own person." He was on the Highway to Success — the MyWay Highway. Livin' in the fast lane. Headin' down the road to Nowhere.

All the while, there was God trying to direct him to the exit ramp. The first stop was the "Worship God in Truth" ramp. Cain gave a passing nod to God at this one; as a matter of fact, he started out doing the offering bit along with his brother, Abel. Although we don't know why Abel's offering was accepted by God and Cain's wasn't, we can surmise a few things. It might be that Cain just threw a few veggies together and went through the motions, while Abel carefully chose the best: "the firstlings of his flock and of their fat portions" (vs. 4). Or it could have been that God had specified that there was to be a blood sacrifice, but Cain figured that his offering, the result of his own works, was good enough regardless of God's instructions. Or it may have been a combination of these things. Heart attitude is most important with God, and works can never open the way to a relationship with Him.

Then there was the "Live According to the Rules" ramp. Cain put the pedal to the metal past this one, and Abel became the first murder victim. He did stop at "Play it Cool" plaza, where he tried to buffalo God in the aftermath of his deed. The Lord told Cain he was going to have car trouble from that time on, but Cain still missed the next exit, "Repentance and Restoration", where the Divine Mechanic could and would have fixed the broken vehicle.

That was the last exit. The MyWay Highway kept going on to spiritual oblivion, out from the presence of the Lord. Cain continued in his ramblin' wreck to the land of Nod (the name actually means "Wandering"). He always could have turned around and come back to the Repentance and Restoration exit which was never far away. But he never did. If Cain's funeral had been held in Hollywood, Frank Sinatra would have sung "I Did it My Way." They probably would have been buddies.

Better to get off the MyWay Highway, and get your kicks on God's

Route 66. That's the JesusWay Highway, and it leads straight to heaven (John 14:6).

"There is a way that seems right to a man, but in the end it leads to death." (Proverbs 16:25)

Genesis 4:23

"Lamech said to his wives, ... 'I have killed a man for wounding me, a young man for injuring me. If Cain is avenged seven times, then Lamech seventy-seven times.'"

This guy let the world know that he was the baddest dude in town. Meaner than a junk yard dog. At least that's what he told his wives. Maybe they were the only ones who were impressed. This is the only time we hear about him in Scripture, so I guess that he didn't leave such a lasting mark on his society that Biblical scholars have been more than mildly interested.

But Lamech is mentioned and his speech recorded in the Bible for a reason. God doesn't have any idle chatter in His Book. Perhaps it's to teach us that we need to pay attention to the spiritual side of our family life, so that our children and their children and their children's children will be sufficiently exposed to God's truth, God's way, and God's character so as to know that the arrogance, pride, self-will and anger that Lamech exhibited is not the norm.

This passage tells us that Cain was Lamech's role model. We found out about Cain in the earlier part of this chapter. His influence extended down through his generational line and surfaced in Lamech. Same arrogance, same violence, same results. Lamech was one of the toxic leaves in Cain's family tree.

We need to tend our family tree with great care. Expose it to the sunlight of God's presence to provide strength of character. Water it generously with the Word of God, so that the roots sink deep into The Solid Rock. Fertilize it with discipline, so that the twig is bent in the way that the bough should be inclined. Feed it with worship of God, so that the leaves are tender and graceful, giving praise to the One Who has created it. Saturate it with the knowledge of the Spirit, so that its fruit is luscious and plentiful. Bathe it in prayer, so that the winds of adversity and the wiles of the devil will not be able to destroy it. And above all, don't forget the love, not only given but expressed; this is the glue that holds it all together, the agent that makes all these other elements interact to produce "something beautiful, something good."

Only when the family tree is able to recognize these characteristics, attitudes and activities in us will it respond to our care. Then it will be like the trees in Eden, "Pleasing to the sight and good for food" (2:9), and it will stand for eternity.

Matthew tells us that, "...every good tree bears good fruit; but a bad tree bears bad fruit.... Every tree that does not bear good fruit is cut down and thrown into the fire." (Matt 7:17) So much for Cain's tree, Lamech included. And that's not friendly fire.

"... and (Eve) gave birth to a son, and named him Seth .... Seth also had a son, and he named him Enosh. At that time, men began to call on the Name of the Lord."

Without a doubt, Eve grieved for Abel, like any mother would do. But there may have been something special about Abel in Eve's heart; God had talked about one of her offspring being the one to defeat the serpent, who had been the initiator of all this sorrow. What would happen now, now that Abel, the godly Abel was dead, and Cain had headed east?

One can almost hear God saying, "Not to worry, Eve, I have a plan. Cain and his progeny will develop their commercial society, their cities, and worship their own gods. I will deal with them in my own good time. But you will have another child and name him Seth. I have appointed (that's what "Seth" means) him to be the start of the line through which that Promised One will come. He will also have a son named Enosh, a humble man, who will lead the people in proclaiming my Name. His children and their children will also be men of God; and My purposes will not be thwarted regardless of man's activity or lack thereof. Cain will build his world, and I will build My kingdom through Seth."

Guess what? That's exactly what happened.

God has His appointed people, regardless of what happens in Washington, Tehran, Jerusalem, Shanghai or Skunk's Misery, Alabama. He is totally in control. He doesn't have any Plan B, because He doesn't need one. Because He lives in the past, the present and the future all at once, there is nothing that takes Him by surprise. He knew Cain before the snake appeared in the garden. He knew Lamech before Lamech was a gleam in his old man's eye. He had appointed Seth before Abel tended his first sheep. In God's plan, Jesus was on the cross, dying for all our sins, before the worlds were ever formed.

In God's plan, all those who belong to Him are "Seths." We are all appointed to do something. There are the Cains and the Lamechs who have no interest in God, and He knows that they never will. They will have to make their own way, bear their own burdens, be part of their own plans, and suffer the consequences. But those who have come to

God through Jesus are appointed by Him to be a part of the final redemption, to be channels of God's blessing and active in the implementing of God's program. Seth was willing and available. So was Enosh. And kazillion others throughout the ages. God will use those who are, right where they are. How about us?

Let's not be late for our appointment!

Genesis 5

"This is the written account of Adam's line. When He created man, He made him in the likeness of God. ... Adam ... had a son in his own likeness, in his own image, and he named him Seth." (5:1,3)

Sometimes I wonder why the Bible has a number of genealogies in it. I suppose that from an historical or societal view they might be interesting or important. But more often than not, they appear to be a mishmash of unfamiliar names that people, especially Christians, cull through in order to find a suitably Biblical but incomprehensible name for a son or daughter. "You named him Jezreel? He looks more like a Mahalalel to me!!"

But there is a reason. Timothy tells us that, "All Scripture is God-breathed and useful for teaching, rebuking, correcting and training in righteousness." (2 Timothy 3:16). Even the several genealogies, and this one is no different.

One of the lessons we learn from this passage is that in the long run, it is most important to be a man or woman of God. Success in this world does not put us in God's hall of fame. A guy might be able to carry a football, but 2,000 years from now it won't really matter. A woman might have a great voice and be the fat lady who sings at the end of the opera, but the headlines won't be there in a generation or two. Jonas Salk will be known in various parts of the world for a few hundred years and then be just a footnote in a medical dictionary. But wherever the Bible is, and that is throughout the world and throughout history and to the end of time, here is Kenan and Jared and Enosh and all the other guys between Adam and Noah. God's men. Part of the lineage of the Redeemer. Heroes of the faith. Check out Hebrews 11 for more.

Everybody in this genealogy had many sons and daughters. We never hear anything about any of the others. God selected these men to be channels for His plan down through the ages. He wouldn't have selected them if they had not been upright and Godly men. Sinners, yes, but with a heart for God. And think about something else. Cain's genealogy in Chapter 4 goes down through Lamech, then nothing further. It appears God wanted us to know how evil was developed, and then its perpetrators are nobodies after Lamech, except for isolated instances

A View of Genesis

and people. In Luke 3, the men found in this passage are part of the cast of characters the whole way from Adam to Jesus Himself.

By the way, who would have ever heard about Pharaoh, if it hadn't been for Moses?

Genesis 5:3

"Adam ... had of a son in his own likeness, in his own image... "

What a difference an apple makes. In Genesis 1:27 it is recorded that God created man in His own image, that is, God's image. Now we find that Adam has a son in his, that is, Adam's image. From perfection to imperfection. From purity to impurity. From righteousness to sin. God's creation is now flawed. Come to think of it, everything of God that man touches gets messed up. And all because Adam and Eve decided to disobey God in the orchard.

Well, God didn't just throw up his hands and rid Himself, either physically or emotionally, of the whole sin-soiled affair. As a matter of fact, this genealogy in Chapter 5 tells us something about God relating to that fact. Remember, He had made a promise to the serpent that the slithery old deceiver was going to get his in the end, and the means by which this was going to happen was through the seed of the woman. So God set the wheels in motion to keep His promise. The lineage to the Messiah was established. Throughout history the devil tried, my how he tried, to derail God's Redemption Train. How many times before Jesus appeared was the Jewish nation in danger of extinction? And how about Herod having all the little Hebrew boys under two years old eliminated? (Matthew 2:16) The devil tried to sidetrack Jesus Himself in the temptation. But God's promise is as good as His word, and events inexorably moved toward the cross, where that promise in Genesis 3:15 was literally fulfilled.

That's what God is all about, keeping His promises. Someone has written a book listing 365 of God's promises to His children from the Scripture, one for every day of the year. And all of them are for everybody. Each one of them available and effective for every day. Not health and wealth and every Wednesday afternoon at the beach, but things like Hebrews 13:5 where God says, "Never will I leave you; never will I forsake you," and the writer responds, "So we say with confidence, 'The Lord is my helper, I will not be afraid. What can man do to me?'" Or how about Philippians 4:19 where Paul (writing according to the Spirit's instructions) assures us, "My God shall meet all your needs according to His glorious riches in Christ Jesus."

God's promises are more solid than Gibraltar, not like men's promises which are made to be broken. As sure as the sun will rise tomorrow. In God we trust, and everybody else pays cash.

"Enoch walked with God; then he was no more, because God took him away."

One can imagine the excitement in the neighborhood when evening came and Enoch didn't make it home for dinner. He was outta here. Gonzo. CNN would have announced the first recorded abduction by space aliens. But that was not the case. Enoch was taking his usual walk with God, and God just invited him home for an eternal dinner.

Enoch is mentioned in a couple other places in the Scripture, notably in Hebrews 11, the Faith Hall of Fame, and in the little book of Jude. He is one of the God Squad that we should be trying to emulate.

In Hebrews 11:5-6, we're told that Enoch was a man of faith in God. He walked so close to God and knew Him so intimately that there was no hesitation in putting his entire present and future in God's hands. Can any of us do that today in this modern, complicated world? Yesirree. Many do. Their knowledge of God is similar to Enoch's; it comes from time spent in the Word and in talking to God.

Not only did Enoch have faith in God, he was a man of faithfulness for God. Check out Jude 14-15. He actually called people "ungodly sinners who were doing ungodly deeds in an ungodly way." The nerve of him. Undoubtedly a zealot, from the dangerous and sinister religious right. Insensitive and politically incorrect. Make sure he never runs for office. God gave him a message and he spoke it. If God had given us that message, most of us would be headed for the chicken coop.

Then Enoch was a man of fellowship with God. Spent a lot of time with God. More than likely he could have made a lot more money if he had paid more attention to his business, but he figured spending time with his Friend was better. He probably missed a few rounds of golf because he was chatting with the Almighty. Hilton Head would have come in a distant second to his walks with Jehovah.

Just another thought. Enoch was probably in great shape. Walking with God is great exercise. It gets rid of weight. The weight of the burdens we try to carry ourselves. God has very broad shoulders and a big heart. He can shape us up better than NordicTrack.

Genesis 5:27

"Altogether, Methuselah lived 969 years, and then he died."

Here is the oldest man who ever lived. Think what he would have done to the Social Security system. 969 years. That's a lot of senior citizen discounts and AARP dues.

He would have had to live that long to get used to his name. Or even learn how to spell it. In the Old Testament, people gave their children names which meant something. Some were named for events that would happen in the future, no doubt at God's direction. It wasn't like today when one or two names such as Allison or Chad or Jeremy or Megan come into vogue, and everybody in the neighborhood comes running when Mom calls the kids home for dinner. Remember "Seth," meaning "appointed"? He was appointed by God to start the lineage to Jesus. My favorite is Mahershalalhashbaz (Isaiah 8:1-3), which means "quick to the plunder, swift to the spoil." But that's a topic for another time.

"Methuselah" means, "after he dies, it shall be sent." People who knew him probably wondered what was going to be sent when Methuselah died. When "it" came, they weren't very pleased, because "it" was the flood. The flood came in the same year shortly after his death, and once again, God proved to be true to His word, right on top of the details.

That's the way God is. He is always true to His word and on top of the details, right down to the last iota. The people in and shortly after Methuselah's time found this out, and those who didn't accept God's message, namely all but Noah and his family, found themselves under water. God has a message for people today as well, which centers around another Person to Whom He gave a name. He told Joseph to name Mary's son Jesus, "because He will save His people from their sins" (Matthew 1:21). "Jesus" means "Savior." Peter, referring to Jesus Christ of Nazareth, told the head honchos in Jerusalem that, "Salvation is found in no one else, for there is no other name under heaven given to men by which we must be saved" (Acts 4:12).

God has the details of this message worked out, too. It's a very simple but profound message. He sent His only Son, Jesus, to die on the cross for our sins. By admitting our guilt and claiming Jesus' death as the only acceptable sacrifice for our sin and the only available means for reconciliation with God, we will receive forgiveness and eternal life from God. Those who don't accept this message, like those living when Methuselah died, will suffer God's judgment.

What's in The Name? Salvation and peace with God! Listen to the message!

"Altogether, Methuselah lived 969 years, and then he died."

Genesis 5:27

"Altogether, Methuselah lived 969 years, and then he died."

You would have thought Methuselah's friends would have gotten tired of him after all those years. He probably would have made a great lead for the movie, "Grumpy Old Men." And what about his wife? What would he have bought her for their 900th wedding anniversary? How many different ways could she have fixed hamburger to keep the old man happy?

Moreover, why would God choose him to be the oldest man to ever live? There were some who came close, like Adam, who lived 930 years, and Jared, who lived 962 years. Others who lived 700 or 800 years were mere children. Probably weren't even allowed to vote. I wonder, though, whether Methuselah claimed the longevity title because God wanted to emphasize His mercy. Remember, Methuselah's name means, "After he dies, it shall be sent," and "it" was God's judgment on man's sinfulness in the form of the flood. God had his message out there for a long time; Noah preached for 120 years, and there may have been others who set up a Gospel tent in the village square. God had mercy on Adam and Eve as well as countless others until Methuselah's time. When that period was over, however, the faucets opened and the local Sam's Club didn't have any life jackets. Maybe God just extended that period until He ran out of patience.

The Scripture tells us that Jesus is going to return to earth to judge the nations. More than that, it also tells us that individual judgment is coming for those who have not accepted God's gift of salvation through Jesus. Many, if not most, people ignore or scoff at these ideas, just like in Methuselah's time. The people when Peter lived were also leery about Christ's coming. Peter told them that God would keep His promise, but was being "patient .... not wanting anyone to perish, but everyone to come to repentance" (2 Peter 3:9). As it was in the days of Methuselah, so it is today. God has His messengers telling people what is going to happen, but thus far He has been very patient, extending His mercy. For those who refuse His offer, judgment will surely come.

Actually, those who have accepted Jesus as Saviour have a better deal than Methuselah. He only lived 969 years. We will live forever. Jesus is coming! Pass the Word!

Genesis 6:1-8

"The Lord was grieved that He had made man upon the earth, and His heart was filled with pain" (6:6).

It was almost like God had been reading the USA Today, then picked up His harp and sang about His achy-breaky heart. On the earth, all hell had broken loose and no one could find the fire engines. Every street corner had its gathering of Sylvester Super-Studs (vs. 4) hanging out, not only watching the girls go by, but also pairing off with the willing ladies and heading for the nearest rent-a-room-by-the-hour hotel.

And it all broke God's heart.

Sex and self-gratification were the main menu items. Bourbon Street would have been the main drag. Whoever the sons of God were in vs. 1, their focus was on females and fun, not on their Father or their future. And it wasn't just a passing fancy, a Saturday night diversion; "every inclination of the thoughts of (man's) heart was only evil all the time" (vs. 5).

And God had holy heartburn.

Before we cluck-cluck-cluck and murmur "My-oh-my-oh-my" and shake our heads at this situation, let's look at our own activities. Do we fall into the same pattern, although not so obvious? Remember, sin-is-sin-is-sin with God. We may not be so preoccupied with sex (at least not publicly), but a lot of us read the romance novels more than we read the Bible, and fellowship more with R-rated movies than with good Christian books. Self-interest and self-gratification are at or near the top of our agendas, whether it be expressed in sexual activity (yes, fantasizing is sexual activity, too), in the pursuit of life-style monopoly (the one who has the most toys at the end wins), or in the I-just-want-to-do-my-own-thing attitude.

In Noah's time, God acted to change the environment. He zapped the whole kit- and-kaboodle. All the men and the ladies and the animals and the birds, except those which He spared to preserve the creation and continue His grand design.

Jesus can change our environment, too, but in a different way. He doesn't zap us literally; He does an internal make-over. He will change our hearts so that we have His interests in mind, rather than our own. If we ask Him to.

The way to avoid putting a break in God's heart is to put a brake on our self- interest. That will give Him cause to sing a happier tune.

Genesis 6:8-22

"But Noah found favor in the eyes of the Lord .... Noah did everything just as God commanded him" (6:8,22).

Fortunately, Noah was not a theological intellectual. He never went to seminary where, very often, people get their minds messed up with isms that create schisms and spasms. He just did everything that the Lord commanded him.

Why did Noah "find favor in the eyes of the Lord?" Was it because he was obedient through his own desire and conviction, or did God select him as a result of His sovereign will? This is an age old theological debate that nobody this side of heaven is going to solve. God's sovereignty vs. man's free will. Calvinism vs. Arminianism. Is man free to choose which path he will walk, or is he compelled to make that choice because of God's irresistible power and grace?

Frankly, I don't think we should worry very much about the whole thing, because it is debates like this that fracture fellowship and friendship alike. We know that God is sovereign, and that "no man comes to God except the Spirit draws him." We also know that "whosoever will may come and drink of the water of life freely." Peter tells us that we are, "chosen (elect) according to the foreknowledge of God the Father" (I Peter 1:1-2). There is enough in the Scripture to support both theologies, and this writer believes that God has worked things out so that His sovereignty and man's free will, His election and His foreknowledge, all work in some irrevocably intertwined way to result in the salvation of those who come to Him by faith.

Noah didn't go through theological contortions while he was obeying God. If he would have laid his hammer down to argue with the Reverend Doctors of the day, the ark would have never been finished. He just went about the business of doing everything the Lord commanded him. Uncomplicated. Non-traditional (whoever built a boat before?) True to God's Word. Preaching and living God's message.

No doubt, theology is important. There are spiritual principles to die for. For instance, a person who wants to argue that salvation is a result of our works rather than or in addition to Jesus' death on the cross, suffering the penalty for our sin in our place, needs to be vigorously challenged and Biblically refuted. One should never compromise the basics. But beyond the basics, there is room for respectful disagreement.

Active obedience was Noah's strong point. He heard the Word of God and followed it precisely. There was no argument about theology. His attitudes and actions were a living sermon. If we do the same, we, like Noah, won't miss the boat.

Genesis 6:22, 7:5,16

"And Noah did all that the Lord commanded him." (7:5)

Noah was sitting around one day talking with God (6:9). If we could have eavesdropped on a conversation between them, it may have gone like this:

God: Hey, Noah! I've got something big coming up, and I want your help.

Noah: I'm on board, God.

God: You're going to be on board longer than you think, Noah. I've had it with the humans, and I'm going to do away with them all, except you, Mrs. Noah, your three sons and their wives.

Noah: Yeah, things are pretty bad. I almost got run down by some drunk dude on a dinosaur at the gospel meeting the other night. And God, it's not getting any better. In the good old days, 450 years ago, it wasn't like this. So what am I supposed to do?

God: I want you to build an ark.

Noah: You want me to do what???

God: Build an ark.

Noah: What's that?

God: It's a thing that floats on water. I've got the measurements all worked out. 450 feet long, 75 feet wide, 45 feet high. Lower, middle and upper decks, with a door in the side. Build it out of cypress wood, and coat it with tar inside and out. It will be a very seaworthy vessel.

Noah: I'm sure You know this, but we're an awful long way from water to float it on. How are we going to get it there?

God: We're going to have a flood.

Noah: A what????

A View of Genesis

God: A flood. It's going to rain cats and dogs.

Noah: Rain? Cats and dogs? We have enough of them around already.

God: Figurative language, Noah. There is going to be so much water around that everyone outside the ark is going to be history.

Noah: I'm sure You know what You're doing, but an ark? Out here? That big? The Mrs. will be sure I've flipped my lid. So will everybody else.

God: You got that right. But it's going to happen, and you gotta have faith.

Noah: You know I'll have to have a building permit. Have You thought about how the DER will react to this? What about the child labor laws? Japheth is less than 100 years old. And what about OSHA?

God: Apply for a variance, and the flood will come in less time than they have to cut through the red tape. Just get yourself a hammer and get to work. And by the way, I'm giving the people a fair chance. I want you and your sons to preach as well as work. Give them the message that judgment is coming. They will hoot and holler, but they need to hear. Above all, don't stop building the ark to argue with them. Your actions will speak louder than your words.

Noah (to himself): It's never rained. No one has ever seen a boat like this. The world hasn't a clue as to what a flood is. Man! I am going to be the laughing stock of the neighborhood. A religious kook, that's what they'll say. Old Noah's ready for the funny farm. He's been chewing on too much peyote root. Whoooeeee! This is going to take a humongus amount of faith! But God said it, I'll do it, and He'll see to it!

And Noah did. So did God. And the world got the message, but too late.

"By faith Noah, when warned about things not yet seen, in holy fear built an ark to save his family. By his faith he condemned the world and became heir of the righteousness that comes by faith" (Hebrews 11:7).

Faith in God gives us the foresight to avoid the situations that we regret by hindsight.

Genesis 8

"When the dove returned to him in the evening, there in its beak was a freshly plucked olive leaf. Then Noah knew that the water had receded from the earth." (8:11)

God is a Great One for illustrations. One picture is worth a thousand words. And man is very adept at taking God's pictures and applying his own batch of paint to keep the image but change the message to suit his own fancy.

This scene serves as one of God's pictures. Noah was on the boat. The water had been God's form of judgment on everything outside the ark. The rain had stopped, since God had accomplished His purpose. He was at peace with Noah and all the passengers. So the dove was sent out, came back with the olive leaf, and Noah knew that God's war against the world as expressed in the flood was over.

The Scripture tells us that all these things happened as examples, as pictures for us. The ark is a picture, a type, of Jesus. The flood is a picture of the judgment which God will wreak upon mankind in the future. (Check out what Jesus had to say about this in Matthew 24:36-39, specifically referring to Noah.) Those who are "in Christ" (i.e., believing in Him for salvation) will be safe. Those who are not will be lost. Just like in Noah's time, the majority of people could care less about their literal future. But also just like in Noah's time, the results will be the same. And it will be forever.

So what about the dove? This was God's sign of the end of that judgment, His expression of peace. The world likes the dove and has adopted it, complete with the olive branch, as its symbol of peace. We have taken God's picture and slopped our own paint on it. It's no longer a symbol of peace between God and man, but a harbinger of hoped-for peace among men, the world as one big brotherhood. Guess what? It has never worked, will never work, and can never work because God is the only One Who can produce peace.

And why has man changed the symbol of the dove from its original meaning? Because we don't want to admit that we are at war with God. We want to live our own lives, seek our own peace and happiness, and hope that God will accept us because we have been basically good people. The truth is that we are all sinners, and regardless of how hard we try not to, we end up fighting against God. We might ignore that fact, but it won't change the outcome. God is the winner, every time.

He still offers Jesus as the Ark. The door is open. When we get on board, we also get the Dove. It's His peace with us, and we then have the complete picture, the original, the real thing. And this Olive Branch makes an eternity of difference.

Genesis 8: 1 5-16

"Then God said to Noah, 'Come out of the ark, you and your wife and your sons and their wives.'"

Noah, his family and his personal zoo had been in the ark for over 300 days. One would think that everybody would have cabin fever, and the cats would be eyeing the mice with something other than kinder and gentler actions on their minds. Noah had looked out the window and seen that the ground was dry (vs. 13); no doubt that news was received by all with something more than, "Goodie goodie gumdrop!"; there may have even been a race to get the gangplank ready. The whole trip hadn't been exactly a Caribbean cruise. But it wasn't God's time yet. He didn't tell Noah to disembark for another 57 days.

Why the delay? Only God knows. It just wasn't His time. If we had been Noah, more than likely we would have been over the side, sliding down the giraffe's neck if we had to. Land! Feet on the soil! No more elephant doo-doo! But it wasn't God's time. And unlike us, Noah was patient. He just stayed put.

God has a time for everything, and it seldom, if ever, corresponds with our schedule. I want patience, and I want it NOW! We want our genie-in-a-bottle God to act in our best interest (as defined by us) right away. This minute. Yesterday. He should have anticipated this "problem" or this "need" and had the solution or the supply waiting — curb service at God's 7-11 store. But that's not His way of doing things.

Some time ago we were in Europe and traveled mostly by train. We soon found out that if the schedule says the train will be there at 8:00, if you get there at 8:01 you are out of luck. The train has come and gone. God is like that. He is always on time. He has never been early or late for an appointment. And the incredible thing is, He has a schedule for each person which He also keeps. Down to the millisecond. We might jump the gun or lag behind or plead with Him to act, but that's not His style. He never sleeps through the alarm or gets caught in a traffic jam.

The writer of Ecclesiastes had a lot to say about God's timing. Check out Ecclesiastes 3:1-8. He starts out, "There is a time for everything, and a season for every activity under heaven." Every event. That's a lot of events. Some good, some bad, some indifferent. God has a time and a purpose for them all. At the end of this portion, Solomon says, "He has made everything beautiful in its time" (vs. 11). Just right. Like the little bear in Goldilocks. Maybe we don't understand or agree, but that's the way it is. He sees it all and makes it work according to His timing. Noah understood this, and waited 57 more days.

It's time we set our clocks by God's timepiece.

Genesis 8:20

"Then Noah built an altar to the Lord ... and sacrificed burnt offerings on it."

Here is a multiple-choice question:

The first thing that Noah did when he got off the ark was to:

a. Vow he would never get on another boat.
b. Look for the local drugstore to get a new supply of dramamine.
c. Chase all the animals off into the bushes.
d. Build an altar and offer burnt offerings to God.

According to this text, (d) would be the correct answer. One can never tell, maybe he did all of the other things as well. Or at least thought about it. If he did, those events were not recorded.

The burnt offering was generally one of atonement, a sacrifice for sin. Through it, the offeror became acceptable to God. Leviticus 1 has all the details and the procedures. One would have thought that Noah and his family would have had little chance to indulge in sinning while being cooped up and tossed around for so long a time. Of course, those conditions may have caused them to think a few unkind thoughts during the voyage. But maybe Noah knew his heart and the hearts of his family.

God knew what was going on, as He stated in vs. 21, "... the inclination of (man's) heart is evil from childhood." This tells us that even though we may not have opportunity to do some heavy visible sinning, or even if we are very respectable on the outside, in our hearts there is a tendency to actively rebel against God and His program. Paul tells us that it is a constant war between our desire to please God and our tendency to fulfill our natural desires.

Obviously, we don't build altars and offer burnt offerings today. Hebrews 10:10 says that, "...we have been made holy through the sacrifice of the body of Jesus Christ once for all." Jesus is our burnt offering, the sacrifice for our sin, and through Him we are acceptable to God.

Noah wanted to be accepted by God, and he knew there was no other way than through the burnt offering. So he did it. For us to be accepted by God, we need only to accept Jesus' work on the cross as the only sacrifice for our sin.

So just do it.

Genesis 8:20 - 9:17

"Whenever the rainbow appears in the clouds, I will see it and remember My covenant between Me and you and all living creatures of every kind." (9:17)

God is a pretty poor negotiator. At least in current circles He would be. Rumor has it that He doesn't have many lawyers in heaven, so He has to handle all this work Himself. In doing so, He seems to always give away the store.

The Hebrew word for "covenant" appears here in the Scripture for the first time. Usually a covenant is made as a result of a deal between two parties, each of whom comes away from the table with something and both of whom are reasonably satisfied with the deal. Unless you're a taxpayer listening to a batch of politicians tell you how the deal they just made on your behalf is going to benefit you. The New Deal, the Fair Deal, the Square Deal, the Shady Deal, etc.

Well, God just made a deal with the whole world in this portion of Scripture. He didn't negotiate it very well, since it is a one-way street. And He made it, even though He says He is aware of all the facts. "I know you all are turkeys," He says, "and have been since you were knee high to a grasshopper. Nevertheless, I am not going to zap the whole scene again. At least not with water. And I am making a rainbow so I'm sure to remember this covenant" (Phinehas Phigtree's paraphrase of 9:11-18). So what does man do for his part of the bargain? Nothing. Just look at the rainbow and marvel at its beauty. Or try to find the pot of gold that's supposed to be at either end of it. Or dream about flying over it for some silly reason.

There are other covenants throughout the Scripture that are similar, in that God offers a deal that is one-sided. Like the one with Israel in Jeremiah 31:33-34. Or the one with all mankind in John 3:16 where He promises eternal life without any action on man's part except to believe in Jesus and accept His redemptive work. No strings attached. It's God saying, "Such a deal I have for you!"

Some people reject this as "easy believism" and say there's no free lunch, even in God's cafeteria. But this deal is real. It also brings about a change in attitude, in desires, in priorities, and in purpose, so that getting in the game in God's ball-yard is a real blast. Paul tells us that even the things he considered as "light afflictions" (some of which might be regarded by us as a ton of bricks), which sometimes come along, are "pure joy" when viewed in the light of God's program. As my friend Tunch says, "Wow! All this and heaven too! If it gets any better, I'll have to go see a doctor!"

Some people dream about rainbows. Some chase the rainbow. Those who love Jesus catch it. And they don't find a pot of gold, they find His covenant, which is as good as *God*.

Genesis 9:6

"Whoever sheds the blood of man, by man shall his blood be shed; for in the image of God has God made man."

God is pro-life. Unequivocally. He started out taking Cain to the wood-shed for Abel's murder, and here He establishes human government to do His retaliation against anyone who takes a life. Some argue that this only applies to Old Testament times, and times and things and God have all changed. Nonsense. Romans 13:1-4 tells us differently. "Every-one must submit himself to the governing authorities.... For (the one in authority) is God's servant, an agent of wrath to bring punishment on the wrongdoer." Last I checked, this passage is still in the Scripture, and God still means what He says. Even if the authorities waffle.

Abortion? It's taking the life which is made by God. Check out Ecclesi-astes 11:5. Or Isaiah 49:5 which says, "And now the Lord says — He who formed me in the womb to be His servant...." How about Psalm 139:13-16, "For You created my inmost being; You knit me together in my mother's womb.... Your eyes saw my unformed body. All the days ordained for me were written in your book before one of them came to be." Of course, we are "enlightened" now. It's not murder, it's "choice." It's the woman's "right to control her own body." Paul tells us that our bodies belong to God (I Cor. 6:12-20). Also Romans 14:7-8. And many other Scriptures. Regardless of what we call it, it's murder.

Euthanasia? Assisted suicide? My, how we like to come up with terms and words that put a candy coating on murder. Even if the person gives his or her permission. Or asks for help. Jeremiah 10:23 states, "I know, 0 Lord, that a man's life is not his own; it is not for man to direct his steps." Numerous other Scriptures, we could go on and on. Soon it will be legal here, but not in God's eyes. "Self-determination" is not in His vocabulary.

With the current state of the political scene and the courts, it's safer to be on death row than to read the Bible in school. When God and His precepts are left out of society, society inevitably suffers. We now reap what man has sown. God still establishes authorities, but, like He did with Israel when they wanted a king, He "gave them their desire but sent leanness to their souls."

A View of Genesis

He is still God, and men will answer to Him by and by. For murder. For failure to properly execute His laws. For doing violence on our bodies, which belong to Him. And maybe for something else, like failing to seek out and help those who out of ignorance or bad advice or intimidation become personally involved in such acts.

Take a stand. God expects it. But like God, let us love the sinner while hating the sin. We may save a life that way. One of those to whom God has given life.

Genesis 9:18-29

"When he drank some of its wine, he became drunk and lay uncovered inside his tent." (9:21)

Noah blew it. Imbibed too much of the vino. He got sloshed. Bombed. Tanked. Here is the guy who preached for 120 years, made a fool of himself in everybody's eyes for the Lord's sake, built an ark when there wasn't any water around and rain was unknown. Someone who had found favor in the eyes of the Lord. If the Washington Post or New York Times had been there, they would have blared out the headlines, "Leader of the Religious Right Found Naked in Drunken Stupor."

So Noah was human, just like us. Subject to letting the Lord and everybody around him down. Maybe there's a certain amount of comfort to us in this; we read about a man like Noah, and he seems to be so super-spiritual, something we could never attain to. And then he falls off the wagon, big time. Just like we do. Do we semi-secretly applaud when something like this happens?

Well, it looks like faithful Noah got a little careless. Perhaps he thought he was beyond temptation after 120 years at the pulpit and in direct communication with God Himself. But the Scripture says, "So, if you think you are standing firm, be careful that you don't fall!" (1 Corinthians 10:12). He planted the vineyard (vs. 20) and thought he could handle the wine. Maybe he should have considered his limitations, either planting carrots instead of grapes or setting the limit before he relaxed on his hammock with the product. At least he should have taken a smaller jug! Certainly he would not have been unaware of the effects of the wine. Remember what God said to Cain? "But if you do not do what is right, sin is crouching at your door; it desires to have you..."(Genesis 4:7). Noah dropped his guard and sin said "GOTCHA!" Noah flirted with the fire and got burned.

Peter tells us to be sober, to be on the alert, because the adversary, that old snake the devil, prowls around like a lion, looking for someone to devour (I Peter 5:8). And there are opportunities everywhere for the devil to eat us alive. Some of us like to push the envelope, walk on the ragged edge. We can handle it. No sweat. Then we find ourselves on the devil's dish. An hors d'oeuvre. Tasty to the devil, but a bitter mouthful for us and a lot of garbage for the cause of Christ.

A View of Genesis

Fortunately, God forgives us, but the damage to us and those around us cannot be undone. Noah probably regretted that afternoon to his dying day. 350 years later. That's a lot of regret. Mrs. Noah probably never let him hear the end of it.

Let's not stir up the pot where sin might be simmering. We might find ourselves in the soup.

Genesis 10

"Cush was the father of Nimrod, who grew to be a mighty warrior on the earth. He was a mighty hunter before the Lord..." (10:8,9).

Here we go with another genealogy, only this time it details how Noah's family started to spread throughout the earth, as they were instructed by God in 9:2. A special mention, however, is made of Nimrod, who not only captured the attention of the writer of this portion of Scripture, but also of a lot of the world at that time.

Nimrod was an in-your-face kind of guy. The Sadaam Hussein of his day. His name means, "Let us rebel." Maybe his father, Cush, had it up to his eyeballs hearing that Canaan's family was to serve the rest of the tribe (9:25-27). If this were the case, he certainly would not have named his son Egbert, Chauncey, or some other wimp name. Nimrod probably spent most of his childhood pumping iron and beating up kids at school.

So he set out to build an empire. Babylon was his first great city (vs. 10). It became the center of power, commerce, and pagan religion in the known world. Babylon is symbolic of the empire and system referred to in Revelation 17:5, "Babylon the Great, the mother of prostitutes and of the abominations of the earth." Billy Graham would not have been welcome. It was at the core of Nimrod's operations to dominate the world and its people. One writer has said of Nimrod:

> "Proud Nimrod first the bloody chase began
> A mighty hunter, and his prey was man."

Here the worship of idols became an art form. Birds, animals, Nimrod himself. And man looked within himself for gratification. The world scene became the basis for Paul's description of God's condemnation in Romans 1:18-32, where "They exchanged the truth of God for a lie, and worshipped and served created things rather than the Creator.." (1:25). Gay pride had its first roots in Babylon.

Nimrod didn't outlast God. Like everything and everybody else who challenges God and His order, he and Babylon are just entries in history books and religious journals, living on in spiritual infamy. We may

56   *A View of Genesis*

set out to build our own empires, whatever they may be, but the Lord will have His way in the end. Better we should click our computers on to His program and follow His instructions, to build His city and not our own.

It's like the plaque which was on the wall in my grandfather's house:
"Only one life 'twill soon be past
Only what's done for Christ will last."

Genesis II

"That is why it was called Babel, because there the Lord confused the language of the whole world. From there the Lord scattered them over the face of the whole earth." (11:9)

Babbling brook. Babbling idiot. Banker babble. A lot of sound and no message, or no understanding of the message. That's what happened at the Tower of Babel, when men decided they were going to marshal all their abilities and forces and build a tower to heaven, according to their own plans and for their own purposes. God got sick and tired of it and threw a wrench into the whole thing. One minute they were all having a profitable conversation, the next minute it was like a modern day committee — everybody was talking, and no one understood what any of the others was saying.

God had told the descendants of Noah to "fill the earth" (9:1). Instead, they stuck around the same general area, becoming stronger and more self-sufficient as a group of people and nations. They finally got to the point where they decided to make a name and a future for themselves (11:4). This is not what God had in mind. So He stopped the whole process in a very effective way. He destroyed their power to communicate with each other. And confusion reigned.

We have a lot of confusion and babble around us. One only has to look to Washington, DC, to hear the political babble from a system that has legislated God out of existence. In our churches, we often get preacher babble. A system of rules, rites and procedures rather than the Word of God; a theology made by men, which changes as men change. And personally, we are experts at babble, sounding off on any given topic without considering what God has to say in the matter. No wonder that people are confused.

The Lord can drown out that babble, however, and replace confusion with order and understanding. He has given us His word, the Bible, to light our pathway. And He has given us Himself, the Spirit, to lead us away from confusion into the green pastures of peace and order.

Tear down the Tower of Ignorance and Ambition, and replace it with the Tower of God's Wisdom and Strength. It's a building where no babble is heard.

A View of Genesis

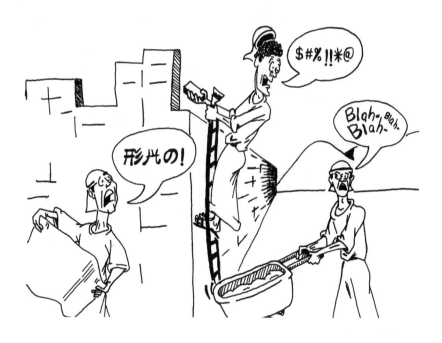

"That is why it was called Babel, because there the Lord confused the language of the whole world. From there the Lord scattered them over the face of the whole earth." (11:9)

"The Lord had said to Abram, 'Leave your country, your people and your father's household and go to the land I will show you'" (12:1).

"The God of glory appeared to our father Abraham while he was still in Mesopotamia, before he lived in Haran. 'Leave your country and your people,' God said, 'and go to the land I will show you'" (Acts 7:2).

If NBC had held a Bible Beauty Pageant in Mesopotamia, Abraham would have been a finalist in the "faith" contest, perhaps even lapping the field in the quest for the crown. "Abe" was sitting in his condo in Ur of the Chaldeans one day, and the Lord told him to gather up his belongings and head for the hills. The Lord didn't give Abe any Trip-Tik, just told him to move on. And it wasn't like Abe was a spring chicken ready to seek out his fortune; he was 75 years old and a member of the Mesopotamian Fortune 500. In effect, he was heading out from a very wealthy and sophisticated pagan city to just-somewhere-out-there. Sort of like leaving a Beverly Hills mansion to go to the uncharted land of the fierce tribe of the Fuzzy Wuzzies. So Abram and Sarai held a garage sale and took off.

That's faith. (The neighbors would have called it stupidity.) As a matter of fact, Abram wasn't even that well acquainted with God. He, his father and his family had worshipped heathen gods (Joshua 24:2). He was no Enoch, walking with God every day. But God energized his faith and, as it says in Hebrews 11:8, "By faith Abraham ... obeyed and went, even though he did not know where he was going. By faith he made his home in the promised land like a stranger in a foreign country; he lived in tents..."

This is the faith that pleases God. An active faith, not just a theological or theoretical faith. Faith that finds its resources, its impetus in the person of God. A living, active faith in a living, active God. A belief that translates itself into action. Actions which are based on the truth that God has a plan for our lives, and we are willing to follow Him to its completion.

Although Abram's move was geographical, our "move of faith" is more often than not one which takes us away from the Land of Our Plans (where the trail is fully mapped out) to the Country of His Will (which is uncharted territory). We need faith like Abram's to make the move. This, too, is a work of God. He will help us strengthen our faith. Like the man in Mark 9:24 said to the Lord, "I do believe; help me over-come my unbelief!"

We can face the future when, by faith, we look into the future in the face of God.

Genesis 12:1

"The Lord had said to Abram, 'Leave your country, your people and your father's household, and go to the land I will show you.'" (12:1)

When Stephen was defending his faith before the Pharisees, he told them that Abraham (God had changed Abram's name to Abraham; see Genesis 17:5) had heard the call of God while he was still in Mesopotamia, before he went to Haran (Acts 7:2-3). Apparently Abram did not respond at once. Genesis 11:31 notes that Terah, Abram's father, took the family out of Ur and moved to Haran. Obviously, Abram did not obey the message until some time later, when God repeated His instructions.

One wonders what was going through Abram's mind between the time he first heard God's instructions and the time he acted upon God's call. Was he afraid? Was he too comfortable? Did Terah or Sarai or his responsibilities in the family business hold him back? Had he heard that Canaan was like the backwoods of Kentucky? Was he waiting for the Haran Hornets to win the Super Bowl? We'll never know. We just know that God told him more than once to get his body in gear and get truckin' out of town.

How many times does God have to tell us to do something? Most of the time the things that He asks us to do are not nearly so piercing as packing up everything and heading out to a place two weeks removed from civilization. "Follow me!" "Love the Lord with all your heart, mind and strength!" "Remember me!" Chances are, he has told us a zillion times, and we still haven't obeyed or, if we have, only in a half-hearted way. But God is patient, up to a point. If we don't obey within His tolerance quotient, He will arrange things so that we don't have much of a choice. Even then, His "encouragement to obey" is administered with love, and with a purpose that is grounded in our best interests.

When the Lord called Peter and Andrew, they dropped everything and followed Him (Matt. 4:20). They didn't even put their tools away. Their father's family business succession plan went in the tank. These untrained fishermen became two of the major figures in the spread of the good news of salvation.

When the Lord calls, let's make sure He doesn't get a busy signal. Otherwise, He may have to cut in on the line.

Genesis 12:7,8 - 13:4,18

"So he built an altar there to the Lord ... and called upon the name of the Lord." (12:7,8)

Just about every time that Abram and his entourage picked up and moved to another place, he built an altar to the Lord and called upon Jehovah's name. He wasn't trying to get God's favor by building the altar, nor did he point his face to the clouds and yell, "Are You still up there, God? Is anybody home?" The altar was built for worship through sacrifice and thanksgiving, and the calling was Abram's reaffirmation of his trust in God for guidance, safety and direction.

Good thinking on Abram's part. There were a lot of foreign gods out there in this unforgiving area populated by Abram's natural enemies. Not that the gods could do anything, but their devotees were less than hospitable to those of different persuasions. And Satan, knowing that the family tree was continuing to grow to the inexorable conclusion of the birth of Jesus, was still frantically trying to chop away at the roots. Abram knew by faith that he was on the winning side, and kept in close touch with God. There were no letters from God to Abram returned with the notation, "No Forwarding Address."

In fact, it appears that the only time he didn't build an altar was when he went to Egypt, where he shouldn't have gone anyhow. (Egypt, in Scripture, is almost always a type or picture of the world, which by its nature is against God.) It's hard to give thanksgiving to God and ask His guidance while doing something contrary to God's instructions or being someplace where God isn't welcome.

As we hurtle on through life with its various stages, times and challenges, it's necessary for us to remember to "build an altar and call upon the name of the Lord." On the altar which we build, we are told to offer ourselves as a living sacrifice to God as a spiritual act of worship, an offering of thanksgiving (Romans 12:1-2). Only by this act can we realize the full effect and the complete joy of our relationship with God the Father through Jesus Christ, who is our Sacrifice for sin. We then can call upon His Name for guidance, safety and direction until we reach our final destination, which Jesus is now preparing for us (John 14:1-3).

By the way, don't take any side trips to Egypt. Satan is the travel agent, and in his motels, they don't leave the light on for ya.

Genesis 12:1-5

"The Lord had said to Abram, 'Leave your country, your people and your father's household, and go to the land I will show you'... And Lot went with him." (12:1,4)

For all the faith that Abram had, for all the confidence he had in God's purposes and His word, he still had a tendency throughout his life to add something of his own ideas to the mix. This was true even in God's first recorded instruction to Abram. He was told to hit the trail without any family baggage; but he took along his nephew, Lot, which turned out to be like taking along the village idiot with you and your date to the high school prom.

Lot continuously gave Abram fits. He was the proverbial guy who is in the family business only because he is in the family. The guy who can't even find his way to the men's room without help, which becomes a greater problem because he sits around all day drinking coffee. When the big deal comes, he messes it up by making a pass at the buyer's wife. He gets rich and powerful on the family coattails, becomes a politician and proceeds to destroy the family name.

After Lot became wealthy through his "Abram connection," his employees started hassling Abram's employees (vs. 7). So Abram told Lot to take his choice of the territory and split and, of course, Lot chose the best of the land (vs. 10-11). Then Lot moved to Sodom, a city which made Las Vegas look like a religious commune. He and all his retinue were carried off by marauding tribes, and Abram had to rescue him (14:12). Then Abram ended up pleading with God to save Sodom, in order to save Lot's skin (18:22 et seq.) He was Abram's Excedrin headache.

We tend to do the same thing as Abram did, adding things to God's instructions. When he tells us to simply live out the Gospel in front of others, we come up with all sorts of extraneous religious hoops we try to jump through in order to appear righteous. When we're told to focus on His kingdom and His righteousness (Matthew 6:33), we think we can do it better with one eye on the cash register (Matthew 6:24). When we're told to trust in His wisdom and follow His directions (Proverbs 3:5-6), we tend to factor in our own faulty judgment and irrelevant experiences. And we end up with a lot of Lots in our lives.

Adding to God's instructions will always add expense and complexity to our daily living. Following His Word precisely yields simplicity and peace.

Genesis 12:2-3

"I will make you into a great nation and I will bless you; ...and all peoples on earth will be blessed through you." (12:2-3)

What a God we have! He chose Abram as an object of His blessing, and through him blessed the entire world to come. Abram was not only the father of many nations, but also the father of the line through which the Messiah Jesus came. Although obedient to God's call, Abram was an imperfect channel. He took Lot with him, although he was told to leave his father's household and his people. He didn't stop in Canaan, which was to be the land for his offspring, but continued through to the Negev, a desert place. He went to Egypt, a country foreign to the worship of the true God, in order to escape a famine rather than depending on God as his provision. He lied to Pharaoh in order to save his own skin, rather than depending on God for his protection. He became impatient for God to act in granting him a son and heir, choosing rather to father a son through Hagar, with disastrous consequences which remain to this day. Yet God chose to bless Abram in his imperfection.

In similar fashion, He chooses to bless us in our imperfections. Yes, like Abram, we sometimes suffer the temporal consequences of our misdeeds. But read Ephesians 1 and count your blessings. Every spiritual blessing in Christ. Holy and blameless in His sight. Redemption through His blood. Forgiveness of sins. The knowledge of His will. The presence of His Spirit. How do we spell R-E-L-I-E-F? It's not through Rolaids! And Ephesians 2:4-9 tells us it's not through our efforts, either. It's all by His grace.

God produced in Abram a heart that honored Him. Although Jeremiah 17:9 points out accurately that, "The heart is deceitful above all things and beyond cure," God will create in us a pure heart if we, like David, so desire; "Create in me a pure heart, O God, and renew a steadfast spirit within me" (Psalm 51:10). A heart that is tuned in to God's way, subject to His will and devoted to His worship. Still imperfect and subject to failure and indiscretions, but full of love for and thankfulness to a God Who is intent on blessing such a heart.

Although we may never be another Abram, we can affect our world. Billy Graham is the most famous and effective preacher of our day, but there was a man with a heart for God who pointed Billy to faith in

Jesus. Through that uncelebrated man the nations of the world have also been blessed.

The spark in our imperfect hearts can be used by God to light a fire which will illuminate the path to Himself for countless others.

Genesis 12:10-20

"Say you are my sister, so that I will be treated well for your sake and my life will be spared because of you." (12:13)

Famine in the land. Growling stomachs. All the troops are getting restless and even the food stamps are gone. Lamech's Tavern is out of brew and the local Food Lion doesn't even have a can of sardines. It's a downer in the desert, a nasty in the Negev.

Hey, there's always Egypt. Plenty of food there. Maybe even leeks and onions and garlic and all that good stuff. To the camels and on to Egypt! We can make it by dinner time! I can taste the wine and cheese already!

Oops. Forgot one thing. Sarai is a real looker, and probably will be approached to be on the centerfold of Playboy, Egyptian edition. If they know that Sarai is my wife, they'll ice me and move in. Funny about those Egyptians. They respect marriage, but have little concern for life. Pharaoh will make sure that Sarai is unattached before she hits the harem.

Come to think of it, there may be a way out. Sarai is really my half-sister, so we can tell them that and it's a little bit true. At least they won't kill me. Take off the rings, and we'll be in good shape. If worse comes to worse, she can tell Pharaoh she has a headache.

They fooled everyone but God. For awhile it worked well. Sarai wowed them all, not only with her beauty, but with her personality and character. (The word "praise" (hallal) in vs. 15 is nearly always used in the Scripture for the worship of God.) Pharaoh's harem recruiters were on their way to Abram's house. And because of Sarai, the locals tried to impress Abram with all sorts of goodies: oxen and sheep and donkeys and servants and even a two-humped camel with a built-in feed bag and four-legged drive.

But a half-truth with God is no better than a bald-faced lie. It has the same results: disaster for everybody. Pharaoh and all the palace people lost their health; Sarai lost her dignity; and Abram lost his reputation. Sure, he got a lot of stuff, but his testimony was kaput. Pharaoh would not have been interested in Abram's God. He was ticked. All because of a lapse in faith (that God would provide their needs in the Negev) that led to a bad decision (going to Egypt) which fostered a worse idea (a half-truth) which created a situation that covered everyone with paint when it exploded. And all the stuff just led to a fight with Lot when they got home.

The whole truth is the last defense against disaster. It may hurt, but in the end it limits the damage and cuts the cost. "Kings ... value a man who speaks the truth" (Proverbs 16:13). So does God.

A View of Genesis

••

Genesis 13:5-13

"So Lot chose for himself the whole plain of the Jordan and set out toward the east.... Lot lived among the cities of the plain and pitched his tents near Sodom" (13:11-12).

There is a fundamental scientific law called the Second Law of Thermodynamics, which states that all systems, if left to themselves, become degraded or disordered. The condition of my desk is proof positive of the vitality of this law. Some would say the same of my mind. Without further comment on that possibility, it can be said that this concept is true with respect to a person's spiritual condition. If it is not carefully tended and vigorously exercised, deterioration will inevitably set in. This certainly was the case with Lot.

Lot started out by hanging around Abram, and in the process became very wealthy. Pretty soon the neighborhood wasn't big enough for both of them. So Abram offered Lot the first choice, and Lot looked around for the best place to set up his digs. He looked east and west, north and south, and decided on the fertile plain of the Jordan. Beautiful country. Loamy soil. Green grass and stately trees. Better Homes and Gardens would have given it the #1 rating.

But it turned out to be near Sodom, which was so evil that even the Mob would have been an improvement. Al Capone would have won the Mister Kleen Citizen of the Year Award. Because Lot chose to get close to Sodom, its influence got close to him. Pretty soon he moved downtown (14:12), and then he became the mayor (19:1). The final straw was his offer of his two virgin daughters to the homosexual mob in order to protect two visitors, which turned out to be avenging angels (19:5-9). He had hit bottom.

We're told that Lot was still a believer (2 Peter 2:7), although if a trial had been held on that issue, there probably would not have been sufficient evidence to convict him. We do know that living in that condition was no fun for Lot; "...for that righteous man, living among them day after day, was tormented in his righteous soul by the lawless deeds he saw and heard" (2 Peter 2:8). His soul was still righteous, but his life was a mess. And he paid dearly for it.

Had Lot stayed close to Abram and his godly influence, participating in

from the Rumble Seat of a Two-Humped Camel

71

the spiritual exercises which were common to Abram, all this would not have happened. The same is true with us. If we pay attention to our spiritual health, we will take the bus right past Sodom and never even stop there. Its attractions, however beautiful, will not suck us in.

Let's not let our spiritual systems become degraded or disordered. Exercise. Eat the right spiritual food. Become a spiritual astronaut and escape the Second Law of Thermodynamics.

····································

Genesis 13:14-18

"The Lord said to Abram after Lot had parted from him, ...'Go, walk through the length and breadth of the land, for I am giving it to you.'" (13:14,17)

The "Me Generation" of this age is nothing new. Lot was a prime example, who put his interests first when given the chance. Come to think of it, so did Adam. Cain. Lamech. Most everybody who has ever seen the light of day.

Abram, however, was different. He was entitled to tell Lot that he, Abram, both as a function of age and family status, was the 800-pound gorilla who takes whatever he wants. But he gave Lot first crack at the territory when the split occurred. In effect, he gave Lot, choosing as a man without God's input, the choice; his faith in God permitted him to do this, knowing that the Lord would make it all work out in the end.

After Lot left, God confirmed Abram's actions and expectations. "Look as far as you can see, Abe. It's all yours. And your descendants. And by the way, you're going to have a bundle of descendants. Like the dust of the earth, with no Dustbuster in sight."

Most of us are like Lot. Cutting across four lanes to get two car lengths in front so we can wait 10 more seconds at the next light. Cut that lady off moving toward the checkout counter with 12 items, because we only have eight and it's going to cost us two minutes. The garage sale opens at 8 AM with no pre-sale? Get there at 7 to make sure we get first look-over. A group home? Not in my back yard.

In the long run, the Abrams prosper. The ones who aren't particularly worried about getting ahead by virtue of greater speed or the all's-fair-in-love-and-war attitude. Or the chop-him-off-at-the-knees-so-he-won't-pass-me-up move. Or the I'm-senior-to-him-so-I-get-the-office-with-the-window declaration. These guys eventually mess up, burn out, run in and go down. But the Abrams, the ones who let God run the show and make the choices, end up with the peace and the health and the good reputation and the measure of prosperity that God gives. You don't need a CPA to figure out that these things add up to happiness and contentment. So it was with Abram.

Paul tells us that we should "[d]o nothing out of selfish ambition or vain conceit, but in humility consider others better than yourselves. Each of you should look not only to your own interests, but also to the interests of others" (Philippians 2:3-4). This kind of attitude is possible only when God is in control. He was with Abram. He wasn't with Lot. The results speak for themselves.

"God opposes the proud, but gives grace to the humble" (James 4:6). Leo Durocher was wrong. Nice guys don't finish last.

Genesis 14:1-16

"When Abram heard that his relative had been taken captive, he called out the 318 trained men born in his household and went in pursuit ... He recovered all the goods and brought back his relative, Lot..." (14:14,16).

Several generations before this occurrence, Cain had asked a question of God, "Am I my brother's keeper?" (Genesis 4:9) Abram didn't have to ask the question. He just gathered up all the available bodies as soon as he heard of Lot's predicament, and off he went to bring him back. And it wasn't like Abram had numbers superiority. He lined up against five kings and their troops, armies that had already swept through Canaan and mopped up everything in their path. Their numbers were similar to the Midianites of Gideon's time, possibly as many as 135,000 men (Judges 8:10). Something like the McKees Rocks Mud Hens going up against the Chicago Bulls, with 50 Michael Jordans on the other side.

Abram didn't even break a sweat. He knew that God was with him, and his duty was to rescue his family. Impossible odds — for the other side. Soon it was all over, and Abram returned with Lot, who, by the way, went right back to Sodom.

Abram was the kind of person Paul speaks about in Galatians 6:9-10: "Let us not become weary in doing good ... As we have opportunity, let us do good to all people, especially to those who belong to the family of believers." Think about what Abram did:

→ He risked his life and his servants to rescue somebody who had taken advantage of his generosity; shown no sign of gratitude for his help; been a constant irritant to Abram and his shepherds; and grabbed the most attractive piece of property at the first opportunity.

→ He left his peaceful existence to fight for a man who had little or no public testimony for God, who was a prominent person in what perhaps was the most wicked city which ever existed, and who appeared to be unrepentant.

But Abram was like his God. Merciful. Forgiving. Loving. Longsuffering.

So off they went, Abram, his servants, and God in command. Lot found himself back in Abram's debt again, a debt which Abram never tried to collect.

Are we our brother's keeper? Yes, we are. Even the ugly brother? They're all pretty in God's sight. Shouldn't he get what he deserves? God hasn't treated us as we deserve, has He?

The hand which we extend to our brother may be the hand which God uses to draw that brother to Himself. Give that Lot in your life a hand!

Genesis 14:17-24

"Abram said to the king of Sodom, 'I have raised my hand to the Lord, God Most High, Creator of heaven and earth, and I have taken an oath that I will accept nothing belonging to you...; so that you will never be able to say, 'I made Abram rich.'" (14:22-23)

Two kings met Abram when he returned with Lot and his entourage. One was from God, the other was from Sodom. God's man brought a blessing; the king of Sodom brought an agenda. The Sodomite knew a good thing when he saw it, and immediately figured out how he could use the situation to his advantage. He had headed for the hills in the battle (14:10), but hurried to the winner's circle to get next to Abram. "You take the goodies, Abe; I'll keep the people. That's a good deal for everybody."

Sometimes the biggest battles in life come after a major conflict is won. Especially when there's a couple of bucks involved. And it all seems so legitimate. The battle was the Lord's, and Abram acknowledged that by his actions with Melchizedek. Now the king of that wicked city appears, and wants Abram to join him in dividing up the spoils of war. "I know what you're up to," says Abram, "and I'm not in any way going to be associated with you. Even if it costs me big bucks. You'll claim that we were in this together, and you made me rich by giving me the loot! Keep it yourself!" He was not going to enter any arrangement with someone who typified all that was against God's character.

We might think that since God won the battle through Abram and his Strike Force, the Sodomite wasn't entitled to anything. It should have been all Abram's. But both the stuff and the people came from Sodom. It was of the world. God had a better reward for Abram — Himself! (15:1). Abram had fallen victim to the "stuff syndrome" before, when he collected the worldly goods from Egypt at the cost of his testimony. This time Abram's faith was great enough to give God the glory and look to Him for his recompense.

What is our expectation from doing God's business? Is it to be used for the glory of God, or for our gain from the hands of men? The gain can be in the form of an augmented pocketbook or an exalted name. Neither is legitimate in the service of the King of Kings. Christendom is littered with those who thought otherwise. It may be that we will be blessed in financial and/or other ways; if it's from the hand of God, we bless Him for it. If it's from the hand of men, like Abram, we reject it. And God will let us know the difference.

When we are involved in God's business, the rewards are usually out of this world.

"Then Melchizedek, king of Salem, brought out bread and wine. He was priest of God Most High, and he blessed Abram..." (18-19)

When I was a kid, my brother and I used to huddle by the radio (this was before TV, if such a time can be imagined) and listen to the Friday night lineup of *The Shadow, This is Your FBI, The Green Hornet* and similar fare. One of my favorites was *The Lone Ranger*. He and his side-kick, Tonto, would ride into a situation just in the nick of time, prevent certain disaster, jump on his faithful horse, Silver, and ride off yelling "Hi Ho Silver, Away!" While those who had just been rescued would breathe in wonder and amazement, "Who was that Masked Man?" It was goose pimple time. When the hero, instead of jumping into the sack with conveniently available women, would kiss his horse and ride off into the sunset. Until the next adventure.

Melchizedek, if I may say it reverently, was the Lone Ranger of Genesis 14. Abram had just won, through God's power, a tremendous battle with impossible odds. All the loot was laid out, ready for claiming. Big bucks. Instead of going back to his tents "near the great trees of Mamre at Hebron" where his altar was (13:18), Abram could have grabbed the gold and built himself a palace. And he had every right to do that. The King of Sodom was about to suggest that he do so.

Enter Melchizedek. "Abram, you have been blessed by God Most High" (El Elyon, which stresses the absolute superiority of the True God over other gods of man's invention). "Abram, get ready. The King of Sodom is about to offer you a deal you can't refuse. Turn it down. It's a trap, designed to get your eyes on the wealth of the world. El Elyon is your great reward." So Abram was prepared to do business with the Sodomite, God's way. He told him to stuff the stuff. Instead of building palaces, he built altars.

Materialism is one of the major, if not the biggest, distractions which we as Christians face. It takes our time, energy, efforts, emotion, and attention and turns us away from God. How easy it is to fall into that trap! We need to be prepared to withstand its siren song. But we have a Melchizedek. It is Christ Himself. "...Another priest like Melchizedek (has appeared), One Who has become a Priest not on the basis of regulation ... but on the basis of an indestructible life" (Hebrews 7:15 -

Genesis 15:1-21

"But Abram said, 'O Sovereign Lord, how can I know that I will gain possession of (the land)?'" (vs. 8)

SHOW ME THE MONEY! Abram must have been an ancestor of Jerry Maguire. God had given him an object lesson when Abram asked for some clue about who was going to be his heir (vs. 2-5), by showing him the stars and telling him that he was going to have to make that many reservations for the future family reunions. But Abram still wanted some assurance about the land, too. Not that he doubted God or His ability to make it work; he just wanted his comfort zone increased a little.

So God put together another demonstration and made a covenant out of it (vs. 18). He also gave Abram a little look into the future of this nation which was to be. There was going to be trouble (vs. 13); deliverance (vs. 14); peace for Abram (vs. 15). But it would take time, and everybody would have to have patience for all these things to occur (vs. 16).

Good old Abram. Just like us. We believe God when He speaks through His Word, but think it would be nice to have something tangible to sink our teeth into. In fact, a lot of people today are so into signs and wonders that when the clock strikes thirteen, they proclaim that a miracle has occurred, if not here, somewhere in the land inhabited by the fierce tribe of the Fuzzy Wuzzies. The rest of us know that it's just time to get the clock fixed.

Thomas had the same problem when Jesus had appeared to the disciples, and he was somewhere else. "Show me the nail marks," he said (John 20:24-25). Jesus gave the ground rules for all of us in His answer when He saw Thomas. "Because you have seen me, you have believed; blessed are those who have not seen and yet have believed" (John 20:29). There it is for us. "Faith comes from hearing the message, and the message is heard through the word of Christ" (Romans 10:17). He tells us through the Scriptures today what He told the people in person 2,000 years ago. "God the Father has sent Me to pay the price for your sin. I died, I rose, I live for you. Trust in Me, and you will live with Us forever!"

That is His covenant with us, His work, our faith. Like Abram's covenant, it won't always be easy for people of faith in this world. But God has provided deliverance, which gives us peace. And we must be patient for God to do His thing. He's in no hurry, and His timing is perfect.

Forget looking for the signs. God has already signed off on His Word. And through our faith, He lets us see everything clearly.

Genesis 16:1-3

"...The Lord has kept me from having children. Go sleep with my maid-servant; perhaps I can build a family through her." (vs. 2)

There are a lot of sincere people in this world. People whose motives are beyond suspicion. People who want to help so badly they try anything to alleviate the problem. Like the person who grabbed the first can of liquid he saw in order to put out the fire, and it turned out to be gasoline. "But he was so sincere," they said at his funeral.

Sarai was sincere. She undoubtedly knew of God's promise to Abram about his seed being as numerous as the stars in the heavens. But Abram was getting old, and she wasn't any junior miss, either. The biological clock wasn't just running out, it already was on sale at half-price in the antique store. Maybe she could help God, Abram, Hagar and herself with one bold, unselfish stroke. God was obviously in need of some assistance in handling His affairs; He had promised a child but hadn't delivered. Abram would get his long-awaited heir; Hagar would be elevated to a more honorable position in everybody's eyes as the "surrogate mother"; and Sarai would have her family, since it was common in that society for the children of a woman's servants to be regarded as her own. Great idea. Wonderful motives. Perfect solution. And Sarai was so sincere.

The results of the union between Abram and Hagar illustrate the disaster of formulating and executing a plan when the plan doesn't follow God's rules, even though everybody is so sincere and it seems so right. Hagar was an Egyptian, typical of the world. The Lord had His reasons for delaying the promised child. Abram's union with Hagar violated the monogamous husband-wife relationship set forth by God when Adam and Eve were brought together, never retracted by God but ignored by men under their "customary-practice" exception. And Sarai preempted God's responsibility to build the family. Disaster. Ishmael became the father of the Arab nations, Isaac the father of the Jewish people. One doesn't have to be a Ph.D. in political science to figure that this didn't turn out very well.

People try to please God today in many ways. Following the "golden rule." Going to church. Giving to the poor. Giving up something for Lent. We're very sincere. These things are obviously good things to do, but pleasing God by doing things, by religious or charitable works, is not His way. His way is the way of faith. Faith in Jesus' atoning sacrifice on the cross. Faith in following Him as He directs in His Word. Any other way, however sincere, will lead to disaster. Only this time, it will be eternal disaster.

If every one who was totally sincere was laid end to end, the line wouldn't reach one inch closer to God.

Genesis 16:5-15

"Then the angel of the Lord told her, 'Go back to your mistress and submit to her... I will so increase your descendants that they will be too numerous to count.'" (9-10)

Go back. Submit. Ugly words to a proud and angry person. "But Lord, you don't understand. I have been abused. I could sue Sarai and Abram for harassment and win big bucks. She has created a hostile environment in her house, and I have my rights. And this is all because of my pregnancy. The old man got me pregnant and she demoted me from the big house to the barn."

But God refused to litigate the case. He just told her to go back and submit, because that was her place of duty. Just because she was moved to a higher place on the social scale by Sarai and sent to bed with Abram didn't alter her position as a servant. As a matter of fact, it all went to her head. When she got pregnant, she became very uppity with Sarai because Sarai was childless. The old "I can do something you can't do" routine. Then she split when Sarai took offense and put her in her place.

Who have we ever met who relishes the word, "submit?" The worker doesn't want to submit to the boss; the wife to the husband; the kids to the parents; the populace to governmental authority. And nobody wants to submit to God. Yet that's what the Scriptures demand. Check out 1 Peter 2:13,18; Ephesians 5-22; 6:1,5; Colossians 3:18,20; James 4:17 and numerous other passages. By obeying this command for submission, we are told, we are doing things "for the Lord's sake." "For it is God's will that by doing good" (i.e, submitting to authority) "you should silence the ignorant talk of foolish men" (1 Peter 2:13,15). God has placed an order, an authority in the home, in the church and in the nations. When that order is broken and that authority disobeyed, chaos results. Just read the paper and view the current state of affairs in Hometown, USA, or anywhere in the world for that matter, and see the results of such rebellion.

God will take care of those who submit. Hagar wasn't being sent back to a warm, fuzzy situation with a benevolent mistress. She was being returned to a jealous and frustrated woman who didn't like her. But God didn't give her a transfer to a different department. He told her to light up her candle in her little corner of the world, and He would bless her.

The Lord has a place in mind for every one of us at any moment in time. We may not like where he has us, or He may be wanting us to go to a place we don't particularly want to go (remember Jonah?). But if we obey, if we submit to Him and to the authority He has placed in that location, we will be blessed. Sooner or later. Like Hagar. And that's a promise.

All God's commands are, in reality, promises to those who obey them.

Genesis 16:7-16

"(Hagar) gave this name to the Lord who spoke to her: 'You are the God Who sees me … '" (vs. 13)

Hagar was on her way home, on the road to Shur (vs. 7), which went from where she had lived with Abram and Sarai to Egypt. Over the desert and through the woods to grandmother's house we go! She would show them; she would go back to her home and her family and her gods; so much for that witch Sarai and the old geezer Abram. They wouldn't abuse her anymore!

But God had different ideas. The angel of the Lord found her and said, "Hagar, servant of Sarai, where have you come from and where are you going?" (vs. 7). Goodness me, Hagar must have thought. This guy knows who I am and who I belong to. How did he find me here in the desert? I better not tell him I'm just on my way to hang out at the mall.

Well, Hagar was right. God knew all about her, who she was, who she belonged to and why she was where she was. He even told her what her son-to-be-born would be named, and predicted his personality and his future. And guess what? He was right on the money, just like He always is. Hagar was impressed. So she gave the Lord a name, "You are the God Who sees me."

Hagar isn't the only one who was or is in God's sight. In Job 34:21 we read, "His eyes are on the ways of men, He sees their every step." Psalm 139 tells us that there is nowhere a man can go out of the presence of the Lord, from the heights to the depths, from the dawn through the darkness, whether in the womb or the grave. From the back of a camel to the driver's seat of a Maserati, from the bowels of a coal mine in Kentucky to the farthest reaches of outer space, there is no escape from the eyes of the One who covers the east to the west, the north to the south, from time to eternity.

The fact that He sees us means more than mere observation. He has a plan for each of us, just as He did for Hagar and her son. Although the pathway to completion of this plan may not always be strewn with roses, it is created in divine intelligence, accomplished by divine power, and designed for divine purposes. And those who are willing to move along this pathway are assured of the divine presence.

Put your camel in God's caravan. There are no curves in the trail ahead around which God has not already seen, and His eyesight is 20-20.

Genesis 17:1-27

"....The Lord appeared to (Abram), and said ... 'I will ... '" (vs. 1)

After God appeared to Abram and announced Himself ("I am God Almighty," vs. 1), He gave Abram fourteen "I wills" to think about relating to Abram and Sarai during the time of their conversation. Mostly, it was God doing the talking, with Abram flat on his face before Him. In reciting all these promises, God revealed a lot to Abram which is instructive to us as well.

If Abram was capable of rational thought while in the prone position, he might have tried to analyze these "I wills" to figure out how his life was going to be impacted from what God was saying. Let's think along with Abram.

The first thing that may have crossed his mind was that this was really happening, and it wasn't something caused by a vivid imagination or too much pepperoni pizza. Here was God Himself, and there was no doubt about it. (This is one of the several "theophanies," i.e., actual appearances of God on earth, which occur in the Old Testament.) And He was telling Abram something about Himself. "I am your God of power and provision, and I'm going to make things happen for you and Sarai, and through you for the generations to come." He was revealing the "Power Facet" of His character to Abram. While we don't have any "theophanies" today, believers have the Spirit of God within them to reveal His power to work in our lives what He has told us in His Word. Paul was a believer in this, as he said, "I can do all things in Christ Who strengthens me" (Philippians 4:13).

Then Abram may have gotten a glimpse of the extent of God's purpose for his life. "God is going to bless the world through me! Wow!" One can never tell how the world will be affected when God is doing His thing through that person's life. Think of Mother Teresa. Billy Graham. Chuck Colson. And a lot of other people whose names we'll never know this side of heaven. When we think of it, just affecting one person's world can make an eternity of difference for him or her.

Abram may also have recognized the demands of God's will while he

A View of Genesis

was there with his nose in the dirt. He got the message that God had spoken, and he was to obey. God's will for us is to obey His communication to us, and trust Him for the results. "Works for me!" is the proper response to His commands.

If Abram stopped to figure it all out, he may also have concluded that it was solely of God's sovereign grace that he had been chosen to be blessed by God. So it is with us. Why have we been blessed? Because it was God's choice to do so. Why did He choose us? Because He calls the shots the way He wants to.

His power. His purpose. His will. His grace. My obedience. Works for me!

Genesis 17:1-27

"This is my covenant with you and your descendants after you ... every male among you shall be circumcised." (vs. 10)

Recently, some billboards have appeared around town advertising a breast enlargement procedure — a complete job for $3,500. There are before and after pictures which illustrate the difference in dramatic fashion. Talk about making a mountain out of a molehill!

I'm told the reason for the demand for this augmentation is "self esteem." Considering the large number of women in silicone implant litigation, there must be a huge scarcity of self esteem around. Too bad someone can't bottle it and sell it. The greater question is why a woman's self esteem would be wrapped up in the size of her breasts; the answer apparently is that breasts make a woman sexually attractive, which is of great importance to her.

Sex is everywhere. It is the primal urge that can't be controlled by law, edict, pronouncement or command. Old as Adam and Eve, new as the latest issue of Playboy. Every society has had its problems with sexual promiscuity, and this present world is approaching the limits set by God for Sodom and Gomorrah.

Have you ever wondered why God chose circumcision as the sign of His covenant with Israel? Why would He not have chosen something more publicly visible? A ring in the nose. A pierced ear. A tattoo on the forehead. But no, He designated a procedure involving the male sex organ. Something private. Intimate. Designed to be sanctified and holy.

Yes, that's what I said, sanctified and holy. That's what God intended sex to be. Something between one man and one woman. No substitutions. No alternates. No varieties. And not just one at a time in successive relationships. Or one night stands. "Within the bonds of marriage" is the operative phrase here. Anything less or more is illicit, illegal (in God's Book) and immoral. Sin. Period.

Back to the covenant. Yes, it's true that circumcision is a hygienic procedure as well as a covenantal sign. God gets the maximum mileage out of His commands. But the primary reason for this sign is that God

A View of Genesis

desired that His people be sanctified and holy, set apart for Himself in a special, spiritually intimate relationship. And this was the best way to illustrate it. The marital relationship was established by God, one man and one woman, physically intimate. The spiritual relationship is now established by Him, one person and one God, spiritually intimate. Not that the procedure established the relationship; it was to be the sign of a committed relationship already established by faith.

There were those when Christianity was first established who taught that circumcision was necessary for salvation. Paul debunks that theory in Philippians 3:1-4. He says, "For it is we who are the circumcision, we who worship by the Spirit of God, who glory in Christ Jesus, and who put no confidence in the flesh" (vs. 3). In other words, those who are truly believers are the present day circumcision, the recipients of the new covenant made with us by God through Jesus Christ. We are to be sanctified and holy before God, in a spiritual and intimate relationship with Him.

The fastest thing that will destroy a marriage relationship is sexual infidelity. That's why the devil has always encouraged sexual stimuli, to denigrate the marital and family relationships and thereby weaken the moral and spiritual foundations of a society. He has been wildly successful throughout the history of man. In the same way, Satan will use whatever he can in order to disrupt the spiritual and intimate relationship each believer has with God. John in his first epistle refers to this as the "lust of the flesh, the lust of the eyes, and the pride of life." All these things tend to turn our attention away from God, to things that are attractive in the devil's domain.

Remember that each believer is a part of the church, the bride of Christ. Spiritual prostitution is a deadly disease. Every Christian must avoid it like the plague.

Genesis 17:1-3

"When Abram was ninety-nine years old, the Lord appeared to Him and said, 'I am God Almighty...'" (vs. 1)

"Abram fell face down" (vs. 3).

Have you ever heard a person exclaim, "Good Mohammed Almighty?" Or "Good Allah Almighty?" Or maybe "Good Maharishi Almighty?"

Not likely. It seems that only God Almighty, El Shaddai in the Hebrew, has the reputation or the clout to have His Name used for emphasis in speech, or as a curse word. Perhaps if men had an inkling Whose Name they were invoking they would be more careful in what they were saying. Abram was impressed. He fell on his face before El Shaddai.

El Shaddai means, "The Mighty One of resource or sufficiency." "El" sets forth His mighty power, and "Shaddai" (which comes from the Hebrew root word meaning "breast") signifies His exhaustless resources, invoking the image of a nursing mother. This was the understanding given to Abram as El Shaddai, God Almighty, appeared to Him on this particular occasion. After God introduced Himself, He followed with nine "I wills" in verses 2 through 8 with respect to Abram's future. God even changed his name to "Abraham," the "Father of many nations." Read this portion to see how Abraham was to be blessed by His El Shaddai. No wonder Abraham almost passed out.

The God of Abraham is our God as well. Scripture tells us that He is the same yesterday, today and forever. Abraham's El Shaddai, his God of power, provision and protection, is our El Shaddai. One writer has said, "What a stimulus to faith it is to know that we serve a God Who is all-sufficient, and Who is strong enough to overpower, able to overcome all obstacles, and equal to every occasion!"

Paul sums up what El Shaddai means to us in Romans 8:31-39. "... If God is for us, who can be against us? He Who did not spare His own Son, but gave Him up for us all, how will He not also ... graciously give us all things? ... For I am convinced that neither death nor life, neither angels nor demons, neither the present or the future, nor any powers, neither height nor depth, nor anything else in all creation, will be able to separate us from the love of God that is in Christ Jesus our Lord."

El Shaddai. If we really get the impact of all this, we, like Abraham, will fall on our faces before Him.

Genesis 18:1-15

"When he saw them, he hurried from the entrance of his tent to meet them... "(vs. 2). "So Abraham hurried into the tent ..." (vs. 6). "Then he ran to the herd." (vs. 7)

Every one is in a hurry. Jumping in line at the super market. Wolfing down a perfectly good dinner with hardly a taste. Cutting in and out of traffic. I don't put a sticker on my car that says, "Honk if you love Jesus," because I'm always in a hurry behind the wheel and my driving isn't a very good testimony! You all know what I mean. It seems like we're in such a hurry to get to the cemetery, we're just dying to get there.

All this is hurry for the wrong reasons. Save a few minutes. For what? To hurry to start or finish something else. For what? To get to some other activity which needs attention. For what? To make some more money or impress someone. Everything is an emergency. Our internal communication system is perpetually pre-set on 911. Someone has labeled it well — the tyranny of the urgent.

Except for one thing. Our commitment to God and to His program. Most of the time we're not very urgent about His business, because everything else crowds Him out. We put Him on the back burner because He doesn't usually turn up the heat. Sooner or later, though, He decides to get our attention. Then some of the other things have to wait. The deadline for this project will pass if we're flat on our backs in the hospital. We won't be able to go out to participate in this critically important function if there's 48 inches of snow on the ground and even the polar bears are staying home. And surprise, surprise! The function occurs without a hitch. The deadline for the project wasn't so rigid after all. Someone else filled in and did a remarkably creditable job.

Abraham had decided that God's business couldn't wait. He hurried. He ran. He told his servant to hurry. He told Sarah to bake a cake, quickly. God is to be served, and served with diligence and dispatch. Everything else can wait. There was more activity around Abraham's tent than ants exert at a picnic. And God's business got done. Both Abraham and Sarah found out that the impossible was going to occur.

We need to hurry to do God's business, too. This world is going to

A View of Genesis

"melt with a fervent heat." Explode. Disintegrate. We won't be here forever, either. Twenty minutes after we're gone and the wake is over, someone else will be doing our job. Probably better. What we hurry about on this earth probably won't amount to a hill of beans in eternity, except for that which is done for God. So relax about the things of this world, and put God's business into high gear.

If God were the IRS, most of us would be prosecuted for task evasion.

Genesis 18:12-14

"So Sarah laughed..." (vs. 12). ... "is anything too hard for the Lord?" (vs. 14).

A lot of people think that God is funny. Not ha-ha funny, but ludicrous. The idea that a Celestial Someone would have any interest in earth or man, when there are millions of galaxies out there bigger than ours and maybe more intelligent life, is preposterous. A figment of the imagination of some uninformed religious nut with a shortage of gray matter. An idea from someone whose elevator doesn't reach the top floor. Part of the dangerous religious right.

And as far as anything being too hard for the Lord, they have a perfect question. "Can God create a stone so large He can't move it?" They also have all sorts of explanations for miracles that Jesus did, as well as those found in the Old Testament. These are called "Fairy Tales" if an explanation can't be given, whether plausible or not. They think that the whole thing is such a hoot.

Other people have a basic belief in God, but snicker at the thought that He is really concerned about individual needs or desires. And even if He is, whether He is able or willing to do much about it. He's got bigger fish to fry, and besides, natural law or happenstance controls every situation. Still others really have a measure of faith but, as one author has put it, "Your God is Too Small." It's their opinion that miracles just don't happen in this multicultural, humanistic age. Yet one doesn't want to laugh out loud at the possibility. That person, heaven forbid, might be considered unspiritual.

Maybe that's where Sarah was, and she laughed. To herself. But God heard. Her womb was dead (Romans 4:19), but with God's touch, the impossible occurred; Abraham, through Sarah, true to God's promise, became the father of the lineage through which the entire world has been blessed.

God hears us as well, when we inwardly doubt the potential of our lives in His hands. We may laugh, snicker or smile at the thought that we can be a force for God. It doesn't escape His attention. Perhaps we have good reason to doubt. Our lives may not have been exemplary

A View of Genesis

Christian lives. We don't feel we have much, if any, ability. The opportunities just don't present themselves. We are in a situation where being forward about our faith would not be well received. We have more excuses than there are mosquitoes in Savannah. The result is that our "Christian Living Mechanism" is on the fritz. But God can fix it, regardless of what state of disuse or disrepair it's in. It's not too hard for Him. He can take that life which is only worth a laugh and make it a hilarious success.

By the way, God isn't interested in building a stone so big He can't move it. He never operates contrary to His purposes. Besides, He's too busy taking the laugh of unbelief and turning it into the laugh of incredible joy. And that's a laughing matter.

Genesis 18:16-19

Then the Lord said, "Shall I hide from Abraham what I am about to do?" (vs. 17)

How would you like to go out to the mailbox every morning and get a letter that says, "Dear Joe (or Suzie), This is what I'd like you to do today .... Love, God." In this letter would be detailed instructions for each minute of the day. Although this sounds like a good idea, we might regret it, because one day we might get a letter that starts, "Today you're going to have to suffer big time for My Name." Whoops. Time to go back to bed and pull the covers up over the head.

But God has a desire to communicate His will to us. We can see that His will is not always going to be a lark-in-the-park for us by looking at Abraham's life and the lives of many of the other Biblical heroes we read about. Nevertheless, we need to have the general gist of what God wants from us and for us and what's going on around us, as well as some specifics from time to time. Life goes along much more smoothly that way.

He can do this, if we are in a condition to hear what He's saying. Abraham was, and that's why God was interested in taking him into His confidence. Abraham was a man with a heart for God. Although he fell on his face now and then, he was a man full of faith, a man who trusted God. He was ready to listen, and ready to do God's will. Because Abraham trusted God, God trusted Abraham. So He told Abraham what He was going to do about Sodom.

So how do we get in this condition of readiness? It's not recommended that we go around living in tents like Abraham did, looking for God to appear to us. But He has given us the Bible, which is His Word. Through this, He gives us both general and specific directions concerning our actions and attitudes. But we have to read it to get the message. It doesn't come through osmosis or by watching a TV evangelist. Then He wants to hear from us in prayer. Not just, "Bless the lunch for all the bunch," and/or "Now I lay me down to sleep, I hope the kids don't make a peep," but talking with God about what's happening, appreciating Him for Who He is, and asking Him for His help and direction in dealing with what's around the next curve. The Bible has a term for this kind of relationship with God. It's called, "Fearing Him." This isn't a wide-eyed, hair-raising, hide-under-the-covers fear, but a proper appreciation of His Person, a ready obedience for His instructions, and a desire for His presence. David talked about this in Psalm 25:12-14: "Who, then, is the man who fears the Lord? He will instruct him in the way chosen for him.... The Lord confides in those who fear Him; He makes His covenant known to them."

Keep the lines open with God. You'll get the straight scoop from His Heavenly Headlines, hot off the press.

Genesis 18:20-33

"Far be it from You! Will not the judge of all the earth do right?" (vs. 25)

Looking at things through our eyes, I suppose we could imagine people on a picket line marching back and forth in front of the Pearly Gates, carrying megaphones and signs and shouting out, "God is Unfair!" After all, one guy who lived on Main Street in Jerusalem went to synagogue, gave tithes, observed all the holy days, didn't beat his wife, but was not admitted to heaven because he had not accepted Jesus as Messiah. But that skunk of a thief and murderer who died on a cross next to Jesus, there he is lounging around his mansion inside the gates, praising God with his harp. And he never even took any lessons.

The same thing happens with people from Chicago. And London. And La Paz and Shanghai. As Rabbi Kushner wrote in "When Bad Things Happen to Good People." Job wondered the same thing. Where is God when people are getting the shaft? When babies get AIDS. When crooks drive away from the probation office in Cadillacs, but guys who sweat and strain and work and struggle have their rusty Chevettes repossessed. When a woman who would be a great mother has a miscarriage, but a prostitute gets an abortion. God must be spending a lot of time at the mall, while the world is spinning out of control.

Well, regardless of how we might see it, the Judge of all the earth is still in His courtroom. But if He dealt out justice in strict observance of His rules, none of us would be here. He would have to be His own executioner, because we all would be on the wrong end of the firing squad. The issue is not God's fairness, it is our sinfulness. Yes, some are more wicked than others and seem to literally get away with murder, but that is a result of our sin and our world system and lawyers like Johnny Cochran. And babies get AIDS because of someone's misconduct, not because God is unfair. One person's sin affects a lot of people.

In this passage, Abraham is pleading with God to preserve Sodom for the sake of the righteous people that might be there, thinking mainly of Lot and his family. He appealed to God's sense of fairness, His moral justice. God really had every right to include Lot in the destruction as well, considering Lot's conduct. But Lot's heart was right (see 2 Peter

100

2:7). God listened to Abraham, but it was more as a result of His mercy than His moral justice.

In the end, the Judge of all the earth does right. Read Psalm 37 for a treatise on this whole matter. He will punish the wicked and save the righteous. The key here is God's definition of wicked and righteous. Those who accept Jesus, like the thief on the cross, are the righteous. Those who don't, even though we might think of them as good people, are the wicked. He has made this perfectly clear. And because He has announced His criteria clearly, He is perfectly fair.

In God's courtroom, Jesus' sacrifice is the only effective plea.

Genesis 18:20-33

"Then Abraham approached (the Lord)..." (vs. 23)

I remember in 6th and 7th grades, when we boys were starting to notice that girls were something other than nebniks to be avoided at all costs, we also started to wonder how we could approach them without our mouths going dry and, heaven forbid, our buddies finding out. The answer was, an Intercessor! Yes! "Psst! Hey, Alice! Jimmy likes you!" "Well, what was her answer???" "She rolled her eyes and stuck her tongue out." Rats. Bummer. Three or four of those experiences, and you decided to become a missionary in the darkest part of Africa.

Remember the story of Miles Standish? He tried this route with a woman named Priscilla. He sent his buddy, John Alden, to propose marriage to her. He found himself with an invitation to John's and Priscilla's wedding in the next day's mail. I don't think he sent an expensive gift. Well, win some, lose some, and some days you just get rained out. Such an intercessor John was.

Abraham was an intercessor, too. Only the stakes were much higher in this particular instance. Sodom and Gomorrah were about to go up in smoke. God had had it with them up to His eyeballs. The daily special was sin du jour. Even Larry Flynt would have been appalled. But Lot and his family were there, and God had shared with Abraham that for everybody in those cities, the fat lady was about to sing. And there would be no curtain call. Abraham approached the Lord, however, and pleaded with Him to save the city, even if only ten righteous people could be found. God said, "OK," but it wasn't even close. The whole place got nuked for the lack of ten people who were acceptable to God.

But Abraham tried. He was out there with a heart for people, pleading for the mercy of God. The Scripture tells us that this is what we should be doing, too. Paul tells Timothy, "I urge, then, first of all, that requests, prayers, intercession and thanksgiving be made for everyone..." (1 Timothy 2:1). What??? Pray for someone else?? What about MY wish list? Praying for ourselves is not God's idea of prayer. His idea is for us, most of the time, to pray and to intercede for others. That He will bless them. That He will spare them. That He will bring them to Himself. That His grace will be evident in their lives. Sometimes the results are not apparent, but that's God's problem, not ours. We are just told to pray.

It's a great privilege to be an intercessor. God comes close to us to listen, and we get farther away from ourselves. And God gives us the joy of seeing Him work in others' lives, in accordance with our prayers. Our hearts are enlarged, our horizons are expanded, our hands are extended.

And do you know what? It's good for relationships. It's awful hard to be angry with someone when you're interceding for him with God!

"Do not be deceived; God cannot be mocked. A man reaps what he sows." (Galatians 6:7)

This is one of the terrible chapters of Scripture. Lot found himself participating in, and next to, the most incredible and basest kinds of sin practiced by men anywhere, anytime. He may have thought he was sowing the good seed for the good times, but all he reaped was poison ivy.

He sowed the seed of "Being Mr. Nice Guy" with the men of Sodom. He ended up sitting in the gate of the city, a place of importance and respect (vs. 1). He called these miserable men "friends" (vs. 7). But when he tried to keep them from homosexual rape, even offering his two virgin daughters to them to satisfy their vile appetite, he found that he got less respect than Rodney Dangerfield (vs. 9).

Then he may have thought he had sown the seed of "Family Leadership" with his sons-in-law. In this culture, "Father Knows Best" was neither an idle statement nor a TV show. But when he warned them about the judgment to come, they sang a chorus of "Send In the Clowns" (vs. 14).

Lot sowed the seed of "Enjoy The World" with his immediate family, his wife and daughters. As a result, his wife had more respect for the things she was leaving behind than God's instructions to beat it out of Sodom and never look back. She ended up like a desert cactus covered with sulfurous salt spray. His two daughters (the same ones he had offered to the men of Sodom for sexual purposes, in order to protect the two men who turned out to be avenging angels) had such a lack of moral fiber that they got Lot sloshed on two successive nights and got pregnant by him (vs. 31-38). The children thus born, Moab and Ben-Ammi, were the line through which the Moabites and Ammonites came, heathen tribes which became the scourge of Israel.

Incredible. What a garden Lot planted. Produced something worse than ragweed to someone with a bad case of hay fever. It brings a question to mind, though, doesn't it? What kind of seed are we putting in our gardens? And even if we're planting the good seed, what kind of effort are we putting forth to cultivate it? Water it? Keeping the weeds and the varmints out?

The good seed (which Jesus says [Luke 8:11] is the Word of God), when planted with diligence and tended with love, will produce a garden that is fit for The King. Don't forget the gardening tools and the elbow grease.

"Now return (Abraham's) wife, for he is a prophet, and he will pray for you and you will live." (vs. 7)

Well, here goes Abraham again, dredging up the same deviousness as he got caught using down in Egypt (12:10-13). "Sarah is my sister." Same old same old. Been there, done that. One would think that God would get tired of the same sin and really whack Abraham a good one up along side of the head. As a matter of fact, this whole charade had been rolling around in Abraham's noodle for thirty years (vs. 13). Probably had Sarah confused, too. "What am I today, his wife, his sister, or his gofer? What dress should I wear?"

Very interestingly, God's view was different. He told Abimelech that if he touched Sarah, he would be history. "Return the man's wife, for he is a prophet..." (vs. 3, 7). Still looking out for Abraham. Why on earth would He put up with all this???

There may have been a couple of reasons.

First, Abraham was a man of faith, regardless of the occasional lapses he experienced. When a man has passed Faith 101, God sees him in a different light. He is one of God's own, one of His people. God saw Abraham as a prophet; Abimelech saw him as a lying jerk (vs. 9). Think about Lot. From our view, he was about as rotten as they come. From God's view, he was righteous (2 Peter 2:7). David was seen by his contemporaries on various occasions as a liar, an adulterer, a murderer, and a wimp. God saw him as a man after His own heart (Acts 13:22). So it is with us. Those who belong to Christ are seen by God through a different lens. As the hymn writer has said, "Dressed in His righteousness alone, faultless I stand before the Throne." Not that these lapses don't have their own consequences; Abraham's and David's produced chaos for generations to come. Ours may as well, and in some instances affect us directly. But God sees us in Christ. Perfect. Spotless. Amazing! That's grace!

Then God may have been strengthening Abraham's faith for the big test, which was coming later. The sacrificing of Isaac. Could Abraham have handled this with flying colors without supreme confidence in God? No way. How about us? Think of all the times God has protected us from the potential results of our sin and unfaithfulness. Even the computer couldn't keep track. It's not because He overlooks it, or lets us get away with something we think He may not see. Maybe He's preparing us for something really really big. Strengthening our faith in His purposes for our life.

Regardless of the reason for God's protection and His view, Abraham didn't take advantage of his position before God. Neither should we. He took instruction from these situations, and gave thanks to God for it. We must do the same.

Genesis 21:1-7

"...The Lord did for Sarah what He had promised." (vs. 1)

Promises, promises. Promises are made to be broken. "I promise I'll never do that again." "Promise me you'll be home at nine." "Lord, if you help me out this time, I promise I'll serve you forever." Most promises are about as reliable as our New Year's Resolutions. If someone says his promise is like money in the bank, better make sure he's not the lookout man for Bonnie and Clyde.

God's promises are different. He always keeps His word. In fact, His promises are often in the form of covenants, with a particular person, nation, or even all mankind as the beneficiary. And His covenant, His promises, cannot be broken. None of them. Paul tell us, "For no matter how many promises God has made, they are 'Yes' in Christ" (2 Corinthians 1:20).

That's what Sarah found out. God had promised a son, and she had laughed as a cynic. Now the son is here, and Sarah laughs again, only this time with joy and amazement. And her world laughed joyously with her (vs. 6); had she told anyone a year previously that she would have a son at her age, they would have laughed Sarah all the way to the funny farm.

God has also made many promises to us, all of which are there in His First Eternal Bank of Promises. The only thing we need to do is make a withdrawal. There are a couple of requirements, however. First, we have to have proper identification. Ever go into a bank and try to cash a check with no identification? It's tough enough to do even with a picture license, two credit cards, a Wheaties box top and an excuse from your mother. Well, our identification in His First Eternal Bank of Promises is provided by Jesus Himself. He knows us. He said, "I am the Good Shepherd. I know my sheep.." (John 10:14). He knows us by name, and He also knows our spiritual condition. He knows if we belong to Him. If we have trusted Him for salvation, we are approved to make a withdrawal. If not, better try the Devil's Bank of Broken Promises down the street. The second requirement is that we have to ask. Just go to Jesus, the Head Teller, and ask for one of His promises. It's right there, in the Inexhaustible Vault. Alone? "I will never leave you nor forsake you" (Hebrews 13:5). Worn out? "Those who hope in the Lord will renew their strength, they will soar on wings as eagles" (Isaiah 40:31). Confused and afraid? "I will instruct you ... in the way you should go; I will counsel you and watch over you" (Psalm 32:8). And on and on and on.

The best promise is eternal life for those who trust Jesus. See John 3:16. Zillions of people have withdrawn that promise, but there's still enough there for everyone. Just make sure you get yours. It's the only legal tender accepted at the Gate of Heaven.

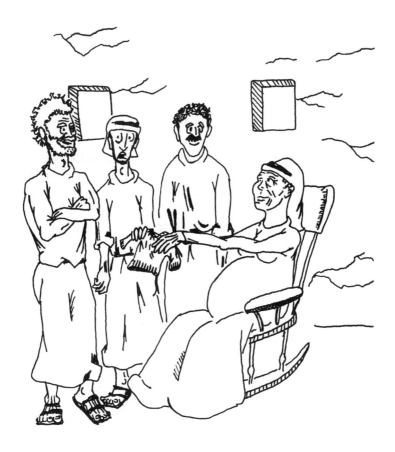

"...The Lord did for Sarah what He had promised." (vs. 1)

Genesis 21:8-21

"The matter distressed Abraham greatly because it concerned his son."
(vs. 11)

Talk about a dysfunctional family. The father is sent to bed with the maid by his wife. The maid gets pregnant and has a son. Then the wife gets pregnant long after she is physically able, and also has a son. The older boy starts to harass the younger boy, because the kid is getting all the attention and he sees his own inheritance going out the window. The maid hates the wife, and the wife hates the maid and her son, and tells the old man to kick them out the door. The new son just lies there, and eats and sleeps and dirties his diaper. The father gets upset, because he loves both his sons. God gets into the act and tells the father, "Do what your wife says and give the maid and her kid the boot. Not to worry, I will take care of the boy." This has more possibilities than "As the World Turns."

God uses all sorts of confused situations to get His point across. Interestingly enough, invariably these situations are created by man since, as the Scripture says, God is not the author of confusion. But He gets mileage out of everything. This brouhaha with Abraham, Sarah, Hagar et al., in which Hagar and Ishmael find themselves out in the cold, ends up as the happening Paul uses to illustrate to the Galatians the difference between trying to gain access to God through ceremonial religion (in this case, circumcision and doing the works of the law, which is impossible) and faith (which is the key to a relationship with Him). The Galatians had been told by certain Jewish teachers, Peter among them (see Galatians 2:11-14), that they had to live according to the law, including circumcision. Paul calls the teachers hypocrites, and then tells the people that because they have been saved through faith, they are like Isaac, who was a son produced by faith. They are not like Ishmael, the son of the slave woman, who was produced by natural means (the flesh). Therefore, in God's economy, the work of the flesh means nothing, and must be cast away (like Ishmael and Hagar) in favor of faith in Christ Jesus. "For in Christ Jesus neither circumcision or uncircumcision has any value. The only thing that counts is faith expressing itself through love" (Galatians 5:6).

A View of Genesis

This illustration is very appropriate for us today. A great number of people are depending on their religion to make them acceptable to God. The question to be answered is not, "Am I keeping the tenets of my religion?" (as the teachers were trying to tell the Galatians). The question is, "Have I received Jesus Christ by faith, and am I depending on His work alone for my salvation?" (as Paul told the Galatians). God's blessing to Abraham came through Isaac, the son of faith, and not through Ishmael, the son of the flesh. Our blessing comes through faith, and not through religion or works.

The Religion Road has a lot of toll booths, and never gets us anywhere. The Faith Highway is free, and leads directly to Heaven.

Genesis 21:14-21

"Then God opened her eyes, and she saw a well of water." (vs. 19)

There they were. Out wandering around in the desert. Hot sun. Food gone. No water. Vultures starting to circle. No road signs to the next service plaza. Nobody to turn to. Road patrol doesn't come this way. No hope. One gets the idea that Hagar and Ishmael were in trouble, big time.

Yes, they were. Except for one thing. God was aware of what was going on. Hagar must have forgotten about the first time she was in the desert (see Genesis 16:7-14). That time, she was running away of her own accord, seventeen years ago when she was pregnant with Ishmael and Sarah was jealous and got ugly. God saw her then, too. "She gave this name to the Lord who spoke to her: 'You are the God who sees me'" (16:13). How soon she forgot!

She forgot about God's presence. She also forgot God's promise made to her at the same time, about Ishmael having a future. And she forgot about God's provision of a well when she was wandering around before, which she had called Beer Lahai Roi - "Well of the One Who sees me" (16:14). Then she forgot how God had protected her out there in the desolation. Must have been spiritual Alzheimers.

It wasn't that God was keeping track of her because He had a guilty conscience about telling Abraham to boot her out of the compound. She and Ishmael brought this on themselves, being uppity with Sarah and nasty toward Isaac. Probably stuck their tongues out at Abraham, too, when he wasn't looking. Not a good idea for slaves, a status they had not lost even though Ishmael was Abraham's son. They doubtless saw that their fortunes were headed south when Isaac arrived, especially since they could see that his birth was by Divine intervention. Better discretion would have suggested that they go along with the program.

But God bailed them out, true to His promises. "Hey! Hagar! Open your peepers! There's water over yonder. Give Ishmael a drink and two aspirins, and he'll be all right in the morning!" And thus it was.

Ever think you're out in the wild and the wolves are getting a little closer? God sees you. Provisions have run out and the golden arches are no where in sight? His hands are not empty. Self-help is not an option any more? His arms have lost none of their strength. Future looks as bright as the bottom of a shaft in a coal mine at midnight on a stormy night in Utah? He still has a purpose for you.

Open your eyes and look for God. He's not hard to see. He glows in the dark.

Genesis 21:22-32

"God is with you in everything you do. Now swear to me here before God that you will not deal falsely ... Show to me and the country where you are living as an alien the same kindness I have shown to you" (vs. 22-23).

Abraham was on display. He was wealthy, famous, and powerful. And that got a lot of attention. But there was something about him that caught the eye of Abimelech, the boss man of the Philistines. Somehow, Abraham had succeeded in demonstrating that God was responsible for his success, and not his own cleverness or his own ingenuity. Sure, Abraham worked at his business; he just didn't sit in the office with the cattle and the sheep milling around, and an angel doing the milking and the shearing. But it was obvious to Abimelech (and no doubt to others) that God was involved. Abraham's life was testimony to that fact.

Seeing that Abraham was tight with God, Abimelech decided to make sure he wasn't going to get on Abraham's hit list. So he proposed his version of the NATO treaty, and Abraham agreed. Was it to Abraham's advantage or detriment to do this? It really didn't matter, since God was with him anyway, and he wasn't compromising his ethics, morals, or spiritual principles by signing. In fact, as a part of the deal, Abimelech returned a well that had been stolen by his servants from Abraham. So everybody lived happily ever after (at least for a little while).

Those of us who call ourselves Christians are on display, too. Everything we say, everything we do. It doesn't matter whether we are in high society like Abraham, or just an everyday-go-to-work-on-the-bus Johnny Bust-your-rump. But it isn't our worldly success which people use to figure out whether God is with us. They will judge that by our attitudes and actions, which, by the way, speak a lot louder than our words. With Joseph, it was apparent that God was with him, even though he was in the slammer on a false charge of attempted rape. With Daniel, it was apparent God was with him, even though he was eyeball to eyeball with some undernourished lions. With Shadrach, Meshach and Abednego, it was apparent that God was with them, even though they went out of the frying pan and into the fire. And in all those cases, the biggies ended up lining up right behind them, trying to hang on to their coattails to get on God's good side.

Paul, in Ephesians, tells us that we should be "walking" in a way that reflects our confession. "Walk ... worthy of (your) calling" (Ephesians 4:1); "walk no longer as the Gentiles walk," i.e., in an ignorant and sensual manner (4:17); "walk in love" (5:2); "walk as children of light" (5:8); "walk circumspectly," i.e., wisely (5:15). In short, letting the Holy Spirit through the Word of God keep our steps pointed in the right direction. Abraham, Daniel, and a whole host of others did. We can, too.

If people are going to read us like a book, we need to make sure that the pages speak volumes for God.

Genesis 22:1-19

"Some time later God tested Abraham ... then God said, 'Take now your son, your only son, Isaac, whom you love, ... and go to the region of Moriah. Sacrifice him there as a burnt offering ... '" (22:1-2).

Wow. What must have been going on in Abraham's mind, heart and stomach when he got this message? *My only son. My pride and joy. I love him so much! Ishmael is history, Isaac is my only hope for the future. Does it have to be Isaac? I'll give all my possessions. Take me instead. But Isaac? How can I tell Sarah?*

What was God doing? Is He such a Supernatural Sadist that He would torture a man who was an obedient servant, a man of faith, His friend? What kind of reward was this for a lifetime of devotion? Does He stay awake nights thinking up these incredible tests for people like Abraham and us to pass? Does He howl with glee when we sweat bullets?

Well, God is not a sadist. Nor does he have a staff of conundrum connivers conspiring to drive us to drink, or like Jonah, head off in the opposite direction. And His heart aches with us when we are hurting. But in order to understand this, we have to know what God's tests are all about.

In the first place, God doesn't test people, wondering how they are going to make out. He already knows. Years ago I taught in a college. I gave tests in order to see what a student knew and to provide a grade for his or her work. I never knew (although I had an idea who was going to do well and who was going to bomb) what the results would be until the test was over. But God has a handle on that before He starts the examination session. His purpose in testing is to prove a point, instruct the testee, and illustrate to those who observe.

In the strict sense of the word, God was not *testing* Abraham, He was *proving* him. If an engineer designs a bridge, he doesn't run a 20-ton truck over it after it is constructed to see whether it will stand under that kind of a load, waiting breathlessly for the results. He runs the truck over it to prove to the observers that it will stand firm. God was hitting Abraham with the 20-ton truck to prove that Abraham had the

116   *A View of Genesis*

faith superstructure to hold up under this most incredible of requests. He was proving that Abraham had such a faith that he was going to do exactly what God said, even though it cut his heart out to do so. Further, He was instructing Abraham in his capacity as the father of many nations; it would be necessary for Abraham to continually and without reservation trust the Almighty to fulfill such a role. And by this event, God was illustrating to the world to come that it is only faith that pleases Him, and that only those who walk in faith are able to handle and overcome any situation which will face them.

Romans 4 designates Abraham as the "Father of all the faithful." Let's join the family, and be instructed by the experience of this proven, faithful father.

Genesis 22:1-19

"Early the next morning, Abraham got up and saddled his donkey. He took with him ... his son, Isaac." (vs. 3)

Abraham didn't procrastinate at all when God told him to do something. Even when it was as tough an assignment as this — the sacrifice of his son. Morning came. The sun peeked over the mountain. Abraham emerges from his tent. "OK, guys, feet on the deck! Up 'n at 'em! Let's get with it!" How could he be so ready to do such an impossible deed?

In a word, faith. Faith that God knew what He was doing. Faith that God had something up His sleeve that was going to make everything come out all right. Faith that God's promise to bless the world through Isaac and his line was yea and amen. Did Abraham have a hint about a resurrection? "I and the boy (will) go over there. We will worship, and then we will come back to you" (vs.5). What did he mean by "we"? He certainly didn't have a canary in his pocket or a dog on a leash.

When we think about it, God had prepared Abraham for this moment. God had been working on Abraham's faith for a long time. From the days in the business world back in Mesopotamia when God had told Abraham to load up the caravan and head south, to the covenant of circumcision (which had to be somewhat of a bizarre experience for him and his household), to the lessons that his failures had taught him in Egypt, to the miraculous conception and birth of Isaac and a lot of other experiences we may know little or nothing about, Abraham was being prepared by God. And now the defining moment was here. The moment which has gone down in the Scriptures as one of the huge highlights of faith that never hit the evening news.

Remember Esther? She had been prepared for a defining moment as well. Haman, the Hitler of his time, had snookered the king into socking it to the Jews. Esther, the Jewish queen, was told by Mordecai, her uncle, to do her thing to save her people. "And who knows but that you have come to royal position for such a time as this?" (Esther 4:14). That's exactly why she was there. She had her Divine preparation for a designed participation.

A View of Genesis

Each one of us has been and is being prepared by God for some purpose. We have good experiences that encourage, difficult experiences that instruct and strengthen. Some laughs, some tears. Some hots, some knots, some shots. But if we really sit back and look at things, we can see how God has steered the ship through the rocks and the shoals, allowing a few scrapes on the hull and maybe a few holes in the side, but always above the water line. Building our faith. Getting us ready for the big show.

So when the curtain goes up and the show begins, don't forget that God has taken you through a lot of rehearsals. As they say on Broadway, "Break a leg!"

Genesis 22:1-19

"Abraham built an altar ... He bound his son Isaac and laid him on the altar" (vs. 9).

"Isaac's momma didn't raise no dummy." So said the preacher. And that was true. Here was Isaac, spending some quality time with his daddy on their way to worship. He knew the routine. Fire? Check. Wood? OK. Something missing here. Where was the sacrifice?

He didn't have to wait very long to find out.

Abraham was 120 years old. Isaac was 20. One would surmise that Isaac was not a 90-pound weakling. Neither had he been kept in a climate-controlled room and fattened up with potatoes and butter, prepared physically, mentally and spiritually for this event. Sarah most likely had explained to him why Ishmael had been given the gate. Doubtless Abraham had told him that he, Isaac, was God's man through whom blessing was to come to their posterity and to all the nations. Most of us, if we had been Isaac, would have thought that the old man had flipped his lid, and taken off like a scared rabbit. No way would we have just sat there while our hands and feet were bound, knowing what was coming next. This was not "playing church."

We don't know what Abraham said to Isaac to make him a willing victim. Perhaps he said nothing, and just quietly went about the process. What we do know is that Isaac could have just said no, and it would have been difficult, if not impossible, for Abraham to physically force him to sit still for this business. But Isaac did, and the rest is history. God commended Abraham for his faith; I wonder what He said to Isaac for his commitment?

There was Another Who sat still for the business of being a Sacrifice. Only that time there was not a ram caught by his horns in the bushes to take His place. Like Isaac, He could have overpowered those who were orchestrating the event. Scripture tells us that He could have called more than twelve legions of angels (about 72,000 of them) to take out a ragtag band of bumbleheads (Matt. 26:53). Like Isaac, He was a Willing Victim. Isaiah tells us that, "He was led like a lamb to the slaughter,

A View of Genesis

and as a sheep before his shearers is silent, so He did not open His mouth" (Isaiah 53:7). Unlike Isaac, He died. Our Sacrifice. Our Burnt Offering.

God did provide Himself a Lamb. His Name is Jesus.

Genesis 23

"(Sarah) died ... in the land of Canaan, and Abraham went to mourn for Sarah and to weep over her." (23:2)

Solomon says in Ecclesiastes 3:1-2, "There is a time for everything, ... a time to be born and a time to die. ..." Death is a reality that each of us must face, not only for ourselves, but also for the person or persons closest to us. Of all life's experiences, death is the most feared. Maybe it's the inevitability of it. Ever since Adam and Eve ate the forbidden fruit, only Enoch and Elijah have avoided the last ride in the long black limousine. Or maybe it's the finality of it. One does not enter the realm of the departed with the expression, "See you on the golf course next Tuesday." Possibly it's because death cannot be understood with our mortal minds. What is out there? Who, if anybody, will be out there? Will there be pain? Happiness? Sorrow? Regret? Or just nothing?

Henry Wadsworth Longfellow wrote, "It seems to me most strange that men should fear that death, a necessary end, will come when it will come." To him, death was as natural as life itself, although most of us might not agree. Perhaps his comment came from his understanding of what death really is: it is a separation of body and spirit, which does not in itself result in a cessation of being, but in the continuance of existence in a different sphere. As Longfellow also wrote in his "Ode to Life," "Life is real, life is earnest, and the grave is not its goal. 'Dust thou art, to dust returneth' was not spoken of the soul."

The Bible agrees. John, in his First Epistle (5:13), writes, "I write these things to you who believe in the Name of the Son of God, so that you may know that you have eternal life." Eternal life. According to this Scripture, we can know that we have it. Without a doubt. For all those who die in faith. Jesus continually talks about those who will not perish, but have everlasting life. Check out John 3:16. And it's there for everyone to read about. The guy with the multi-colored hair and the sign at the sporting events sure knows about it.

So where is this eternal life lived? Paul tells us in several places that the departed believer goes "to be with the Lord." In Heaven. For the unbeliever, physical death brings another separation. The second death. Sepa-

A View of Genesis

ration from God. In the lake of fire, forever (Revelation 20:14-15). Those whose names are not written in the Lamb's Book of Life. Who depended on something or someone else, other than Jesus, to gain acceptance before God.

Heaven and hell are real places, where real people go. Jesus spoke more about hell than He did about heaven. Sarah died in faith (Hebrews 11:13). She trusted in God, and lives there with Him today. Abraham mourned, but he knew he would see her again. He also died in faith, and is in heaven, too.

Make the right choice for your forwarding address. Eternity is a long, long time.

Genesis 24:1-67

"(Abraham) said to the chief servant in his household ..., 'Go to my country and my own relatives and get a wife for my son Isaac.'" (24:2-4)

Everybody loves a love story. This is God's Harlequin Romance Novel. Only it isn't a novel, and there isn't any explicit sex. But this account of Isaac's getting his wife must have been very important to God. It took Him 31 verses to tell about the creation of the universe and man (Genesis 1:1-31), but it takes Him 67 verses to give the details of "The Courtship of Rebecca." Men may argue like crazy about creation, but they get all misty eyed when they visualize Miss Mesopotamia hopping on a camel for the long hot bumpy ride to Canaan and Mr. Wonderful. Could have been a Norman Rockwell original.

But there's something deeper than a love story here. This is one of God's illustrations that even Rockwell couldn't have painted. Here is a servant who goes off to get a bride for his master's son. He meets a woman who is an incredible beauty and pure as the driven snow (vs. 16). The woman, when asked if she will go to be married to this unseen man, says, "You betcha!" (vs. 58). Without even seeing a picture. Without knowing for sure whether she's going to Canaan, or to a third story walk-up on the south side of Chicago. She just gets aboard the camel and heads out with a guy she just met. Is that faith, or what?

Yes, that was faith. And this is the application of the illustration to us. The Spirit of God has come to tell us about Jesus, the Son of the Father. We have never seen Him. But the Spirit of God, through the Scripture or whatever way He chooses, continues to tell us all about what life can be as part of the believing church, the bride of Christ. Then He asks us if we will go. Will we leave all that we have in order to become all that we can be in Christ? Will we respond in faith, and like Peter says (1 Peter 1:8), "Though you have not seen Him, you love Him; and even though you do not see Him now, you believe in Him and are filled with an inexpressible and glorious joy..."?

Rebecca's faith was rewarded. She became the matriarch of Israel, the mother of Jacob, God's woman through whom the line of Christ was continued and preserved. She didn't have a clue as to what was in store for her, except what the servant had told her. But if she had said "No way, Jose" to the servant, she would have missed a life of blessing from God. Probably would have ended up as the wife of a Philistine bookie.

So do we want to be the central figure in a love story? The Holy Spirit wants to cast us in that role. And if we say "Yes," it will take God a lot of space to print this story, too. After all, we're much more important to Him than creation.

He sent His Son to Calvary to tell us that.

Genesis 24:1-14

"Then he prayed, 'O Lord, God of my master Abraham, give me success today, and show kindness to my master Abraham ... By this I will know that you have shown kindness to my master.'" (vs. 12-14)

The servant had a big job. Bring back the bride. With him, it was not to be as the song goes, "Que sera, sera. Whatever will be, will be." Better he should keep on going with his camels than come back with a dog. As the Proverbs say, "Better to live in a desert than with a quarrelsome and ill-tempered wife" (Proverbs 21:19). And the servant would be the one in the dog house.

So he prays to God, and asks Him for some guidance. Not just any guidance, but real specific. "I'll just sit here by this well, God, and You bring the right woman to me. When I ask her to give me some water, she'll volunteer to water the camels, too" (vs. 14). He may also have been thinking, "Oh, by the way, she needs to be a real stunner, from the right family, wonderful personality, a great cook, not a member of the Mesopotamian NOW, a strong work ethic and somebody that Sarah could have gotten along with if she were still alive." Now this was no small request. Just think about watering the camels. There were 10 camels (vs. 10), and each camel, after a long journey, would require up to 40 gallons of water. God had His job cut out for Him on this one.

Was God listening? He heard even before the servant had come up with the criteria. Rebecca was on the way before the camels came over the last dune.

What about this servant? Was he being presumptuous in putting God to the test? Throwing out the fleece, a la Gideon? Was this a lack of faith on his part? Not necessarily so. Remember, he wasn't sent out to acquire something for his own pleasure. He was commissioned with the job of finding the right woman for the master's son, the woman who would become the mother of Israel. It was something terribly important to God, as well. It was for His ultimate glory. The servant needed to be sure he was moving in God's direction.

How about us? Should we be calling for specific actions on God's part,

126   *A View of Genesis*

and setting out the conditions so that we know it's God Who is on the other end of the telephone? Some think that God is too busy to listen to our laundry lists. But He isn't. He is a God of specificity. One Who delights in detail. He's got the whole world in His hands, but He also has all our hairs counted, and His eye is on the sparrow, too. We need to be careful with our requests, however. James tells us we don't have things because we don't ask God for them. But then he also adds that we may not get the things we ask for, because our motives are wrong (James 4:2-3). How about the fleece? In Scripture, one sees such actions only on special occasions. Faith in what the Bible says is usually sufficient.

People who look for a sign may get fleeced by the devil.

Genesis 24:1-14

"Then the servant took ten of his master's camels and left ... " (vs. 10)

Many Old Testament passages have three specific facets: an historical event, a typological teaching, and one or more practical applications. This chapter is one of the most vivid examples of this truth. Historically, it is an honest-to-goodness real life love story. Typologically, it sets forth the New Testament relationship of Christ and His church; Abraham represents God the Father, Who has sent His Servant, the Spirit of God, into the world to bring out a bride, the church, for His Son. And one of the practical applications of this account has to do with the service performed by Abraham's servant. Let's look at that facet for a moment or two, so we can see what our service for God should be like.

First, we need to understand the circumstances of this servant's assignment. He was leaving a cushy existence to herd a batch of camels across 500 miles of desert and wilderness to find the perfect woman, if in fact she did exist, with no air conditioning and nary a Marriott Hotel along the route. And did you ever try to ride a camel, even down to the end of the block? They don't have a great set of Sears shock absorbers or a JBL Surround-Sound stereo system. Also, if you drink a glass of milk before you get on, by the time you pass the first mile marker it would be cottage cheese. And forget breaking the speed limit. A three-speed camel would be creep, crawl, and lie down. If the servant had had any sense, he would have called on one of his snuffies, since he was the boss (vs. 2), and then retired to the officers' club. Or asked for a transfer to another outfit.

But he didn't. The master asked him, and he responded without argument. He was careful to understand fully his assignment (vs. 5-8). He committed himself fully to carrying out his assignment (vs. 9). He was careful to ask for guidance in the process of his assignment (vs. 12-14). He followed the instructions for his assignment exactly (vs.17 et seq.). He completed his assignment without delay (vs. 33, 56). And he was careful to give thanks and glory to God for the success of his assignment (vs. 26, 52, 56).

We can also serve God in the same manner. God has given us His

"How-to-Serve Book of Instructions." It's called the Bible. He tells us to be "FAT" Christians; Faithful (1 Corinthians 4:2); Available (Isaiah 6:8); and Teachable (Matthew 11:29). All the other instructions are in there, too. More than likely, God will call us to service right in our own back-yard, where there aren't any camels. But He may send us to suffer for Jesus on the beaches of Hawaii. Or in the jungles of Peru. In any event, if we follow His Word, communicate with God in prayer, and do what Abraham's servant did, we can be sure the file on our assignment will be stamped "Mission Accomplished," and God will get the glory.

When He calls, let's make sure our answer isn't, "Here am I, but please send Harvey." Harvey isn't cut out to do the job God has for us to do.

Genesis 24:57-61

"They called Rebekah and asked her, 'Will you go with this man?' 'I will go,' she said." (vs. 58)

Talk about a fast worker. Here is the servant, arriving at Nahor in Mesopotamia in the afternoon, making his pitch for Rebekah in the evening, and getting up in the morning to head back with the bride-to-be and her entourage in tow. You can almost hear the groans of the guys who were with him. "Oh, man! Not on those camels again already! We didn't even get a chance to get into the pool!"

Rebekah's relatives weren't too thrilled with this arrangement, either. "Give us ten days or so to get used to this idea, and say our good-byes" (vs. 55). After all, she wouldn't be hopping on the USAirways commuter for a weekend home anytime soon. But the servant was insistent. Rather than argue, Rebekah's mother and brother decided to let her make the decision.

From her response, it sounds as though she had spent the night packing her bags. We don't know why she made her decision so quickly, but make it she did. I doubt if it was all the goodies that the servant brought (vs. 53); this would not have been unusual, and besides, Rebekah's family wasn't exactly on the welfare list or getting food stamps. Neither would it have been that Rebekah had no other opportunities. She was a beautiful and resourceful woman. The woman of Proverbs 31, who hadn't even read that chapter yet. Probably she decided because Isaac had already won her heart, just from the description of him that the servant gave her. She was in love.

But there were a lot of reasons to delay her response. Her family wanted her to take her time. This was so sudden, so unexpected. She was going to experience a whole new life style, and maybe she should ease into it. Maybe Isaac himself could come to see her, so she could make a more informed decision. Besides, she was young, and had a lot of life to live before she settled down. Not so with Rebekah. She heard about Isaac, and that was it. Off to Canaan!

The Spirit of God has told us about Jesus, the Son of God, the One

Who died for us, our only hope of salvation. Many hesitate to commit themselves to Him. We're still young, with so much living to do. We haven't seen Him, and need more facts to decide. Our families may not like this. It involves a whole new life-style. And there is time ... time... lots of time! We don't know what the servant would have said if Rebekah had delayed. Perhaps he would have decided that she was not the one. But we do know that God has told us to make our decision without delay. "I tell you, now is the time of God's favor, now is the day of salvation" (2 Corinthians 6:2). The Spirit of God calls us to come to Jesus at once. We may not have the opportunity to respond in the future.

The "I will go!" of today avoids the "I wish I had gone!" of tomorrow.

Genesis 24:1-67

"The Lord ... will send His angel with you and make your journey a success" (vs 40); "...I praised the Lord ... Who had led me on the right road" (vs. 48) "... the Lord has granted success to my journey." (vs. 56)

When I was taking plane geometry in high school, I was told that the shortest distance between two points is a straight line. Then I got confused, because I was told later on that the arc of a great circle is the right answer. Maybe it didn't make a lot of difference anyhow, because my life's pathway has never followed a straight line. Or the arc of a great circle. It's more like the Burma Road, which has so many curves and bumps and squiggles it would break a snake's back.

Abraham's servant read all the right road signs, however. He made sure that he got the right map; constantly referred to it; kept good track of his check points; and didn't put it away until the end of the journey was reached. His road was like the straight line, or the arc of a great circle, whatever. He got there quickly, safely and successfully. Even though he had to ride 500 miles on a camel through the wilderness with a batch of complaining buddies to do it. Not exactly your generic Sunday afternoon scenic drive. The key to his success was that He depended on the map's Author to not only show him the way, but also to ride with him and lead him along.

Makes a lot of sense, doesn't it? Here we are on our "Road of Life," trying to get on down the highway with a minimum of breakdowns, sideswipes, side trips, flat tires, wrong turns, and head-on collisions. Most of the time, we're hanging on to the wheel for dear life. Sometimes we try the automatic pilot. Regardless of what mode we're in, the potholes keep coming, broader and deeper, and we hit them with amazing regularity. And interestingly enough, we hit them so often that it may seem normal, and we don't realize the car's in trouble until the wheels fall off. Or we get hit by an eighteen-wheeler we never saw coming. But just like Abraham's servant, we can cruise down the highway safely, if we take on the Divine Pilot as our guide. He tells us that if we don't depend on our own knowledge and experience, but acknowledge Him in all our ways, He will direct our paths, headed in the right direction (Proverbs 3:5-6). Although the territory we're going through may still be rugged country, the journey will go a lot more smoothly.

A View of Genesis

We'll also reach the desired destination in one piece, and hit the SUC-CESS sign right in the bulls' eye.

Jesus isn't into car-jacking, however. We have to stop the car, open the door, invite Him in, and follow His directions to the destination. Do it and enjoy the ride!

"...Abraham breathed his last and died at a good old age, an old man and full of years; and he was gathered to his people. His sons Isaac and Ishmael buried him ... with his wife Sarah." (vs. 8-10)

Isaac and Ishmael got together again to bury their father. It would appear that they had buried the hatchet, at least for this occasion, and restored fellowship with one another to some extent. Let's listen to a possible conversation between the two brothers.

Isaac: Hey, Ish! Good to see you!

Ishmael: Yeah, Zack! It's been awhile! How're things goin'?

Isaac: Not too bad. Did you hear about Rebekah?

Ishmael: Sure did! Like to meet the missus one of these days. I understand she's quite the lady, and old Eliezer (*probable name of Abraham's servant - see Genesis* 15:2) brought back a beauty!

Isaac: You got that right! When my mother died, she was right there for me! (*24:67*) How's everything with you?

Ishmael: Fair to middling. Dad set me up pretty well with a business (*vs. 6*), and it's doing good. You remember I married the Egyptian lady? We have a bundle of kids, and it's pretty wild. They fight all the time! (*vs. 13-18*).

Isaac: I know what you mean. Rebekah and I have twins, and they are so different! They really don't understand each other and are so competitive.

Ishmael: Yeah, brothers can be difficult. I'm glad we're back together, even though it's for Dad's funeral. We had a good father, and although I didn't have regular contact with him in later years, I remember him well and fondly.

Isaac: You know, Ish, he was a great man. He taught me so many things. I guess the most significant thing I learned from him was all about <u>faith</u>.

134   *A View of Genesis*

He was so in touch with God, so tuned in, it's almost like he had a direct line to the Almighty.

Ishmael: That's for sure. And one of the things I appreciated most about him was that he explained to me all about <u>God's plan</u>. For his life, for your life, for my life. I guess it was a problem for me at first to understand that you are to be his sole heir *(vs. 5)* but he was so forthright in explaining that whole process, and he let me know that God was going to provide for me and my family as well.

Isaac: Well, I guess that would be hard to understand, but Dad was so convinced of Who God is and what He is doing, that he <u>followed</u> His instructions to a T. I'm glad you realize that his last will was not my idea.

Ishmael: Yes, I know that. Dad kept talking about <u>God's purpose</u>. He told me that there is a real purpose in everything that God does and, although I'll have to admit that it's difficult to relate some of the experiences I've had with any purpose, much less God's purpose, I'm comfortable with Dad's thoughts on that matter. When Mom and I were out in the desert and we thought we'd had it, God's purpose was pretty far away from my mind! *(21:15-18)*. But we've made out all right.

Isaac: Yeah. Dad told me all about that. In fact, I've spent some time at Beer Lahai Roi, where your mother was shown the well that saved her *(16:14, 24:62)*. I had some difficult moments on Moriah as well. If God hadn't provided the ram caught in the thicket, I'd have been history! *(22:10-13)*. But that gave me a great lesson in Dad's <u>fear</u> of God. Not that he was scared silly of Him, but he had a great reverence for God and <u>His power</u>. He told me later that he had every confidence that God would have restored me to life. It was still pretty scary!

Ishmael: Man, that must have been a dilly of an experience! What were you thinking about when Dad was building the altar? *(22:9)*. Didn't you put two and two together?

Isaac: I did, but I didn't come up with four until a little later. He was always building altars. He built more altars than Sodom had sinners! He was really into <u>fellowship</u> with God through worship. It really worked for him, and I'm hoping I can follow his example in my life.

Ishmael: Yeah, me too. But he was a special guy for God and for us, and it'll be hard to wear his shoes. He had a full life, a happy life, great respect from friend and foe alike. And he had your respect and mine, too.

Both: God, we commit our father's spirit to his people, and his body to the ground. May we know Your <u>plan</u>, Your <u>purpose</u> and Your <u>power</u> as he did; and may we walk in his <u>faith,</u> <u>following</u> You as he did, in Your <u>fear</u> and in <u>fellowship</u> with You. Then, like our father, we will also be Your friend *(James 2:23)*.

ABRAHAM - THE FRIEND OF GOD
Born in Ur of the Chaldees
Died in Canaan
175 Years Old

If a man has "A Friend of God" inscribed on his tombstone, his influence will be inscribed upon the lives of all with whom he comes in contact in this life. He will go to live with God his Friend, and take many of his friends with him.

Genesis 25:19-34

"Isaac prayed to the Lord on behalf of his wife, because she was barren. (Rebekah) went to inquire of the Lord ... ." (vs. 21-22)

Isaac and Rebekah had been trying now for twenty years to have a child. But it wasn't happening. He was getting old, and Rebekah wasn't far behind. He also had been around long enough and had seen and heard enough to know that God's plan for the future of the nations was going to happen through him. And Isaac remembered well his father's experience with Hagar and Ishmael. To look for a substitute for Rebekah was a no-no.

So what to do? Pray! What a good idea! Remind God about His promises and the situation. Tell Him that he and Rebekah are just not connecting. Let Him know that he still trusts God, but this waiting is a bummer. So that's what Isaac did. And guess what? In a short time, Rebekah was getting morning sickness. Then the morning sickness graduated into what felt like a full scale war-in-the- womb (vs. 22). So what to do again? Pray! What a good idea! Ask God what is going on, since He is the author of life. What is happening? Is this normal, or is Rebekah going to have a couple of Tasmanian Devils rather than sweet little boys? So that's what she did. And guess what? God laid out the landscape for her so she got the whole picture. Better than a sonogram.

Sometimes we look for things in life that just don't happen. Then there are other things that do happen that throw us for a loop. Our most frequent expression becomes, to quote a well known celebrity, "What's up, Doc?" And Elmer Fudd can't give us an answer. Confusion. Frustration. Disappointment. Despair. Anger. Our emotions run the gamut. These times especially occur when we think that God should have acted in a way we expected. Or when we think He is acting in a way we didn't expect. Everything has been planned out from the budget to the business to the babies to the biscuits to the beach. Then blooey! "Gone With the Wind" isn't just the name of a novel and a movie. It's real life, and Mount Saint Helens has just erupted at our address.

So what to do? Write to Ann Landers? Buy a book on self-help, situational ethics, or a horoscope? Maybe try hypnosis? Well, Isaac and

Rebekah have just told us what to do. Pray! What a good idea! And guess what? God knows about our situation and our problems already. And He also has the solutions. Perhaps He just wants us to depend on Him more than we have been doing. Perhaps He wants to be the Playwright, rather than having us write the script. Perhaps His timing doesn't correspond with our schedule. Maybe He just wants to let us know that He is still in control.

Like the song says, "I'm gonna have a little talk with Jesus; gonna tell Him all about my troubles ... and just a little talk with Jesus makes it right."

A View of Genesis

Genesis 25:23

"And the Lord said to her, 'Two nations are in your womb ... and the older shall serve the younger.'" (vs. 23)

When I was in officer's boot camp in the Marines, there was this guy named Albert who was also in training. The DI's chose not to like Albert. They picked on him all the time, finding fault with everything he did. It was inevitable that when we were commissioned, Albert was already on his way to some other role in the Grand and Glorious Corps. He never made the grade. Probably spent the rest of his career cleaning latrines and peeling potatoes. Not what heroes are made of.

Why did the DI's pick on Albert? Who knows? They could have run any of us out of the program if they wanted to. But Albert had drawn the short straw. They just decided that he wasn't going to make it. And he didn't. Was that fair? No one ever thought to ask the question. It wouldn't have mattered if they did. No discussion would have been forthcoming. The DI's were like gods to us. They didn't have to give an account for any of their actions. It was like you didn't exist unless they willed it so. In fact, sometimes we even thought that God Himself snapped to attention when they gave the command.

Esau was someone like Albert. God just decided that Jacob would be the top dog, and Esau wouldn't even get the bones. Why did God pick on Esau? Who knows? And more so than the DI's, can anyone question God? He doesn't have to give any account for His actions, either. Job wondered out loud more than once why he was being whacked over the head with an ugly stick. But he never got his explanation. God just told Job it was none of his business and made him feel lower than a snake's belly. God had His reasons, and that was that.

Paul talks about Esau and Jacob in Romans 9. He concludes that God chose Jacob and rejected Esau simply because He is God, had every right to do so, and knew exactly what He was doing. Was this fair? Not to worry, says Paul. Don't even think about asking the question. He is the Creator and, unlike the DI's, who didn't have the capacity to will something in or out of existence, He does. Isaiah had the right perspective when he said that God sits on the circle of the earth, and the inhabitants thereof are as grasshoppers (Isaiah 40:22). And even that gives us a greater stature than we deserve.

But God's choice still didn't relieve Esau from responsibility. Paul states this clearly in Romans 1:18-20, where he points out that all are guilty of their own accord before God. That includes Esau along with the rest of us. How does personal responsibility and God's choice fit together? We can't really tell, but we can be sure that God has it all worked out. After all, He is the Author of it all.

God has a reason for everything, but His reasons are beyond our reasoning.

"And the Lord said to her, 'Two nations are in your womb ... and the older shall serve the younger.'" (vs. 23)

A View of Genesis

"Isaac, who had a taste for wild game, loved Esau." (vs. 28)

John Wayne. The Marlboro Man. James Dean. Humphrey Bogart. Clint Eastwood. All these guys were men's men, and Hollywood and the advertising people knew it. How to sell a product? Tell the public that real men use it. Not some wimp that gets sand kicked in his face at the beach. Show the stud that flexes his muscles, and even his muscles have muscles and all the girls come running.

Esau was that kind of guy. He was "a skillful hunter, a man of the open country" (vs. 27). You can almost picture him in his sheepskin jacket and leather Nikes sneaking up on some wild animal and bringing it down before it ever knew what was happening. No desk job for him. Running around the range, sleeping under the stars, a stranger to Lifebuoy Soap and Mennen's Shaving Cream. He even smelled like the outdoors (27:27). And he was his father's favorite (vs. 28).

Why was Esau Isaac's favorite? There may have been several reasons. Esau was the firstborn. Jacob was quiet, contemplative, a home boy, much like Isaac had been; maybe Isaac admired Esau's free-spirited personality and rugged life-style, something which he never had experienced himself. This passage also tells us that Isaac had a taste for wild game. He loved the meat that Esau brought back from the country. Lamb chops are too tame; gimme that great venison steak! It didn't really matter that Esau's heart was not right before the Lord, and his life was the life of a rebel. He provided Isaac with something that pleased his palate, and thereby captured his soul. In short, Isaac's heart followed his stomach, his affection followed the things of this earth.

A lot of us are like Isaac. We eat too much, drink too much, and spend too much time in front of the TV. Others of us don't do those things, but spend most of our time at the office and the rest at the spa, making money and making muscles, building a bundle and building a body. The goal is to live the good life with the beautiful people. Paul spoke about this kind of thing in Philippians 3:18-19, "For, as I have often told you before, and now say again even with tears, many live as enemies of the cross of Christ. Their destiny is destruction, their god is their stomach, and ... their mind is on earthly things." Most of the time it ends up with big stomachs and little minds. And a soul that is lost somewhere along the way.

Paul also tells us in Colossians 3:1-4 to "Set your hearts on things above, where Christ is seated at the right hand of God. Set your minds on things above, not on earthly things ... When Christ, who is your life, appears, then you will also appear with Him in glory."

Prudential may want us in this life to have a "piece of the rock"; but we can have the peace of The Heavenly Rock by setting our hearts and minds on Jesus.

Genesis 25: 29-34

"'I am about to die,' Esau said. 'What good is the birthright to me?' ... So Esau despised his birthright." (vs. 32, 34)

You've heard of DARE and SCORE and MADD and CLEAN and all those other groups with acronyms that represent a cause of some sort. It seems like there's one for almost every real or perceived inequity or disadvantaged group. Wouldn't surprise me to hear next of BARF — The Brotherhood of Acrimonious Refuse-collection Facilitators. Fair treatment for angry garbage men.

Well, if the ACLU had heard about Jacob and many of his Jewish brethren, they might have started another one. SABRE. The Society for Acquisition of BirthRight Equality. They could have rattled the sabres big time over this one. The firstborn was Top Banana in the Jewish family, and the rest were Second Siblings. He got the majority of the goodies from Father's estate (Deuteronomy 21:17), and also became the head of the family, the spiritual as well as the economic leader. Through no fault of their own, the other brothers had to serve the eldest, and the girls really didn't matter. They came in after the camels. NOW would have had a conniption. And Esau was Isaac and Rebekah's first born.

Jacob wasn't particularly pleased about this whole arrangement, and started his campaign for the top spot while still in the womb. He lost the birth race, even though he tried to grab Esau's heel and get to the starting gate in first place (vs. 26). He got his name as a result — Jacob means, "Conniver," or "Deceiver." It appears that Jacob lived up to that name throughout his career; and getting that birthright from Esau was on the top of his caper list.

One day Esau came back from a hunting trip, hungry enough to eat the back side of a horse. Chef Jacob was mixing up his specialty — red stew. When Esau's nostrils got a whiff of that, his stomach hummed and his brain went numb. Jacob saw his chance. He had lived for this moment. Before you could say "Such a deal I have for you," the birthright was his. Esau had bargained it away for a light lunch, and it proved to be the unhappiest lunch break of his life.

There is a birthright available to us, which most people, like Esau, consider to be of little or no value. Unlike Jacob, though, we don't have to connive or deceive anybody to get it. It becomes ours when we are born by faith into the family of God. All that God has for us comes into our possession: eternal life, peace with Him, all His resources and His blessings. Read Ephesians 1. But most people would rather have their plate of red stew — something tasty for the flesh right now. This spiritual birthright is spurned or ignored, and just like Esau, the privileges are lost. Eternally. And the regret will never be abated in a living hell.

The light lunch served up by earthly pleasures ends up as devil's food cake, and it produces eternal indigestion.

"(Isaac) moved on from there and dug another well, and no one quarreled over it. He named it 'Rehoboth,' saying, 'Now the Lord has given us room, and we will flourish in the land.'" (vs. 22)

Remember Hansel and Gretel? Snow White and the Seven Dwarfs? Goldilocks and the Three Bears? Where the wicked witch always gets it in the backside and the porridge ends up just right and everybody lives happily ever after? A lot of people will tell us that the Christian life is just like that. The devil gets run off into the great beyond never to be heard from again, and peace and prosperity and popularity and pleasure fall all over the happy believer for ever and ever.

As the kids say, "NOT!"

In this Chapter, Isaac gives us a good illustration of what we can expect as believers, and how (and how not) to respond to these things.

First, he finds himself in the middle of a <u>famine</u>, and heads south to avoid the consequences (vs. 1-6). "Hold on!" says God. "Stay right where you are. Things ain't any better in Egypt, and I'm going to make it work for you right here." Isaac demonstrates <u>strength of conviction</u>, that <u>God will provide</u>, remains in Canaan and passes this test. We sometimes run into famines — not a shortage of bread and milk and Tollhouse cookies and pizza, but a shortage of good, solid spiritual encouragement and support in our environment. (Maybe it's because we're not exerting the effort to find it!) Rather than running off to another venue, if we look to God in faith, the spiritual chow wagon will soon appear.

Then Isaac finds himself in the middle of <u>failure</u>. A chip off the old block. Like father, like son. Tells the same sister-story about Rebekah as Abraham did with Sarah. With the same results (vs. 7-11). He should have read his father's diary. He didn't have the <u>strength of character</u> that <u>God would protect</u>. Should we tsk- tsk about Isaac? Look in the mirror and decide. Like Jesus said, "if any one of you is without sin, let him be first to throw a stone ..." (John 8:7). We're always devising schemes instead of trusting God. Usually with disastrous results. But even then, God usually sooner or later gets our chestnuts out of the fire.

Isaac next is in the middle of <u>frustration</u>. He is the envy of his neighbors (vs. 14), and they steal his wells as soon as his servants get them dug. More than once. Water was arguably the most important commodity in that area (vs. 15-21). But he didn't dig his heels in and scream, "MINE! MINE!" He showed <u>strength of commitment</u> to the fact that God <u>would produce</u>, and that's what happened. God gave them room, and they flourished in the land (vs. 22). When we prosper spiritually, we exhibit a joy that others get jealous about. When we're used by God for a spiritual purpose, someone else wants to take the credit. They try to steal our results, they try to steal our reputation. It's not only frustrating, it's real ugly. How should we react? Throw bigger stones back, only harder and faster? Demand our recognition rights? Hold the halo up higher, heartier, haughtier, and holier? Don't even think about it, says Paul, in Hebrews 6:10: "For God is not unjust so as to forget your work and the love which you have shown toward His name ..." God will give us our room, and we will flourish in His land.

Then Isaac finds himself in the middle of God's <u>favor</u>. God would bless him and increase his family, fame and fortune (vs. 24-33). The world around him saw the blessing, and wanted to get on the bandwagon. They came up with their version of "Let's Make A Deal!" Isaac showed his <u>strength of conduct</u>, and his conviction that God <u>would proclaim</u>. He didn't have to toot his own horn. His life-style was enough testimony and evidence that his God was a winner. Maybe we won't end up with the equivalent of all Isaac's wealth when we are in God's favor, but our testimony of love, joy, peace, etc. (read about the fruit of the Spirit in Galatians 5:22) will prove to others that we have a God worth seeking. That's God proclaiming Himself through us, and it's a powerful sermon.

God has a <u>future</u> for us, like Isaac, as we demonstrate a <u>strength of confidence</u> (otherwise known as faith) in Him. God <u>will promote</u> us from this world of pleasure and pain, fortune and failure, triumph and tragedy to His everlasting presence where, as the Psalmist has said, "You will fill me with joy in your presence, with eternal pleasures at your right hand" (Psalm 16:11).

When God gives us room, the earth isn't large enough to contain it.

146   *A View of Genesis*

"Rebekah said to her son Jacob, '...take (some tasty food) to your father to eat, so that he may give you his blessing before he dies.'" (vs. 6-10)

There is an ever-increasing (perhaps now almost universal) school of ethicists which has embraced the concept of "situation ethics." In simple terms, this means that there isn't any black and white, there are no ethical absolutes, but that the circumstances dictate what ethical path should be followed. One example I have heard poses this dilemma: A frontier mother, hiding with a group of other settlers from a band of marauding Indians, is holding a baby. The baby starts to cry, endangering the lives of the entire group by threatening to expose their hiding place. In order to protect the others, she smothers the baby. Because this act is for the greater good, is it excusable under "situation ethics?" Another more common question might be, is it acceptable to steal food for a starving child, if there is no money to pay for the food?

Some people might think that all this is modern thought, but Rebekah was the mother of all situational ethicists. Isaac, her numbskull and misguided husband, was going to go against God's will by giving Esau the blessing which attached to the birthright. Esau was on her nasty list because of his marriage to a couple of women from the wrong side of the tracks (26:34-35). Besides, Jacob was her pet; and hadn't God told her that Jacob was His man? (25:23). So she hatches this convoluted plot of lies and deception to secure the blessing for her favorite son, so risky that even a super-schemer like Jacob gets a case of the willies over it (vs. 11-12). And they pull it off. Isaac gets his dinner, Jacob gets the blessing, Esau gets the well-deserved shaft. The situation demanded action, and the ends were justified by whatever means were necessary to get there. Deception and lies were all right, as long as the proper result was obtained. OK?

No-K! What a price Rebekah paid! She caused an irreparable breach between her sons; Jacob had to flee for his life (vs. 41). She never saw her beloved Jacob again. And it's safe to say that her relationship with Isaac was strained, to say the least. Also, I'm sure that Esau didn't say, "That's OK, Mom! I understand." She is never mentioned in Scripture again, except for the place of her burial. Her epitaph might have read,

"Died of a broken heart."

Paul puts to rest the situation ethics argument in Romans 3:5-8, where he pronounces a pox on those who would say, "Let us do evil so that good may result" (vs. 8). The Bible is full of instructions to follow righteousness and truth, and avoid that which is contrary to God, Who cannot tolerate evil. He can protect the baby and the group from the Indians, and provide food for the children. Situation ethics requires our judgment. God's help requires our faith.

We may color the facts and situation, but God sees things in black and white.

Genesis 27:1-4

"When Isaac was old and his eyes were so weak that he could no longer see, (he) said, 'I am now an old man and don't know the day of my death.'" (vs. 1-2)

Isaac was just sitting around waiting for the undertaker. He had retired, mentally, physically and spiritually. The same guy who was such a worshipper of God that he was willing to be a sacrifice (22:9); who was meditating on God's things in the field when Rebekah came over the horizon (24:63); who had sufficient faith in God to stay in Canaan in the middle of the famine (26:1-2). He was on spiritual social security. The only thing he thought about was a good dinner before dying (vs. 4). His version of the last supper. A steak dinner, then off to Dr. Kevorkian.

He had been the child of promise. God's miracle child. Destined to be the spiritual triple crown winner. He started well, maintained superbly, but apparently stumbled around the clubhouse turn and limped across the finish line, far back in the pack. Blind, both physically and spiritually. Out of touch with God and His purposes. In fact, he didn't even know where the finish line was. After this little supposed pre-mortem scene with Esau and Jacob, he lived 43 more years (35:28). You would hope he didn't plan to spend his last cent in Esau's Cafe.

What happened? Probably the same thing that happens to a lot of Christians. The majority of us go from A to Z in our Christian lives, only in the wrong direction. Z to A. Zeal to Apathy. Sizzle to Simmer. Dazzle to Dabble. And why is this so? If I knew, I'd write a book, go on the rubber chicken circuit and make a zillion. But looking at my own life, I have a couple of ideas.

First, we start to think about Jesus as the Absentee Boss. We go to work, but don't see any immediate benefits. We get little recognition and less respect. In fact, we often get a lot of grief from our co-workers. Criticism, some of it real nasty. And not only that, most of the other people are downright vicious. We actually might have to suffer some. Maybe a lot. And where is Jesus? It seems like He isn't helping us in a tangible way. Or even intangible. So who needs it? It's easier to keep in the middle of the group where we'll not be noticed too much, if at all.

Then we get away from reading the Manual. And talking to the Boss, even though His answers may appear to be few and far between. Different things start to be more important, different pursuits appear to provide greater satisfaction. Making it in this life without a lot of hassle and with a few bucks left over at the end of the month. Settling into a routine that may be unexciting, but is predictable and steady. Going comfortably through the stages of life toward the final exit. Losing communication with Jesus, forgetting Who He is and what He's done. That's when we end up like Isaac. Starting with determination, ending up with disappointment. Starting with vitality, ending up with vacillation. Starting with a blast, ending up with a bloop.

But it doesn't have to be that way. Jesus said that He had come so that His people would have life, life to the fullest extent (John 10:10). Paul tells us that he considered everything rubbish for "the surpassing greatness of knowing Christ Jesus my Lord, for whose sake I have lost all things" (Philippians 3:8-9). He was therefore able to say immediately before his death, which, unlike Isaac, he knew was just around the corner at the executioner's booth, "I have fought the good fight, I have finished the course, I have kept the faith. Now there is in store for me the crown of righteousness, which the Lord, the Righteous Judge, will award to me on that day — and not only to me, but also to all who have longed for His appearing" (2 Timothy 4:7-8).

Is it all worth it? Maybe tomorrow it won't seem like it. Maybe the day after it won't either. But the Lord has a way of letting us know, even in this life, that He knows all about what's going on. Peter tells us that, "... after you have suffered for a little while, the God of all grace ... will Himself perfect, confirm, strengthen and establish you" (1 Peter 5:8-10). And that's worth working and waiting for.

Let's not be like Isaac, looking for the undertaker. Instead, let's be vigorously pursuing our spiritual goals, following after God, watching expectantly for the Uppertaker.

Genesis 28:1-9

"Esau then realized how displeasing the Canaanite women were to his father Isaac, so he ... married ... the daughter of Ishmael ... in addition to the wives he already had." (vs. 8-9)

Many of us are pretty hard on Jacob because of his shyster activities, especially exhibited in his successful campaign to get the birthright from Esau and the attendant blessing from his father. We should note, however, that God never has a hard word to say about Jacob, and even changed his name to Israel, which means, "He persists with God" (Genesis 32:28). Although his methods were inadvisable, Jacob's heart apparently was focused on the proper goals, and that was to "be all that he could be" in God's army.

Esau, however, was a horse of a different color. After he lost his birthright and the blessing due to his own lack of spiritual interest, his focus changed. He became determined to recapture at least some portion of the benefits of the privilege he had frittered away. He first decided to put the hit on his brother (27:41); perhaps with Jacob out of the way, that would make him the top dog. Not a good idea. Cain had already gone that route with less than desirable results. Then he heard that Isaac had sent Jacob to his own people to get a wife, instead of the Hittite women Esau had married. Much to his father's and mother's disgust (27:46). Aha! The light bulb came on. He would do the same thing. So he looked around and spotted Ishmael's family nearby. That would do. Not really the immediate family, but close enough for government work. Let's see. There's Mahalath over there, she's a likely prospect. Ta da! Here comes the bride!

Well, Esau was a spiritual Charlie Brown. Every time he flew his kite, it ended up in the tree. One difference between Charlie Brown and Esau, however. Charlie Brown is sincere; Esau had an agenda. He wanted it both ways. His father's blessing and his own worldly desires. But he blew it again. He had climbed the wrong family tree. Ishmael had already been passed over by God in favor of Isaac, and bringing home one of his daughters was like bringing Suzie Six-Pack to a Sunday School picnic. And Esau didn't send the Hittite women packing when he latched on to Mahalath, either. He just added another plate to the table.

Many of us are like Esau. We want it both ways with our Father, God. We want His blessing, but we have our own agenda, too. We try to please Him with what we perceive as good works or pious activity, when we're not really willing to give up our own self-interest and worldly desires. Like Esau, we find out that this doesn't work. God's blessing comes when we operate according to His rules.

There is only one way to reach the fruit from the Tree of God's Blessings, and that's to go up the Steps of Faith on the Ladder of His Purposes.

Genesis 28:10-22

"When Jacob awoke from his sleep, he thought, 'Surely the Lord is in this place, and I was not aware of it.'" (vs. 16)

There was Jacob, trudging through the wilderness on his donkey. Heading for Haran, just like his grandfather's servant when he went hunting for a wife for Isaac. Only this time, there wasn't a whole retinue with a batch of camels and gifts and good food, where they would sit around the campfire at night on their journey toasting marshmallows and singing Kumbaya. Just Jacob and his donkey. Five hundred miles with a dumb animal that couldn't even help pass the time playing Battleship or "Knock Knock! Who's There?"

One night when Jacob pulled in to Bethel, without a Motel Six or McDonald's in sight, (more than likely the same place where Abraham had built an altar [Genesis 12:8]), he must have wondered whether all this was worth it. "I got the birthright, but it's only gotten me a bushel of trouble. I got the blessing, but Esau's back home sticking pins into a little doll that looks like me. He's having fun with the family, and I'm running scared with the donkey. God must be pretty ticked with me for all the garbage I've thrown around, and He's putting it to me pretty good." So with a stone for a pillow (vs. 11), he heaved a big sigh and went to sleep.

Well, God saw Jacob right where he was. Away from home and his support system, out under the stars far from Mother's cooking, running away from Esau, tired, hungry, maybe a bit discouraged and so alone. So He gave Jacob a dream. And what a dream it was. Angels running up and down a ladder that reached from heaven to earth, with God Himself at the top. He must have eaten too much feta cheese and green olives. But no, God was speaking, it was so real, and He was saying that Jacob was His man. All this time when Jacob was hightailing it out of Beersheba looking over his shoulder for fear of his life, God was up there in His heaven, looking down on Jacob's shoulder to firm up his life. And Jacob, with his mind on his circumstances, didn't have a clue that God was anywhere in the vicinity.

Sometimes we find ourselves out in the wilderness, heading off for who knows where and running rapidly out of gas. Oh, there may be a lot of folks around us, but the support system has disappeared or isn't helping. There may be a lot of advice being given, but the panic's roar is drowning it out. There may be a lot of crutches being offered, but none of them seem to have legs. Well, instead of looking backward in bewilderment, forward in fear and all around in anxiety, we need to look upward in faith. God is still in His heaven, and He is ready to take the knocking knees, churning tummy and swirling brain and calm things down, firm things up, rein things in and work things out.

When we don't have a clue, God has already worked out the puzzle. He has fit the pieces all together that will give us an awesome picture.

A View of Genesis

Genesis 28:10-22

"Taking one of the stones there, he put it under his head and lay down to sleep. He had a dream ... ." (vs. 11-12)

When I was five years old, I experienced the first day of Miss Johnson's kindergarten. I had been well prepared for this occasion, with great assurances of what a wonderful time I would have, how much fun it would be, how super it would be to play with other kids, etc. etc. So armed with my new box of Crayolas (96 colors), my bag lunch (PB&J on Mom's homemade wheat bread), my hair combed (except for the renegade curl that never would stay down until it departed, along with most of its brethren) and my blankie, I was off to school. The car and my mother pulled away. I started to scream. Bloody murder. A clear case of child abuse. I'm sure they heard me 40 miles away.

This night in Bethel was Jacob's matriculation into God's school. At the end of this first session, after he figured out where he was, he was terrified, too (vs. 17). And in his educational experience (many of the details are found in the next 20 chapters of Genesis), he not only attended God's elementary and secondary schools, but also went to God's university and took continuing education courses throughout his 147 years of life (Genesis 47:28). He was a bright fellow, but a slow learner. He had to repeat a few grades, but finally graduated magna cum laude.

All God's children go to school. Some, like Jacob, take a long time to learn the curriculum. Others, like David, have regular appointments in the woodshed. Then there are the Pauls, who are disgustingly brilliant, but are also beat up by the local neighborhood bullies from time to time until the Schoolmaster intervenes. But this education is compulsory. There's no exception. Like Miss Johnson's kindergarten, where even a terminal case of pants-wetting wouldn't have gotten me out of there. (Believe me, I tried.)

And God has several ways of instruction. First, there's the manual, the Bible. Lots of instruction in there, all that is really needed. Some students don't crack that book, however, so God has to use other methods. Like counsel from other more experienced students. That may not work either, because most of God's students think they're pretty smart themselves, and fluff it off. Then God may have to go to experience, which can be pretty painful. If that doesn't work, then comes the wood-shed of His direct tutoring. Generally not a pretty sight.

Proverbs 1:7 tells us that, "The fear of the Lord is the beginning of knowledge, but fools despise wisdom and discipline." Solomon doesn't talk about a "scared silly" fear here, but a recognition that God is the Teacher, accompanied by the proper respect for and attention to Him and His curriculum.

That will get an "A" every time.

Genesis 28:10-22

"... and (the Lord) said, 'I am the Lord, the God of your father Abraham and the God of Isaac.'" (vs. 13)

It was Jacob's first day in God's school. Actually, I guess you could call it night school, with the dream and all that. All through his life he had lived under his father's and mother's home schooling, which left a lot to be desired. Some of the instruction was downright bad. The National Education Association and the teacher's union would have screamed to high heaven. But now he was in the celestial classroom, and it was time to get on with his lessons.

The first order of business was to get to know the Teacher and His qualifications. So God starts out by telling Jacob just Who is holding the hickory stick. "I am the Lord!" I don't think Jacob had any thought of asking what degrees God had earned. "Works for me!" was his probable response. God continues, "the God of your father Abraham and the God of Isaac!" Without a doubt, Jacob had heard a lot about God's activities in the lives of these two men. About Sodom and Gomorrah. The doings on Mt. Moriah. The details about his father's birth. Eliezer and Rebecca. Abraham rescuing Lot. Melchizedek. He didn't need any further introduction. So instead of finding an apple for the Teacher, he set up an altar.

Most of us are not very knowledgeable about our Instructor, God the Holy Spirit. He is the one of Whom Jesus said, "The Counselor, the Holy Spirit ... will teach you all things ..." (John 14:26) and, " ... when He, the Spirit of Truth comes, He will guide you into all truth" (John 16:13). He helps us understand about Jesus and His work for us. Through the Gospels, He tells us about Jesus' birth, His life, and His atoning death for us. In the Epistles, He reveals Jesus' excellency and His character. In Hebrews we're told of Jesus' eternal priesthood. The Revelation describes Jesus' crowning day. Using the Scriptures as a textbook, the Holy Spirit teaches us everything we need to know about time and eternity.

God knows that we fidget and fuss a lot while we're in His school, so he tells us in Psalm 46:10, "Be still and know that I am God." Slow down. Sit for a spell. Cool it. Quit jabbering. Think about eternity. Read the Book. Get better acquainted with Him. Paul says something similar to the Ephesians, "I keep asking that the ... Glorious Father may give you the Spirit of wisdom and revelation, so that you may know Him better" (Ephesians 1:17). When we contemplate His greatness, we get a good picture of our smallness. But we're too often like the person who is so enthralled with the trickle of water from the faucet he just installed that he misses the whole ocean just outside his door. Our small vision misses God's grand designs. Our small minds lose sight of His immensity.

Get to know the Teacher. He's the subject of the final exam.

Genesis 28:10-22

"I am with you ... will watch over you ... will bring you back to this land ... will not leave you ... ." (vs. 15)

In the university where three of my children attended, there is a course which all incoming freshmen must take called "University 101." It is a course which gives the new student an orientation to the University; what it is all about, where to go for student needs, helpful hints for student success (going to class and studying is recommended, etc.), and general information concerning the academic and social environment.

In these verses, Jacob had just matriculated into God's School. He had left his parents' home schooling and was beginning his education under the direct tutelage of God Himself. The Teacher had identified Himself in vs. 13, "I am the Lord, the God of your father Abraham and the God of Isaac." Jacob was now enrolled in God's School 101, where he was to find out about student services.

First, he found out that he was to benefit from the Teacher's *provision*: "I will give you and your descendants the land..." (vs. 13). Next, he learned that he would always be in the Teacher's *presence*: "I am with you"; under His *protection*: "and will watch over you wherever you go"; and the object of His *preservation*: "and I will bring you back to this land" (vs. 15). Further, Jacob received the Teacher's *promise*: "I will not leave you until I have done what I promised you" (vs. 15).

Jacob may have been a slow learner in many ways, but he caught on to this course in a hurry. "... How awesome is this place! This is none other than the house of God; this is the gate of heaven" (vs. 17). Without a doubt, Jacob would refer back to his course notes from this class many times before he graduated.

All those who have come to Jesus for salvation have also been enrolled in God's School 101. Most of us act like we slept through the class. It's a good thing there's no exam, and that we're not graded on class participation. Regardless of what we have learned in class or applied in our lives, however, the course principles still hold true. We are the beneficiaries of God's *provision*: "I give (my sheep) eternal life ..."; His *preservation*: "and they shall never perish ..."; and His *protection*: "no one can snatch them out of my hand" (John 10:28). We are always in God's *presence*: "I will never leave you or forsake you" (Hebrews 13:5). And as Paul notes, "For no matter how many *promises* God has made, they are 'Yes' in Christ" (2 Corinthians 1:20). And do you know what? The tuition for this course has already been paid by Jesus, 2000 years ago at Calvary. There's not even an activities fee. Is this a great school, or what?

We need to study the Textbook for God's School 101. It will help us do better in our course work through the rest of life's curriculum.

"(Jacob) had a dream in which he saw a stairway resting on the earth, with its top reaching to heaven." (vs. 12)

There's an old camp song which goes, "We are climbing Jacob's ladder (repeat two times), soldiers of the cross." A couple of later verses start out, "Every rung goes higher, higher," and "We are climbing higher, higher." It might be a good ditty to sing while toasting marshmallows and making S'mores, but Jacob sure wasn't whistling this tune. He was so freaked out, he was hunting for a place to hide underneath the stone he was using for a pillow. And it's also bad theology.

Actually, God was in His teaching mode; the class was Grace 101, the ladder was His visual aid. May we sit in with Jacob as he learns this lesson? Sure can.

"Jake, today you're going to learn about GRACE. You don't understand what that means? OK. Here it is, plain and simple. I'm going to give you something of great value that you don't deserve and could never earn. It's free. That's grace. Now look at this ladder. You could never make or do anything to reach from earth up to heaven, so I have set this ladder here to reach from heaven down to earth. Don't bother trying to climb it; you don't have the strength. I have come down to you. About 3,000 years from now, Jesus will come down to earth to become the sin offering for men. They will be big time sinners like you, so Jesus will have to enter their world. We call this 'condescending grace.'" "OK, Lord, I got that."

"Another bit about grace, Jake. Do you know why I chose you for this? Didn't think you did. It's because I decided to. Like your Dad used to answer when you asked 'Why'? He said, 'Because I said so.' Not because you're pretty or smart, because you're not. Not because you're good or religious, either. Remember the shenanigans with Esau? We call this 'sovereign grace.'" "Can't argue with that, Lord."

"Hey, Jake. You're on the lam from Esau, aren't you? If he gets his hands on you out here, you're an hors d'oeuvre for a buzzard. Well, more grace, Jake. I've told Esau to buzz off. He's out to do you in, and I'm standing in his way. In the future, you and countless zillions after you will be running from your respective dirty deeds, and I will help all of you. That's 'overruling grace.'" "Works for me, Lord."

"Oh, one more thing, Jake. You, you rascal! You're going to blow it mucho times from here on in. You and the generations after you. But the grace doesn't run out. We'll have to help you smooth off the rough edges, but that won't affect My grace to you. Or those that come after you. This is 'long-suffering grace.' So, you dig it?" "Got it down in my class notes, Lord, so I don't forget." "For you know the grace of our Lord Jesus Christ, that though He was rich, yet for your sakes He became poor, so that you through His poverty might become rich" (2 Corinthians 8:9). GRACE - God's Riches At Christ's Expense.

Genesis 28:20-22

"Then Jacob made a vow, saying, 'if God will be with me ... The Lord will be my God ... and I will give (Him) a tenth.'" (vs. 20, 22)

Some people just don't get it. After a girl slams down the phone for the 14ᵗʰ time, the poor guy dials for the 15ᵗʰ. Charlie Brown still tries to kick the football with Lucy holding. And the Chicago Cubs still go to spring training with high hopes.

Well, Jacob didn't get the message, either. Here is God, standing at the top of the stairway to heaven, telling Jacob that He, God, was going to bless Jacob out of his britches (vs. 12-15), and Jacob wants to sit down at the bargaining table. "If you'll do this for me, God, I'll do this for You." It's a wonder that God didn't throw up His hands and look for a lightning bolt. Imagine! Here is a guy who is running for his life after tricking his brother and lying to his father, and he is going to impress God with his promises? Sort of like the street person who finds himself at a buffet in Bill Gates' mansion, and assures Bill that he will leave a reasonable tip after dessert.

Before we're too hard on Jacob, though, we need to look in the mirror. We're constantly trying to make deals with God. Our relationship with Him has become an "iffy" proposition. "If You get me out of this mess, I'll be your main man, God." (Hanging out at all the stores on Main Street.) Or, "If I could just win the lottery, Lord, I'd support Your work all over the world." (And inspect it all in my new 90 foot yacht.) But just like with Jacob, God smiles His omniscient smile, and blesses us in accordance with His own will. To be perfectly honest, God doesn't need us one bit. In the 50th Psalm, God tells us that the cattle on a thousand hills and every animal of the forest are His; "if I were hungry I would not tell you," He says, "for the world is Mine and all that is in it" (Psalm 50:10-12). The fact that He uses us or even acknowledges our existence, is a matter of pure grace and love.

The thing that Jacob (and we as well) had to learn (and he ultimately did) is that God doesn't make a deal with anybody. He has His plan, and it will come to fruition. And His plan is not only global, universal and eternal in scope, it is also local, personal and time specific. Jacob fit into His plan at a specific time in a specific manner at a specific place. So do we all. He has it all planned out. And we can try to nego-tiate what we think is a mutually satisfactory deal with God, but we may as well be a woodpecker trying to make a home in a steel piling. God has already set our paths; the thing we need to do is follow Him and be thankful.

In God's dealings with us, we should remember that there are no ifs, ands or buts about it.

● ●

Genesis 29:1-35

"Then Jacob continued on his journey ... ." (vs. 1)

Jacob had just had an encounter with God. After a night which had started out with a stone for a pillow and ended up with the same stone as an altar, Jacob got on his donkey and headed east. The Hebrew phrase here translated "continued his journey" literally means, "lifted up his feet." In the Hebrew colloquial sense, it means that Jacob got the lead out, put on the jets and hightailed it to Haran. No more lollygagging along. Forget dinner at the Cracker Barrel. Even the Road-runner (Beep-Beep) would have eaten his dust.

After this encounter, he was a <u>changed</u> man. No more the deceiver, he became the deceivee. Instead of the cheater, the cheatee. His Uncle Laban socked it to him real good. Laban's daughters, his wives-to-be, went along with the ruse. His children lied to him again and again. But it didn't matter, because God made it work. Funny. Laban may have laughed up his sleeve, but God saw to it that Jacob ended up with Laban's shirt. Later on, God would even change Jacob's name to Isra-el — "He persists with God." Instead of doing the shady deals, he took God on as a Partner and made the Haran Fortune 500 in record time. Donald Trump would have been green with envy.

He also became a <u>challenged</u> man. He had a more focused desire. He became fully aware of his mission, his destiny. And he set out to accomplish that mission without delay or distraction. It's true, Laban & Co.'s actions cost him some time, but Jacob took the matter to the Lord, and God made that time worthwhile and productive. All the roadblocks which appeared became God's opportunities. More than likely the discussion was, "What are we going to do about this one, Lord?" "Not to worry, Jake, it's in the bag." And it always turned out that way.

Then he became a <u>consecrated</u> man. He had a continual sense of the Divine Presence. Oh, yes, from time to time he still had his doubts and booted a few easy ones, but after Bethel and later on Peniel (Genesis 32:24-32), he didn't get up in the morning wondering if God was going to make it to work today. God was on his mind, in his life, by his side and on his case. And Jacob prospered.

An encounter with God will do these things for us. No, it's not generally a dream like Jacob had, a vision like Isaiah's, or a bright light that brought Saul (Paul) to his knees. But the Spirit of God will reveal Himself to us when He decides it's time. Then comes the <u>change</u>. Like David said, "...renew a steadfast spirit within me, ... grant me a willing spirit" (Psalm 51:10,12). And the <u>challenge</u>. As Paul said to Timothy, "... fight the good fight, holding on to faith and a good conscience" (1 Timothy 1:18-19). And the <u>consecration</u>. Again, Paul: "That I may know Him, and the power of His resurrection, and the fellowship of His suffering" (Philippians 3:10). When God steps into our path, our path will turn to follow in His steps.

Genesis 29:1-14

"Yes, we know (Laban) … and here comes his daughter, Rachel." (vs. 5-6)

The 400 miles or so from Bethel to Haran went quickly. Jacob was on a mission. Thoughts of Esau had disappeared, replaced by the promises of the Almighty. Without the benefit of Rand McNally or the Triple-A, Jacob managed to end up in Paddan-Aram in the right place at the right time. Here was a well. Three shepherds were hanging out, even though it was earlier than the usual time of day for watering sheep. They knew Laban. And wouldn't you know it, here comes Rachel with the family flock. A real doll! From the right family. Whoooee! Jacob's hormones went into high gear. (After all, he was 75 years old at this time, and the hormones had had time to work up into a real lather!) It was love at first sight. "Hey, you cats! Water your sheep and bug off! I've got some serious business to take care of!" (vs. 7).

Some people call it fate, some call it a happenstance, some call it the smile of Dame Fortune, or it's in the stars. Nonsense. When God brings about an event, it's a planned development. In Rachel's and Jacob's case, God was the ultimate "schatchen" — a marriage broker. Laban messed up the works by his scheming, but God brought things back to His original intention, threw in a few things to settle Laban's wagon for good measure, and made the whole thing a part of His eternal program. When the dust settled, Jacob had his wives and children, beaucoup more flocks than Laban and his clan, and a three-day head start on his way home (vs. 22). And the line which would produce the Messiah was intact.

God doesn't waste any events in our lives. There are instructive events, corrective events, directive events, life-enriching events, life-changing events, life-challenging events. Some start out disastrous, but end up distinguished. Some start out as fractious, and end up as fortuitous. Some start as disappointments, but soon turn out to be His-appointments. What we think are ordinary events are really ordained events. Whatever is going on, God is fully in charge. Sometimes we end up in the deep end of the pool without water wings as a result of our own stupidity, cupidity or rigidity, but God will pull us out after we have learned what He wants us to learn.

"And we know that in all things God works for the good of those who love Him, who have been called according to his purpose" (Romans 8:28). Just like Jacob at the well, and Rachel coming with the sheep at an unusual time of day. All things, good, bad and indifferent. God has the puzzle all worked out.

We may minimize the importance of events, but God will maximize His purposes through each one of them.

"When morning came, there was Leah! So Jacob said to Laban, ' ... Why have you deceived me?"' (vs. 25).

Genesis 29:15-30

"When morning came, there was Leah! So Jacob said to Laban, ' ... Why have you deceived me?'" (vs. 25).

Unbelievable! Jacob went to bed thinking he had married Claudia Schiffer, and in the morning he found out it was Tugboat Annie! What a revolting development! If the face of Helen of Troy could have launched a thousand ships, Leah's face would not have gotten a row-boat out of the New York harbor. Jacob was not pleased. But Laban was ready for the fallout. The master spinmeister already had concocted his story. "Can't marry off the younger before the older, buddy boy. Finish off the festivities with Leah, then Rachel is yours, too. Oh, by the way, she'll cost another seven years in the barnyard."

Jacob might have told him to stuff it, Leah included. Sue the schmuck for fraud, breach of contract, alienation of affection, unauthorized use of Tollhouse cookies at a reception, whatever. But he didn't. He must have been in love, because he agreed to the deal. At the end of Leah's time in the seven-day nuptial sun, Jacob claimed Rachel as well. I'll bet this time he peeked beneath the veil before the vows, to make sure that Laban didn't substitute his decrepit Labrador retriever.

Or maybe he didn't. God had adjusted his attitude in Bethel, and he believed that God was on top of his situation. Or perhaps he also re-membered his last act with his father. "Yeah, Pops! It's really me, Esau! Feel the hair on my arms! Smell the clothes! Taste the venison! I know I sound like Jacob, but Mom has told you that you need to get a hearing aid!" (Genesis 27:19-29). Bingo! Been there, done that. What goes around, comes around. Then, too, Leah really loved him, and she may have pleaded her case effectively, or even promised to wear a gunny-sack over her head.

Whatever the reason, Jacob stayed with the program. And he and all the family were blessed because of it. Leah became the mother of Judah, in the Messianic line. Rachel finally had her two sons, although the second birth claimed her life. It was the beginning of the twelve tribes of Israel, affecting mankind for all time.

What happens when we get the shaft? Is it time to hire the Seven Bar-racudas Law Firm? Oil up the .354 Magnum? Call the guys that fit the cement shoes before the boat ride? Not according to Scripture. Jesus Himself is our Example. "... Christ also suffered for you, leaving you an example ... When they hurled their insults at Him, He did not retaliate; when He suffered, He made no threats. Instead, He entrusted Himself to Him Who judges justly" (1 Peter 2:21-23). Whatever the provocation, a Sovereign Judge will make things right, sooner or later. Our godly reaction will result in a Godly action.

Besides, they make some pretty keen designer gunnysacks.

Genesis 29:31-30:24

"When the Lord saw that Leah was not loved, He opened her womb ... Then God remembered Rachel ... and opened her womb." (29:31; 30:22)

"(God) has made everything beautiful in its time." (Ecclesiastes 3:1 1)

Jacob was in a pickle. Laban was putting him on, Rachel was cutting him up, and Leah was turning him off. He was being messed with at work, and messed up at home. Leah was desperate but unsuccessful in her attempts to win his affection (vs. 31-34). Rachel was desperate but unsuccessful in her attempts to have children (30:1). The two ladies were like two lionesses after the same carcass. Throw in a couple of concubines a la the Sarah/Hagar formula, and Jacob had a real jungle in there. The Horrible Harem of Haran. Jacob may have sent for a French Foreign Legion brochure.

Maybe if Jacob had taken charge of things it would have been different. He should have sat Laban down and made a deal that didn't change every time the sun went down. But he didn't. He should have sent Leah back the morning after the fraudulent nuptials and told the conniving crowd that the party was over. But he hadn't. He should have told his two wives to knock off the nonsense, work out a schedule and forget the competition. But he wouldn't. He should have been more in touch with God's instructions in all these matters. But he wasn't.

Regardless of the chaos in Haran, everything was cool in Heaven. God was still in the picture and hadn't lost control of things. So He gave Leah some happiness and some honor through the six sons she bore to Jacob (30:20). And He took away Rachel's despair by giving her a son, and the promise of another (30:24). It is not recorded that they squabbled any more; in fact, they were of the same mind when Jacob decided to head back for home (31:14-16). With another four sons by the concubines and a daughter by Leah thrown in, probably everybody was too busy changing diapers and baking cookies to fight. And Leah was blessed as the mother of the Messianic line through Judah; Rachel was blessed through Joseph, given to the ages as an extraordinary type of Christ. So in God's time, everything was beautiful, and there was "a garment of praise instead of a spirit of despair" (Isaiah 61:3).

Sometimes things at home and things at work are going in the wrong direction. Maybe it's because we did something we shouldn't have, or vice versa. Maybe we should have acted or reacted in a different manner than we did. Whatever the problem, God is watching, and He can turn that jungle into Central Park. Sometimes He acts on His own to pretty up the area. But it's better if we ask Him to be the Facilities Director. The environment becomes much more friendly, and the natives become much less restless.

And it helps us stop and smell the roses along the way.

"Leah ... said (to Jacob), 'I have hired you with my son's mandrakes.' So he slept with her that night ... and she became pregnant." (vs. 16-17)

I saw a fellow the other day who was wearing suspenders along with a belt. Seemed to be a little overkill. Maybe one time his belt broke and his pants fell down when he was giving a speech on modest behavior before the Benevolent Bevy of Bashful Baptist Beauties and several of them passed out. Whatever the reason, it appears that he needed both in order to feel secure.

Leah and Rachel were also hunting security; in fact, they were in a contest for security and satisfaction. For her part, Leah wanted Jacob's affection; Rachel desperately wanted a child. So anything that might help was eagerly sought after. One day Reuben, Leah's eldest son, found some mandrake plants. This herb was commonly thought to be an aphrodisiac. He brought them to his mother, and Rachel saw them. Thinking that this would fan the flames of fertility, Rachel asked for some. After some negotiation, Leah traded the mandrakes in return for exclusive access to Jacob for the night. As a result, she became pregnant with her fifth son. And Rachel formulated her Midnight Madness Mandrake Mother Mixture for future reference.

What straws people grasp after when they are seeking for security and meaning! Mandrakes may make a good salad addition, but it's doubtful if they are an effective pregnancy potion. But Rachel was convinced, and agreed to go to a movie while Leah produced her own entertainment center. Poor Jacob. He comes in from the field and finds out he is being bought and sold like a share of AT&T (vs. 16). I guess in this instance, it paid a dividend for Leah.

If only Leah and Rachel had turned to God with their desires! It was God Who opened their wombs (29:31, 30:22). It was God in Whom their security and satisfaction could be found. But you know, we're not much better. We have the testimonies of literally thousands before us, plus the assurance of the Word of God that, if we trust Him, He will bring about His perfect will for our lives, which will in His time produce the greatest blessing for us. But we also look to other things to find this happiness and security. Money. Prestige. Position. Booze. Sex. Food.

Makes about as much sense and is about as effective as the mandrakes.

The Lord dresses us up in security and happiness far better than Rodeo Drive could ever imagine. For security, He has "clothed (us) with garments of salvation and arrayed (us) in a robe of righteousness" (Isaiah 61:10). We can also find happiness at His exchange desk: "a garment of praise instead of a spirit of despair" (Isaiah 61:3). And He doesn't need to give us any suspenders, just in case.

God has His own private label, and it's real haute couture. And it was paid for by Jesus at Calvary.

A View of Genesis

Genesis 30:25-43

"Jacob said to (Laban), '...The little you had before I came has increased greatly, and the Lord has blessed you wherever I have been.'" (vs. 29)

Jacob had left his home with hardly more than a donkey, his Nikes and a kiss from his mother. If he hadn't gotten a job with Laban, he'd have been looking for the Golden Arches to flip burgers. And he didn't go in with a key to the executive washroom; he did what was in that society, "women and children's work" —tending sheep. "Israel served to get a wife, and to pay for her he tended sheep" (Hosea 12:12). Hardly an auspicious start for a guy with a Ph.D. in skulduggery.

But regardless of where he was, where he came from and what he was doing, Jacob was in the will of God and under His direction. He was a prima facie example of God's Sovereign Grace and His Divine Determination. It was almost like he could have tangled with a skunk and come out smelling like wintergreen, because God blessed everything he touched.

And Laban knew it.

So when Jacob wanted to start hatching his own nest egg, Laban wanted to keep him in his own henhouse (vs. 25-28). Laban's fortune teller had told him that his bank account was bulging because of Jacob (vs. 27). So he tells Jacob to write his own check, and he'll sign it. (Of course, he had no intention of honoring his commitment, but that's another story — 31:4-9).

Have you ever noticed that some people who have little interest in God often want to hang on to committed Christians, because they see the blessings of God and think they may get some of the fallout? These may not be financial blessings such as Laban coveted, but good marriages, stable children, peer respect, just a general satisfaction with life. An aura of peace. And no fear of death. But even when things are not going well from an earthly perspective, there's a certain attractiveness about the person who trusts in God for strength in the present situation as well as for the outcome. In either scenario, testimony is given to the goodness of God. For this reason, Peter tells us, "Always be prepared to give an answer to everyone who asks you the reason for the hope that you have ... with gentleness and respect" (1 Peter 3:15). Blessing will result every time.

Sometimes people are on the periphery, hoping for some fallout from God's blessings on His people, and end up having a falling in with Jesus. It is through Him that God's blessings score a direct hit.

Genesis 30:27

"Laban said to (Jacob), ...'Please stay. I have learned by divination that the Lord has blessed me because of you.'" (vs. 27)

Many of us thought that Nancy Reagan was two hot dogs shy of a picnic when it was revealed that during her husband's presidency she consulted with an astrologer, and tried to control his daily movement and meetings to conform to "favorable signs." But there may have been as many, if not more, who supported her actions or really didn't care. Astrologers and psychics and witches and warlocks have proliferated in this present age like dandelions on a suburban lawn before Scott's Weed & Feed ever made it out of the lab.

Nancy was a piker compared to Laban. He had his own household gods (31:30), and regularly consulted them for direction. And sometimes he even got correct answers. On this occasion, when he was doing the "Mirror, mirror on the wall, who is the shrewdest of them all" bit, he was properly informed by his occult sources that he was making the big bucks because Jacob was being blessed by Jehovah. And he better keep Jake around for continued success in the farm futures market.

Laban was related to Abraham, and certainly knew about Jehovah. But he chose to hitch his spiritual wagon to dimwit deities which may have been aware of what was going on, but were powerless to do anything to change the results. After Jacob and his family left, Laban is never mentioned in Scripture again. He had many years of exposure to the Person and power of the True God through Jacob's work and witness, but continued in his idolatry. He wanted God's blessing on his own terms. God's work but not God's way.

Well, there are a big bundle of Labans around today. Ever watch the "Psychic Network" on TV? See the ubiquitous horoscopes and astrological forecasts in newspapers, magazines and similar media? Notice the exploding impact of satanic influence in modern society? The rise of eastern mystic religions with their mantras and polytheistic nature? It's here, it's ever increasing, it's demonic and it's deadly. Dabbling in these activities exposes the participant, however innocent, to occult influence and turns him or her away from Scripture and the knowledge of Jesus. God's Word consistently prohibits and condemns any participation in these things (see, e.g. Deuteronomy 18:9-14).

Although such illicit spiritual pursuits are increasing in an alarming manner, God is not about to relinquish His authority over all the universe. Satan himself can operate only within the limits set by God. And those, like Laban, who choose the gods of this world and reject Jesus, will ultimately perish along with all the elements of that choice.

I read the end of the book, and God wins.

• •

Genesis 30:25 - 31:13

"Every dark-colored lamb and every spotted or speckled goat ... will be my wages." (30:32)

Jacob must have been chewing on too much peyote root. Here Laban had given him a blank check, and he tore it up. "Just give me the ir-regulars, the seconds, Laban. Forget the cash. And if you have any more daughters, I'll pass on that, too." Laban must have gone nuts. "What's he up to? Is he going to open a 'slightly irregular' department at the Sheep and Goat Bazaar?" He was so freaked that Jacob was going to get the best of him, that he picked all the streaked, speckled and spot-ted animals out of his herds, made a separate flock and moved them three days' journey away from the main group, so Jacob wouldn't have any access to them for breeding purposes (vs. 35-36).

Well, God gave Jacob a crash course in genetics and pharmacology. In addition, He told Jacob in a dream that He was fed up to His eyeballs with Laban's compensation practices, and was going to make Jacob rich and get him outta there (31:10-13). In animal genetics, there are "heterozygous" animals which contain genes for different colored prog-eny. By selective breeding, Jacob could eventually develop a flock of predominately spotted and speckled animals. One scientific writer has said that even today there is so much unknown about the transmission of hereditary factors that Jacob may have learned certain things about these animals which modern scientists have not yet even approached. (Even if Jacob hadn't learned it, God knew it anyhow.) Then Jacob put branches from certain types of trees in the watering troughs when breed-ing season came around (vs. 37-39). (Boy, if Laban had seen this going on, it would have driven him to the Batty Barnyard!) But it's not as goofy as it may seem. These trees have a chemical substance which is commonly used in both ancient and modern times in animal husbandry as an aphrodisiac and fertility promoter. And it all worked. So Jacob learned his lessons well, listened to the Lord, and chuckled the whole way to the First National Bank of Haran (vs. 43).

So Jacob got rich and Laban got frustrated (31:1-2). But that's the way it is when God's principles are followed. When somebody is getting the best of us and we get angry, it doesn't solve the problem. Better to talk to the Lord about it and listen to what He says. More than likely we won't need to hit the big books in the library, but God will teach us all that we need to know for the situation. We may not make regular visits to the deposit window like Jacob did, but the withdrawals of peace and satisfaction from God's ATM machine will more than suffice.

And do you know what? Maybe the guy who is the itch under our saddle won't be a dunderhead like Laban. God may give us a bonus and make us a friend.

We may all get a charge when God is in charge.

"Every dark-colored lamb and every spotted or speckled goat ... will be my wages." (30:32)

"Laban's sons were saying, 'Jacob has taken everything our father owned and has gained all this wealth from what belonged to our father.' And Jacob noticed that Laban's attitude toward him was not what it had been." (31:1-2)

Genesis 31:1-55

"Laban's sons were saying, 'Jacob has taken everything our father owned and has gained all this wealth from what belonged to our father.' And Jacob noticed that Laban's attitude toward him was not what it had been." (31:1-2)

Everybody loves a winner. Success breeds success. Jump on the front runner's bandwagon and everybody sing a happy tune. Except there's always the guy who sounds a sour note because he's jealous. In this case it was the whole Laban family. They sang such a sour tune, they should have taken their show on the road as the Lem'n-Blends.

God had blessed Jacob big time. One of the reasons for this was that Laban was such a shyster (vs. 6-12). He would have stolen the Mona Lisa's smile if he could have. In fact, even his daughters were fed up with his shenanigans (vs. 14-16). But God had decided that it was time for Jacob to go back home and get on with his life. And God had also decided that it was time for Laban to sit in the corner and suck his thumb over all the wealth that was going over the hill with Jake when he headed back to Isaac's pad.

Sometimes we're a lot like Laban. The person we're trying to witness to at work gets the raise and the promotion, and we force a smile that's green around the edges. Or the one at church gets the applause for his singing, or for her pies at the bake sale, and we get mad at them and God because our voice would cause a screech owl to run for cover, and the last time we made a pie crust someone mistook it for a man hole cover. Success and applause are wonderful as long as it's directed toward us, so that we can say, "Aw, shucks, it's really nothing," and be appropriately humble. Unfortunately, God sees through all the facades.

Paul talks a lot about being happy with and for those who succeed. In Romans 12:15, he says, "Rejoice with those who rejoice." Then in 1 Corinthians 12:26, he notes that, "if one part (i.e., person who belongs to Christ) is honored, every part rejoices with it." Even when he was in prison, knowing that he was about to meet the guy in the black hood with the big ax (and not for the purpose of helping him negotiate his contract), Paul told the Philippian church that he was rejoicing with them because of their faith, and that they should rejoice with him (Philippians 2:17-18). And there is a reason for all this; it's because Paul knew that it is God Who prospers people and gives them success and happiness, and jealousy and anger at those recipients is really anger at God. The writer of Ecclesiastes said, "Moreover, when God gives any man wealth and possessions, and enables him to enjoy them, ... this is a gift of God" (Ecclesiastes 5:19).

So let's not sing a sour tune at the party God throws for someone else. Be happy. Enjoy the shindig. Tasting God's Tollhouse cookies, even if our name isn't on them, is a lot better than sucking on our own lemons.

Genesis 31:19-55

"God came to Laban ... and said to him, 'Be careful not to say anything to Jacob, either good or bad.'" (vs. 24)

Laban was ticked. Here he was out shearing his sheep, and he gets word that Jacob has headed for the hills three days ago. He had already talked himself into the erroneous notion that everything Jacob owned belonged to him (vs. 43), even though Jacob had worked for Leah and Rachel for 14 years, plus another six years beyond that, and Laban had messed with his wages so often that even the NLRB couldn't have straightened it out (vs. 41). All that didn't matter. All Laban could think of was that Jacob had absconded with the goodies, so he organizes a posse and heads out after him (vs. 23).

God knew that Laban saw an opportunity here, and that was to leave Jacob swinging from a tree, and take all his daughters, grandchildren and all Jacob's flocks and herds back to the compound. So He tells Laban in a dream something like, "Look, fella, if you mess with My man Jake any more, I'm going to whack you on the top of your noggin so hard you'll be shining your sandals with your mustache" (vs. 24). You better believe that Laban didn't enjoy his breakfast. His agenda had been changed. Of course, when he caught up with Jacob, he had to put on the big front ("I have the power to harm you" [vs. 29] and "We could have had a whingding of a going away party" [vs. 27-28] Phinehas Phigtree translation), but he had to admit that God had told him, "One misstep and you're history" (vs. 29, PP translation!).

Perhaps Laban had some reason to be upset because of the way Jacob had left (as well as for the fact that his good luck gods had disappeared [vs. 30]), but his motives for pursuing Jacob were basically mercenary. God, of course, knew all this, and Jacob was under His orders and protection anyway (vs. 3). So Laban was powerless to do anything other than kiss his daughters good-bye, and cry in his beer as he watched all that wealth disappear over the sand dune.

When we as believers are paying attention to God's program, we could be surrounded by every Indian ever assembled in a wild west movie and still come out with our scalps intact. The Lord has committed Himself to our protection, within the boundaries of His overall plan. Although Jacob may have said when he saw Laban and the gang coming

184   *A View of Genesis*

over the hill, "Uh oh! This is not going to be a good day!," he had nothing to fear. Neither do we, when the ogres appear on our radar screens. Solomon tells us, "When a man's ways are pleasing to the Lord, He makes even his enemies live at peace with him" (Proverbs 16:7).

Our marching orders are in the Scripture. God gives us power to accomplish our mission if we are willing to get out on the trail. And even though it may seem like the trail is going through the wilderness, it's really a protected area.

And the Labans in our lives will have to live with it.

Genesis 31:17-55

" ... Rachel stole her father's household gods." (vs. 19)

I have a friend who was in the Navy at the same time I was in the Marines. He had just come back from a Med cruise when we got together. "If anybody makes it to heaven," he told me, with tongue in cheek, "it's going to be me. I was just blessed by the pope in St. Peter's Square; I've been saved; I'm circumcised, and my cousin has been baptized by proxy for me in the Mormon Church. I've got a lot of tickets to present to St. Peter at the Pearly Gates!"

If getting into heaven were a matter of having the right ticket to show Peter at the proverbial Pearly Gates, it would be interesting to be his assistant ticket taker for a few hours to see what aspiring entrants would dig out of their pockets and purses. "Hmmmm. Here's a ticket that says, 'My family was a Christian family.' Sorry, the bus leaves for the other place right over there. What's that you have on your ticket, sir? 'I gave up bingo for Lent.' Nope. Doesn't make it. Yes, ma'am, I'll look at your ticket here. 'I was baptized into such-and-such church.' That's very nice, lady, but that doesn't mean anything here. Over here, sir, let's see your ticket. 'I was an elder, sang in the choir, served regularly at the pancake breakfast, loved my neighbor and gave generously to the mission.' Wow! You were busy! They'll be able to use you at the other place. Bus leaves in fifteen minutes. What's on your ticket, sonny? 'Complimentary ticket. Paid for by Jesus at Calvary's cross.' Hey, Peter! Open the gate! We've got a live one here!"

Rachel may have thought her father's household gods had some clout. Although she was a worshipper of Jehovah, it appears that she wanted something else on her ticket, too. But the only things that she accomplished by taking the little images were to make her father angry; almost get Jacob into the soup; and put her own neck in the noose (vs. 32). She then had to lie to get out of it (vs. 35). Better she should have left them on her father's armoire.

The Scriptures are clear that there is only one way to God the Father, and that is through Jesus, God the Son. He said, "I am the Way, and the Truth and the Life. No one comes to the Father except through me" (John 14:6). And He is the exclusive way. No other person, no other method, no other god, no other image, no other sacrifice, no other

A View of Genesis

intercessor, no church, no work, no heritage, no merit of any kind will open the gate of heaven. It is Jesus, and Jesus only. Complete faith in His sacrifice, His atoning work on Calvary's cross.

"For there is one God and one Mediator between God and men, the Man Christ Jesus, Who gave Himself a ransom for all men ..." (1 Timothy 2:5).

Make sure your ticket has the right price for admission on it!

Genesis 32:1-2

"Jacob also went on his way, and the angels of God met him." (vs. 1)

Laban and his entourage had gone back to Paddan-Aram, and Jacob continued on his way home. Another problem was on the horizon — Esau! The victory over Laban was soon forgotten, and all the old fears came back. Esau would have had twenty years to chew on the loss of his birthright and blessing, and he had to be waiting with all sorts of novel tortures to inflict upon Jacob.

But who was this in the path? Angels! A whole host of them! Jacob had seen them before at Bethel (28:16), up and down the ladder. And what did this mean? Well, maybe Jacob had forgotten that God's promises to bring him safely back to his father's house and to multiply his family like rabbits and to bless all the nations through him were backed up with God's version of the U.S. Marines. Angels! All over the place! Esau may as well run up the white flag if he had any nasty ideas.

Jacob was the only one who saw the angels, but they were there protecting his entire group. At another time, Elisha and his servant were surrounded by the forces of a king who wanted Elisha's head on the business end of a sword. The servant had the panic button at the full depress position, but Elisha went on sipping his coffee and checking out the results of the chariot races. When the servant kept on wailing, Elisha asked God to open his eyes and give him the big picture. He saw angels and horses and chariots of fire (2 Kings 6:13-17). Although he couldn't see them before, they were there, ready for whatever.

One could go on for pages about angels. Billy Graham has written a book about them. Suffice it to say that they are "... mighty ones who do (God's) bidding ... who obey His word ... who do His will" (Psalm 103:20-21). They are "ministering spirits sent to serve those who will inherit salvation" (Hebrews 1:14). In simple terms, angels are who God calls on to get on with His program, everything from socking it to Sodom (Genesis 19:13) to gearing up with Gideon (Judges 6:12) to meeting up with Mary (Luke 24:4) to building up the believers (Hebrews 1:14 and many other places) to implementing any other idea that God comes up with.

They were there for Jacob, even though his actions in dealing with Esau made it seem like he thought they were just decorations. And they are also here for us, for those who are children of God through faith in Jesus. To guide, protect, deliver, assist, serve. Not to carry us to Acapulco and feed us bonbons and lemonade by the pool, but to help accomplish God's program in our lives.

If we think that guardian angels are just a myth, we're mything out on one of God's great comforts for our lives.

Genesis 32:3-21

"In great fear and distress Jacob divided the people who were with him into two groups... ." (32:7)

There is a saying that goes, "Trust in the Lord, but keep your powder dry." In other words, don't sit around waiting for the Lord to bail you out of every situation which may come up. He expects us to be prepared and use our noodles.

But sometimes using the noodle gets us into a pot of noodle soup. Mostly when the noodles are home made, with none of the ingredients coming from God. Completely ignoring His recipe book. That's what happened to Jacob here. He wasn't even allowing God into the kitchen, although he had just seen God's assistant chefs, all the angels, ready to help mix up the sauce (32:1-2).

Although Jacob prayed to God (vs. 9-12), it was a panic prayer, and he probably had his gift list for Esau made out before the last "Amen." "God, I really, really need Your help." "Man, I hope that Esau grooves on all these goodies." "God, do you remember that Esau is a bad dude who will whack up the women and carve up the kiddies?" (vs. 11). "Maybe if I call him 'my lord' and 'your highness' and 'here am I your humble servant' he'll forget he doesn't like me." "Don't forget your promises, God, to bring me home and make me a great nation" (vs 12). "If I divide up the gang, maybe Esau won't see them all and some of them can slip through" (vs. 8). But God hears panic prayers, too, and Jacob, ever the manipulator, went through the gift and groveling bit for zilch. God already had Esau wired.

All of us get into these panic situations. Those that don't are already residents of the local cemetery. And God does, as before stated, hear the panic prayer. In fact, He already has help on the way before we hit the knees to the carpet. "Before they call I will answer; while they are still speaking I will hear" (Isaiah 65:24). But He also expects us to "keep the powder dry." Be ready. Read His Word. Pray before panic time. Trust. Associate with His people, where His message is preached and heard. Make sure our plans are consistent with His purposes and Word. And when the crisis comes, ask for His wisdom to deal with the matter, rather than crying out for Him to transport us to an abandoned village in Antarctica where trouble can't find us. Right away, anyhow.

A View of Genesis

Jacob could have avoided his loss of sleep and sour stomach and dry mouth and knocking knees if he had remembered God's promises and power, and prayed for God's principles to permeate his plans. So can we.

If we trust in prayer more than our plans, God will provide His plans in response to our prayer.

Genesis 32:22-32

"So Jacob was left alone, and a man wrestled with him till daybreak. When the man saw that he could not overpower him, he touched the socket of Jacob's hip so that his hip was wrenched ... ." (vs. 24-25)

When I was a kid in school, I was a pretty good speller. We used to have spelling bees in our classes, and my friends used to marvel that I could almost keep up with Martha DiFonso, who was so good she could spell words that weren't even invented yet. (She was great in Latin, too.) She won all the contests, and she never even had to buy a vowel.

Occasionally we had community spelling bees, too. Most of the time, my Dad and I were the last ones standing. And I always beat him for the prize, which was inevitably a fresh cooked apple pie. My Dad just couldn't win. He always choked in the finals. But I usually graciously let him have a piece of my apple pie.

Well, here was Jacob, wrestling with God Himself. The WWF would have drooled over this match. It lasted all night. (This is one of the "theophanies," where the Lord appeared to people at those times as a man.) And the Lord couldn't win (vs. 25). Jacob knew he wasn't wrestling some native bonzo who jumped out of the bushes, and he hung on for dear life until he prevailed and got his prize — a blessing (vs. 29).

So why couldn't God win? The same reason my Dad couldn't win. God could have vaporized Jacob if He had decided to, just like my Dad could have spelled twenty words to every one that I knew. The Lord wanted Jacob to win, so that He could bless him; He loves to bless those He loves. And my Dad made sure that I won, because my joy was his joy. Their love prevented them from winning.

There was another time when Jesus couldn't do something. The Jewish leaders and rabbis had it right when they said in derision, "He saved others ... but He can't save Himself! ... Let Him come down from the cross, and we will believe in Him!" (Matthew 27:41-43). Oh, there were gazillion angels standing by ready to crush these mockers like an elephant would crush an ant, and Jesus would have just had to say, "Come!" But Jesus "endured the cross, scorning its shame" (Hebrews 12:2). Why? It was a demonstration of His incredible love for us. Our blessing was His goal; our joy is His joy. His love kept the angels at home.

The Lord touched Jacob's hip, and Jacob limped for the rest of his life. When we accept Jesus' sacrifice as the payment for our sin, the Lord touches us, too. But this touch doesn't cripple us; it takes a soul which is dead because of sin, and gives it life (Ephesians 2:1-6). Eternal life. A gift of love which cost Jesus His life.

And apple pie tastes so much better when it is love and joy a la mode.

Genesis 32:30-32

" ... I saw God face to face, and yet my life was spared." (vs. 30)

If the National Enquirer would have been around in Jacob's time, he would have made a zillion bucks for this story. Can't you see the headline? "Itinerant Farmer Wrestles God to a Draw! Lives to Tell About It!" And he would have never escaped the paparazzi following him on their supercharged camels, waiting for the rematch to get a picture of the Almighty.

It wouldn't have happened. God wasn't in the habit of showing up in the Canaanite coffee houses. He did kibitz with a couple of other people from time to time; He and Moses had a regular kaffeeklatsch (Numbers 12:8; Deuteronomy 34:10), and Isaiah got a private audience which left him practically breathless (Isaiah 6:1-5). But very few mortals have ever had the privilege of seeing the Immortal One without being carried out feet first.

Until Jesus came. He told His disciples, "Anyone who has seen Me has seen the Father" (John 14:9). And He told the Jewish crowd, "I and the Father are one" (John 10:30). But very few people believed Him. Wasn't He just Jesus, a poor carpenter's son from Nazareth? And "Nazareth! Can any good thing come from there?" (John 1:46). Certainly not the Father. So the paparazzi put away their cameras. It wasn't even worth following Him to Calvary, where He was put to death along with a couple of incorrigibles.

Paul was another one who saw the Lord (1 Corinthians 9: 1). He was cruising on down to Damascus from Jerusalem (when he was anti-Jesus, to put it mildly), and got stopped in his tracks by Jesus Himself (Acts 9:1-9). From that time forward, he saw, lived and preached "the light of the knowledge of the glory of God in the face of Christ" (2 Corinthians 4:6). And Paul tells us that someday we will see Jesus face to face (1 Corinthians 13:12).

At that time it will be a different picture. Calvary and the cross will be in the past. Some will see Him as the Lamb of God, those who have accepted His sacrifice on Calvary for their sin. "They will see His face, and His Name will be on their foreheads .... And they will reign for ever and ever" (Revelation 22:4-5). Others will come face to face with Jesus, sitting on a great white throne, the Judge of all the dead. The books will be opened, and, "if anyone's name was not found written in the Book of Life, he was thrown into the lake of fire" (Revelation 20:15).

One who doesn't face up to his sin and accept Jesus while he's on this earth will face some very heavy music when he sees Him face to face, wearing His judge's robe of absolute righteousness.

There won't be any wrestling match to determine the winner.

"So Jacob was left alone, and a man wrestled with him until daybreak ... Jacob replied, 'I will not let you go until you bless me.'" (vs. 24, 26)

"(Jacob) struggled with the angel and overcame him; he wept and begged for his favor." (Hosea 12:4)

It's a good thing God can't get sick. He would have been in intensive care by now from all the nausea created by haphazard prayer. When's the last time you were at a prayer meeting in which the major features were not a recitation of the church's S. L.& L. Platoon (sick, lame and lazy, as we used to say in the Corps) and the latest juicy gossip disguised as a pious request, "Please pray for our poor sister Phoebe, whose husband just ran off with the mailperson?"

Then there's the "Program Prayer," known by the acronym "ACTS." "Adoration" must be first, "Confession" next, some "Thanksgiving," and finally "Supplication." All these things are well and good, but some people seem to think that God might be confused if a little Thanksgiving gets in before the Confession. And, of course, there's the Lord's Prayer, which in some instances has become so mechanical in the Sunday Service that it should have an inspection and oil change every 3,000 words or three months, whichever comes first.

Jacob in essence gives us a lesson in prayer in this passage, which is confirmed by the Lord in His treatise on prayer in Luke 18:1-14. Jacob got alone with God, and struggled until he got results. Not just five minutes and off to the mall; it was an all night session. Not just a few words to God like, "Bless my house and kids and car, and help me not to stray too far;" it was an all-out struggle for help in a very difficult situation. Nor did Jacob arrogantly tell God that it was His responsibility to meet Jacob's needs; here was a focused man who, when his strength was gone, hung on to God for dear life. And it wasn't a "season of prayer" that had more snoozing than praying; Jacob was really into it, spiritually as well as literally wrestling with God to get the blessing.

The Lord gives some of the same principles for prayer in Luke 18, in His parables of the woman who wouldn't give up, and that of the publican and the sinner. Read them to get on the same page with God when it comes to prayer time. Find out that prayer time is all the time; consistent, earnest, focused, humble, penitent prayer to a God Who delights, as He did with Jacob, in granting the petitions of prevailing prayer. As Paul says, "Do not be anxious about anything, but in everything, by prayer and petition, with thanksgiving, present your requests to God. And the peace of God, which transcends all understanding, will guard your hearts and your minds in Christ Jesus" (Philippians 4:6).

When we wrestle with God in prayer, we have a better chance of winning than when we are wrestling with our problems and circumstances.

Genesis 33:1-20

"So that day Esau started on his way back to Seir. Jacob, however, went to Succoth, where he built a place for himself...." (vs. 16-17)

Everyone thinks that Jacob was a farmer and a rancher. Actually, he was a politician. This chapter proves it. Look at what happened.

First, remember that he had used fraud and deceit to get Esau's birthright and blessing. Then he took off to another district to avoid the consequences. In the previous chapter when he was about to come back home with all the wealth he had acquired (Genesis 32:13-23), he made up a gift package that would hopefully make Esau forget the fact that he had gotten the shaft, or at least soften him up somewhat. It was sort of like they do in Washington — take away your assets and then give a little bit back to you just before they have to face you again, so you feel like they're on your side. Of course, all this was to be accompanied by fawning speeches — "I am your humble servant;" "here is a gift to my lord Esau;" blah blah blah. The only thing missing was, "Ah feel yore pain."

Well, regardless of what had happened in the past, Esau was happy to see his brother again (vs. 4). So after they had had a good cry and a cup of coffee, Esau suggested they all go back home together. Jacob had no intention of heading in Esau's direction, so, like any good politician, he came up with a plausible excuse why that wouldn't work (vs. 13). Then Esau offered to leave some of his men with Jacob for protection (vs. 15). "Oh, that's most kind of you, Esau, but please don't trouble yourself. Your friendship is all I want. See you in Seir" (vs. 14-15). And as soon as Esau was out of sight, Jacob took off in a different direction.

So why did Jacob say one thing and do something else? Who knows? Maybe he really didn't trust Esau. Maybe he thought Esau would be mad if he said he was going elsewhere. But it was another demonstration of Jacob's difficulty with the truth, when he felt it was to his advantage to be less than candid.

Lest we be too hard on Jacob, however, do we not all have a tad of the politician in us? Fibbing a little when we think it might help us. Trying to buy favor with someone with a well timed gift. Lathering up our public with a flowery speech. Promising to do something and not following through. We all fit the mold.

The Lord is not impressed. Read the 15th Psalm, in which David describes the kind of person who finds favor with God; one who is honest in all his attitudes and relationships. "He ... who speaks the truth from his heart; ... who keeps his oath even when it hurts; he who does these things will never be shaken" (Psalm 15: 2-5). Jacob really didn't have to lie again to Esau. God had already proven His faithfulness, and He didn't leave it behind at the border of Canaan.

Although the truth may hurt, it doesn't cause the lasting pain that lying does.

Genesis 34

"Now Dinah ... went out to visit the daughters of the land." (vs. 1)

"It's nine o'clock. Do you know where your children are?" Some time ago, that was a question which was asked on the radio in connection with a campaign for good parenting. And they didn't mean nine o'clock in the morning.

This chapter is a primer on ineffective parenting. Jacob's daughter Dinah was hanging out at the oasis with the other girls of Shechem (vs. 1). The then-current answer to Sylvester Q. Studley (vs. 2, 19) bopped in on his convertible camel, and before you could say Doctor Ruth, he had bundled her off to his bungalow and done the dirty deed. Now Dinah was about 15 years old, it appears that she was forced, and her father and brothers were not very pleased, even though Shechem wanted desperately to marry the girl he had defiled. And they expressed that displeasure in a very definitive manner, as the remainder of the chapter relates.

So what was so bad about Jacob's parenting?

In the first place, he had set a bad example for his children over the years. He had two wives and two concubines. Even though that was socially acceptable, it was contrary to the law of God. And no doubt they had observed his duplicity in his reunion with Esau, as well as his obsequious behavior in preparation for that meeting. His sons may well have wondered, if Jacob's God is so great, why is he going to all these lengths to mollify Uncle Esau? Great parenting involves a personal walk of faith and obedience with God, rather than social acceptability.

In addition, Jacob had settled in a place which was not God's choice. He had been told to go back to Bethel, where he had first met God (31:3). But he turned aside to Shechem, bought property and built a house there. It was the wrong place, and when Dinah went off with the girls, it was the wrong crowd. Great parenting involves creating the right environment for children, as much as is possible. Inattention to God's choices is not helpful in this endeavor.

Then, it would appear, Jacob had not instructed his sons effectively in the truths of God's covenant. To use the act of circumcision, a holy sign

200   *A View of Genesis*

of the relationship with God Himself, as a ruse to exact revenge in what was by all measures an overkill (vs. 14-17), was outrageous. It would be like inviting the whole village to a Billy Graham evangelistic film, locking everybody in the building and setting fire to it because one guy in there was a child molester. It demonstrated the fact that Jacob's sons were not sufficiently familiar with what was holy and pleasing to God, as well as seeking His counsel to deal with this situation. Great parenting involves constant teaching of spiritual truths. Read Deuteronomy 7 in this regard.

Want to be a great parent? Stay in His Word, speak out His principles, stand for what is holy and just, and spend a lot of time on your knees.

Genesis 34:30

"Then Jacob said ... 'You have brought trouble on me by making me a stench to ... the people in this land.'" (vs. 30)

God must have had an Excedrin headache by now. Here is Jacob, who He has not only tolerated but blessed clear down to his shoes, cheating here, conniving there and fibbing over yonder, and he, Jacob, is worried about his own reputation for what his sons have done. He's sweating that the Canaanite Cartel might come and fit him with a set of concrete boots (vs. 30).

You can almost hear God speak. "Hey! Jake! What about MY reputation? Do you and your gang think you can go to the next village and tell them what a wonderful God you have? Do you? I got news for you, chum. They ain't gonna listen!"

No, they wouldn't have listened. Jacob and his sons were terrible representatives for the Almighty. And God couldn't just fax the rest of the tribes living around the area and tell them that He regretted what Jake and the boys had done, and here's a little foreign aid to make it all right.

You know what? We may be giving somewhat the same impression about God to those around us, only not in such an obvious or violent manner. The Bible tells us that, "We are therefore Christ's ambassadors, as though God were making His appeal through us" (2 Corinthians 5:20). And if He is making His appeal through us, how are we coming across?

Some of us are so self-absorbed that we are totally insensitive to the spiritual, emotional and physical needs around us. Others who call themselves Christians are less than honest in their business affairs, less than civil with their neighbors, less than loving with their families, and downright nasty when it comes to others in the church. Then there are those that if they were accused of being Christians, there wouldn't be enough evidence to convict them. And some are so rigid they could hold up a circus tent. People notice, believe me, they notice.

The job of an ambassador is to tend to the affairs of his or her Sovereign State. In our case, we are charged with representing God Himself. Because He is righteous we are not only to stand for righteousness, we are to practice it as well. Because He is loving, we are to exemplify that love to all around us. Because He is merciful, we are to be channels of mercy and care to those in need. Because He is the only true God, we are to make Him known to our world. Not many (if any) of us will be another Mother Teresa, but we can make a difference in the lives around us, if we are true to our King.

Since how people view us may be how they view Jesus, let's make sure we're not showing them a junkyard.

Genesis 35:1-15

"Jacob said to his household ..., 'Get rid of the foreign gods you have with you, and purify yourselves and change your clothes. Then come, let us go up to Bethel, where I will build an altar to God'... Then they set out, and the terror of God fell on all the towns around them so that no one pursued them" (vs. 2-5).

After the Shechem disaster, it would appear that God had had enough of Jacob sitting in a place where he shouldn't have been to begin with. Oh, yes, Jacob had built an altar there (33:20) but, like today, just because a person goes to church doesn't mean that he's keeping the Almighty happy. And God wasn't happy with Jacob. So He told him, "Hey, Jake! You and I are out of touch. I'm the One Who appeared to you when you were running from your brother. Remember? Well, rent yourself a U-Haul and get yourself back to Bethel where you belong" (vs. 1).

But first, there were a few things that had to be taken care of. When a person gets careless with God, he picks up habits that affect his relationship with the Almighty. And it usually rubs off on the people around him. That was the case with Jacob and his household. He had tolerated Rachel bringing pagan idols with her when they left Laban's house (31:19). He had been less than diligent in training his sons in the fear of God; they were stained with the blood of the Shechemites as a result. His inattention to Dinah's associations had led to her defilement. All this had to be changed. So Jacob, now under God's direction, gathered up all the idols, Rachel's beloved teraphim and the lucky charm earrings included, and buried them under a tree (vs. 4). Then there was a ceremonial bath, signifying a change of heart (vs. 2). And they left for Bethel.

And because he was back in fellowship with God, what Jacob feared didn't happen. God spooked the people around Jacob so much that they stayed in their tents, rather than coming after Jacob to avenge their buddies from Shechem.

Some of us, like Jacob, gradually get out of touch with God. Things and habits just sort of slip in, and pretty soon there's so much static on the heavenly line that God just can't get through. But He just doesn't hang up the phone; sooner or later He'll get the line open, one way or the other. He lets us know that it's time we clean up our act, change our attitudes, and get back to where we belong. And all the idols have to go. Things we worship. Material desires. Personal pride. Power grabs. Anything that gets between us and God.

And do you know what? The things we fear the most won't happen. More than likely we won't be burned at the stake as a religious zealot. Nor will we have to go to the mission to get a square meal. People might roll their eyes and say, "Joe (or Suzie) has religion," but God will keep them in their tents.

God will not remain idle with His people who fiddle around with their own idols.

"He called the place El Bethel, because it was there that God revealed Himself to him when he was fleeing from his brother." (vs. 5)

How would you like to get up in the morning, and there sitting on the edge of the bed would be God Himself? "This is what I'd like you to do today." He would say. "And here is a little blessing to go along with it." Life would be a little different, wouldn't it? Like the Seven Dwarfs of Snow White fame, we would whistle while we worked. We would know that everything was cool between us and God, and a screaming boss and deadlines and messy desks and overflowing in-boxes and really ugly coffee wouldn't make a whole lot of difference.

But it's more likely that if the Almighty made such an appearance, we would faint dead away, and our wives would think that we were getting too old for the excitement of watching Monday Night Football. Or Baywatch. Or Lassie reruns.

There were three times that God made such an appearance to Jacob. The first time was at Bethel (23:12) when he was hightailing it out of Canaan with Esau nipping at his heels, and Jake almost had a heart attack. But he recovered in time to hear God's blessing, even though he didn't believe it. If he had, he more than likely wouldn't have been afraid of Esau anymore and would have gone back home. He'd have saved himself 20 years of working for Laban and all the grief that went with it. Then God appeared to Jacob at Peniel, after he had run away from Laban and was dreading meeting up again with Esau (32:24). This time he got a bad hip out of it, but also another blessing. He still didn't get the message, though, because he came up with all sorts of convoluted schemes to mollify and then avoid Esau, and wasted yet another ten years of his life.

Finally, back in Bethel, he got the message after God told him again (vs. 9-12). "Hey! Jake! El Shaddai here. Remember me? The God of power and provision? Here's the deed to the turf, it's all yours. You and your descendants will possess it until the end of time." And even though Jacob was to experience a good many trials and sorrow in the years to come, he never ran from anything or anybody again, and was able to pass the blessing on to his children and grandchildren.

A View of Genesis

Come to think of it, God is available to meet with us every morning, and He brings His briefcase of blessings along. He appears when we open the pages of His book, and we see Him with the eye of our faith. And even though He doesn't give us specific instructions like, "Go easy on the doughnuts today, call your mother— she misses you, avoid the boss because he's going to have a bad day and don't forget your wife's birthday tomorrow," He has enough instructions and encouragement in there to guide us through the problems and keep us out of the hands of the Philistines. And bless us with the knowledge of His presence.

You can leave your Nikes at home, since you won't be running from anybody.

Genesis 35:8-29

"Now Deborah, Rebekah's nurse, died..." (vs. 8); "So Rachel died..." (vs. 19); Then (Isaac) breathed his last and died. ..." (vs. 29)

First his mother's faithful servant, who apparently had come to live with Jacob and his family. Then his beloved wife, Rachel. After that, his father, Isaac. All of them gone over a short time. Pretty tough pills for Jacob to swallow. Was God mad at him? Was his past catching up with him? Did the blessing run out?

None of the above. Even though it may come at any time to anybody in any stage of life, death is the natural termination of life in this sphere. Only Enoch and Elijah made it out otherwise. It's one to a customer. Everybody gets a ticket and goes through the gate. Unless Jesus comes again before our gate opens. In that case, we get the Uppertaker instead of the undertaker.

So Jacob wasn't being punished for his past deeds. If that were the case, he would have been hit with everything in the book a long time before this. It's true that those who sow trouble will also reap it (Job 4:8; Proverbs 22:8; Galatians 6:7-8); but that may not come until they stand before God (see Psalm 73). Jacob's sorrow was just another series of life experiences for him to take to God for solace and comfort. And there wasn't any way for him to connive himself out of any of it.

Some people seem to think that the recipe for Christianity is like a Duncan Hines cake mix: just add Jesus to whatever we are, stir, and everything will come out smooth. Unfortunately, it doesn't work that way. Believers still go through life's experiences, good, bad and indifferent. But just like God was with Jacob through the loss of his "nanny," wife and father, He is also with us as we walk through the land mines of life. Sickness. Death. Job loss. Family pain. Financial ruin. Loss of reputation. Betrayal by friends. God feels our pain. Really, He does. And that's something more than a political sound bite. Read Psalm 22 to find out how much Jesus suffered. Pain and grief were not just academic exercises to Him.

Hebrews 4:14-16 tells us that we have a High Priest, Jesus, Who understands all the things that we will experience in this life, and that we should, "draw near with confidence to the throne of grace, that we

A View of Genesis

may receive mercy and find grace to help in time of need." No, He doesn't generally dispatch a heavenly helicopter to pluck us out of our circumstances, but He Himself comes along side to pick us up and carry us through.

Rachel, as she was dying, named her son Ben-oni, "son of my sorrow." Jacob, even in his grief, was able to change his name to Benjamin, "son of my right hand," or "son of strength" (vs. 18). God gave him strength to see through his great sorrow to the promise of the future.

And there is great strength in God's futures market.

Genesis 35:16-29

" ... Reuben went in and slept with his father's concubine Bilhah" ... . (vs. 22)

It wouldn't have made many headlines today, but it hit the local gazette back in Canaan. Reuben did a no-no. As a matter of fact, incest was labeled as a detestable act by God and was punishable by death (Leviticus 18:8). By the way, so was homosexual conduct — see Leviticus 18:22. I guess that's what's wrong with God today. He's not politically correct. He would be labeled a homophobe.

Perhaps Reuben didn't get the ax right away because the tables of the law were not yet given. But that wasn't an acceptable loophole. God took notice of this act, and so did Jacob (Israel) (vs. 22). And it affected Reuben's life, as well as his posterity throughout the annals of the nation Israel. "You will not excel" (literally, "you will have no preference") was Jacob's deathbed "blessing" to Reuben, referring specifically to this sin (Genesis 49:4). It was the reason why he lost the three privileges of the firstborn— the priesthood, which went to Levi; the birthright, which went to Joseph; and the kingdom, which went to Judah. Reuben's tribe never rose to prominence, and was one of the first tribes to be carried into captivity (1 Chronicles 5:26). There was never a prophet, a judge, or a national hero which came from his lineage.

Was God being too tough on Reuben? After all, his father was a liar, a thief, a conniver, and probably even cheated on his income tax. Compared with Reuben, he got away with murder. Besides, this was only a one-night stand, and everybody's entitled to one little indiscretion here and there. Well, God has different ideas than we do, and since He is the Final Judge, even the 800 pound gorilla lives by His rules. While any kind of sin is still sin to Him, it seems that God is especially intolerant of sexual sin. Proverbs 5 through 7 talks a lot about the evil, the hazards and the consequences of lust, fornication and adultery. Samson, David and numerous others whose lives were devastated bear witness to the lasting effects of sexual immorality.

In Ephesians 5:31-32, we're told that the marital union is the earthly illustration of the relationship between Christ and His church. When we love the things of this world more than we love Jesus, we are committing spiritual adultery (James 4:4- 5). Perhaps this is why God is so

210   *A View of Genesis*

hard on sexual sin. He wants to let us know that intimate relations are special, because of the spiritual relationship with His Son that it exemplifies. He didn't create sex for the benefit of Hollywood or the tabloids. It is the expression of a sacred union, and He expects it to be kept pure.

And speaking of creating sex, God also made it for Adam and Eve, not Adam and Steve. He doesn't give a bag of beans for political correctness.

Genesis 35:23 - 36:40

"These were the sons of Jacob..." (35:26); These were the chiefs descended from Esau ... the father of the Edomites." (36:43)

After Isaac's funeral, the two brothers went their separate ways, more than likely never to see each other again (36:6-8). And the separation was not only geographical; Esau married into the Canaanite society (36:2-3) and drifted further and further away from God, while Jacob (now Israel) took his place as the patriarch of God's chosen people, the nation through which the entire world has been blessed.

In the succeeding generations, the Israelites and the Edomites made the Hatfields and McCoys look like bosom buddies. Although they were blood relatives, the only blood Edom was interested in was Israel's blood flowing in the streets. Edom was a constant source of irritation and conflict to Israel. One of its greatest acts of savagery was when Herod the Great, an Edomite, had all the male children of Bethlehem who were two years and under killed, in order to get rid of the Baby Jesus (Matthew 2:13-16).

An interesting fact in the genealogy of Esau in Genesis 36 is that when one king or chief died, generally there was a king or chief from a different tribe that took over (36:31-39). They apparently had no family succession plans. Or else they got kicked out by someone bigger and badder. There was a lack of national discipline and cohesiveness that destroyed the unity and the life of the nation.

Edom was the ultimate dysfunctional family. And a Christian family, or a local church body, can easily find itself in a similar condition. It all starts with a lack of leadership. Carelessness in the things of God. Allowing the spiritual termites to gnaw away at the foundation. When the four letter word heard on Sunday morning is "Fore!" instead of "Amen!" Drifting. Floating down the Undisciplined River until the roar of the Falls of Forgetfulness is heard, and it's too late.

There's one major difference, however. Edom had been on God's hit list from the time Esau was hassling with Jacob in Rebekah's womb. A Christian family or a local church body, even though it may be floating along with the current, is never rejected by God and can be pulled out of the river before terminal disaster is reached. There's a life boat called

A View of Genesis

Repentance, and it's always on duty. It turns everything around. It's powered by a Grace Engine that has enough power to get right to the edge of the falls, pick up the floater and return safely to shore.

A family or a church needs to be spiritually disciplined, so that God doesn't have to discipline it spiritually.

Genesis 37:1-10

"Joseph ... was tending the flocks with his brothers ... and he brought their father a bad report about them." (vs. 2)

I guess Joseph never went to the Dale Carnegie course, "How to Win Friends and Influence People." Or the graduate course in the School of Life, "Learn to Keep Your Mouth Shut Before Someone Stuffs a Dirty Sock in It." He was out there with the sheep and the brothers (the four sons of the two handmaidens). Apparently they were engaged in activities other than sheep-tending. Joseph saw what was going on with the Boyz in the 'Hood, and he snitched to the old man. Not a good idea. The brothers would have loved to have arranged a necktie party for Joey, with one end of the necktie tightly tied around his neck and the other end thrown over the limb of a tree and pulled smartly downward.

Or was it a good idea? Let's think about it. Joseph is one of the few personalities about whom Scripture says nothing derogatory. In fact, in Genesis 39:3 we read that, "The Lord gave (Joseph) success in everything he did." Instead of going after the babes like Samson did, Joseph ran away from opportunities. Instead of lying like his three ancestors Abraham, Isaac and Jacob did, he told the truth regardless of the consequences. And he was totally moral. After all the garbage God had put up with from Adam to Jacob, He must have been thrilled to have someone like Joseph to work with. Morality and the truth. A rare commodity in those days, and even less in these. Joseph saw that things were not right at the office, and he became the patron saint to all whistle blowers.

There was a difference to his whistle blowing, however, than what we see today. Joseph didn't think about what big bucks he could get for his efforts. Whether he would be seen on CNN or interviewed by Larry King. Maybe even get to that pinnacle of success, an appearance with Oprah. He was motivated by honesty, morality and truth. Whether or not his brothers liked him was not an issue. And even though the Scripture passage doesn't say it, my bet would be that he confronted his brothers about their conduct before he went to the old man.

Ecclesiastes 3:7 says, "There is a time to be silent and a time to speak ..." And even though today in most circles it is unacceptable to speak

A View of Genesis

out against sin, dishonesty and unrighteousness, we need to be shouting it from the rooftops. Sure, we are labeled as the "sinister religious right," homophobes, unloving and judgmental, but if we "speak the truth in love" (Ephesians 4:15), hating the sin but loving the sinner, we will be fulfilling our responsibility in God's eyes, and that's what really matters.

Jesus said in Matthew 5:13, "You are the salt of the earth." Salt is that which hurts in a wound, but ends up healing it. We are the salt shakers.

There ought to be a whole lot of shakin' goin' on.

Genesis 37:1-10

"Now Israel loved Joseph more than any of his other sons   ... and he made a richly ornamented robe for him." (vs. 3)

Joseph was in a real pickle with his brothers. Israel showed open favoritism for him over the rest of the gang. Took him out to Brooks Brothers for a coat, when the others' coats came from the Salvation Army Thrift Store. Put him in charge of the sheep herding crew, even though he was the youngest in the field. Joseph had snitched on the others for messing up on the job. And then came those dreams (vs. 5-9). "This brat is telling us that we're going to kiss his big toe? He better watch his flanks, or he'll end up as part of the lamb barbecue." He was about as popular as tomorrow's mother-in-law at tonight's bachelor party.

But Israel's inappropriate favoritism wasn't the real source of the fire which burned in the brothers' bellies. There were other things. Joseph was the original Mr. Kleen. He was impeccably behaved; color the brothers troublemakers. He was industrious to a fault; color the brothers lazy. He was totally truthful; color the brothers disingenuous. He was on the same wave length with God; color the brothers tuned out. He was without a nasty bone in his body; color the brothers merciless. Maybe it was the brothers who should have had the coat of many colors, rather than Joseph. They would have worn it to Guilt City. And they knew, just like Israel did, that Joseph wasn't chewing on too much peyote root when he told them the dreams. These were from God, and they didn't like it one bit.

They were flat out envious. They were envious of his character and his conduct. They were envious of his status in the family and his status with God. They were envious of his abilities and his success. They were green from their nose to their toes. And it wasn't Joseph's fault, it was their fault.

Maybe before we agree that the brothers were real jerks, we ought to take a look at ourselves. What happens when we're struggling, especially financially, and one of the brothers drives up to church in his new Cadillac and says, "Hey! Brother Joe! See how the Father has blessed me? Praise the Lord!" About that time we hope a flock of pigeons will ruin his paint job. And also hit him directly on his toupee. Or when Sister Suzie's perfect kids in their perfect clothing sit like perfect angels in Sunday School, and we just get told for the third time this month our own wild banshees knocked over the Kool Aid. Are we jealous?

Well, if we're in tune with God, others' successes won't bother us. And we'll know that even though the Father might seem to have dumped a 30-ton trailer of blessings in someone else's back yard and only a wheel-barrow full in ours, He knows what He's doing. Some day we'll know the reasons. He doesn't play favorites. We should thank Him for what He's done with us, in us and for us.

In the meantime, it's a real blessing to be able to bless God for blessing others.

Genesis 37:12-27

"I'm looking for my brothers. Can you tell me where they are grazing their flocks?" (vs. 16)

Joseph was tending to his knitting around the family compound one day, when Israel asked him to go and find out how his brothers were doing with the flocks. They had gone out to Shechem to graze the sheep. With all that had transpired, the dreams, the coat, and all the anger of his brothers, if I had been Joseph, I'd have asked for a platoon of marines for protection. Not Joseph. He put on his tennies and headed for Shechem.

Well, they didn't have cell phones and smoke signals were not yet in vogue, so Joseph had to wander around trying to find the brothers. "They went to Dothan," he was told (vs. 17). Dothan was about 20 miles away, and there was no Greyhound bus leaving any time soon. He had to walk. Again, if I had been Joseph, I'd have gone back home. "I tried, Dad. But if I'd have gone to Dothan, they'd have probably already taken off for Chicago." Not him. He was diligent to do His father's business, and loved his brothers (45:15) regardless of their feelings and actions toward him.

When the brothers saw Joseph coming, they were less than delighted to see him. This was their chance to send him off to Permanent Dreamsville (vs. 18-20). It was no contest, ten against one. In great distress he pleaded for his life (42:21), but they threw him into a desert cistern, with all but Reuben figuring he would be history in a few days.

Joseph is one of the greatest types of Jesus in the Old Testament. (One writer has come up with 141 points of similarity.) He was an upright and righteous man (even though, being human and in this point unlike Jesus, he certainly sinned like all the rest of us). He loved his brothers, even though they hated him. He went searching for them, even though they were far off in the wilderness. They sold him for twenty shekels of silver, the price of a slave, and considered him as good as dead. He ended up, after much suffering, being their salvation from famine and death. And he freely forgave them for their sin (50:21).

Jesus, like Joseph, was diligent to do His Father's business (Matthew 26:39; Luke 2:49). He loved his brethren, even though they hated

218

Him (John 15:23-25). He was sold for thirty pieces of silver. He died, after much suffering, in order to become our salvation from eternal death, the penalty for sin. And He freely forgives us for that sin, when we acknowledge Him as our Saviour.

Like Joseph was exalted in Egypt, Jesus is now exalted over all the universe. Like Joseph's brethren owed everything to him, we now owe all that we have and are to Jesus.

Genesis 37:31-36

"Then Jacob tore his clothes, put on sackcloth and mourned for his son many days. All his sons and daughters came to comfort him, but he refused to be comforted. 'No,' he said, 'in mourning will I go down to my grave. ...'"(vs. 34-35)

Jacob's world had fallen apart. He grieved for his beloved son, as he had grieved for Rachel, Joseph's mother. All the Hallmark sympathy cards in Canaan, all the words of comfort, all his other children, all his wealth, couldn't put Jacob back together again. He went around looking like death sucking on a pickle. He never recovered until he saw Joseph again.

Joseph's world had fallen apart, too. Here he was in Egypt, away from his father, betrayed by those he loved, in a different culture and language, sold as a slave. It was enough to make him hunt for the nearest bridge. But, as the Scriptures tell us, Joseph made the most of his new world. God had His hand on him, and Joseph knew it. And even though he had a rough row to hoe on his way to the top, Joseph worked at it and made it with God's guidance and protection.

No doubt we will all agree that life is not a perpetual vacation in Hilton Head. And Monday morning comes around with too much regularity. With most of us, it is just a matter of time until our world falls apart. There are very few exceptions, if any. The question is, what do we do when it happens? Are we like Jacob, who had at least four appearances by God Himself to tell him he was going to be blessed out of his shoes, but still got lost in his black cloud? Or are we like Joseph, who was able by faith to look beyond his circumstances and discomfort to God's purposes?

I imagine it was hard for Joseph to see God's face from the cistern; or from the back of a Midianite camel on the way to Egypt; or while he was unjustly sitting in a prison for years. But his eye of faith had 20-20 vision. And his foresight was as sharp as his hindsight. When Joseph got to heaven, he probably gave God a high five and said, "You and me, we had 'em all the way!" When Jacob got there, God may have said, "Jake, if you would have kept the faith, you would have smiled a lot more than you did and drunk a lot less Pepto-Bismol."

What's God going to say to you and me?

220

" When Judah saw her, he thought she was a prostitute ... (He) went over to her and said, 'Come now, let me sleep with you.'" (vs. 16)

Sometimes you wonder what God was doing when He inspired the writers of Scripture to write what they did, and how and when it appears. Here we are, right in the middle of Joseph's problem and Jacob's sorrow, angry at the brothers and wondering how Joey and Jake are going to handle things, and then comes this account of Judah's indiscretions. Did God think we had to have a little bit of spicy material to keep us interested? Did He think we needed more evidence that the brothers were the worst by giving us the lowdown on another one of them? Did He just think that now was the time to make a comment on birth control methods as practiced by Onan (vs. 9-10)?

None of the above. One of the great things about God is that He tells it like it is. You might think that since the nation of Israel was and is God's chosen people, that He might have spruced them up a little bit, so that we don't think that God needed some help in making choices. But He lets it all hang out. People are people and sinners are sinners wherever they are. And God doesn't participate in any coverups.

Actually, this sordid chapter tells us more about God, His faithfulness and His grace. If we had been picking a nation to sponsor and through which redemption was to be provided to the world, we would have thrown Israel to the sharks a long time ago and made another selection. But not God. He made His choice, and although Israel has suffered incredibly through the years because of her sin, God has protected her from sure annihilation time and time again. So one of the things this chapter does is show how the line of the Messiah was continued. Jesus is referred to as "The Lion of the Tribe of Judah" (Revelation 5:5). And it shows how God uses ugly people and social low-lifes, dressing them up in His garments of righteousness solely by His grace, to achieve His purposes. Judah didn't have to go to seminary and become His Eminence the Most Reverend Doctor Judah before he was tapped for such a lofty role as the ancestor of the Savior Himself. Check out the genealogy of Matthew 1. And Tamar, who played the part of the prostitute (vs. 15-18) was one of the five women mentioned in that genealogy (1:3). Actually, when we look at the other four women there, only one had any spiritual credentials. Rahab (1:5) was a heathen prostitute; Ruth (1:5) was an alien; Bathsheba (1:6) was an adulteress; only Mary (1:16) had the right stuff. Is all that grace, or what?

And by the way, Onan was zapped not because he practiced birth control, but because he was selfish, dishonest and refused to participate in what was then "the rule of the levirate," in which the next oldest brother was responsible to produce children in a dead brother's name, to continue that brother's line. Onan wanted the birthright and all the goodies that went with it for himself. Bad choice.

Genesis 38:13-30

"As she was being brought out, (Tamar) sent a message to (Judah). 'I am pregnant by the man that owns these...' Judah ... said, 'She is more righteous than I, since I wouldn't give her to my son Shelah.' And he did not sleep with her again." (vs. 25-26)

A scene from "As the Old Testament World Turns:"

The crowd was gathered, ready for the execution. The stake was in place, the sticks piled at its base, the fire ready. "Who is it?" whispered a woman in the crowd. "A young girl named Tamar," said a bearded man nearby. "She is an adulteress. She was betrothed to one of Judah's sons, and got pregnant." "Who is her lover?" asked a young fellow standing next to the bearded man. "Don't know," was the reply. "She refuses to tell."

Slowly, Tamar walked between two men toward the center of the square, where the stake was waiting. Occasionally her step faltered, but she held her head high. Her eyes seemed to be riveted on Judah, whose scowling countenance followed her every move. It was he who had ordered Tamar to be burned to death. Judah, the tribal chief. She was pregnant, an adulteress. The law demanded her life. Only he could spare her, and he had no mind to do anything like that.

He remembered when he had first seen her, a beautiful woman, both of body and spirit. "Tamar will make a wonderful wife for my son," he had said. But shortly after the marriage, his son Er mysteriously died. It had to be the Lord's hand, Judah had thought. But then, after she had married his second son Onan, according to the law of the levirate, he also died suddenly. Was God displeased with Tamar? Was she a curse on his family? Was there something she had hidden from Judah that caused these terrible tragedies?

Only his youngest son Shelah was left to continue the family line. Judah's wife had become hysterical. "If Shelah marries that woman, he will also perish!" she had screamed. "God is against her, and He has punished us as well!" Judah had tried to calm her, but he, too, was afraid. "Shelah is young," he said. "I will send Tamar home to her father and tell her to wait until Shelah is older. By the time Shelah is ready for marriage, perhaps the truth will be known."

Perhaps the truth was now known. It had taken several years, during which time Judah's wife had died and Shelah had reached marriageable age. But the truth was now clear to Judah. Tamar had hidden a lustful spirit which had brought this condemnation on Judah's family, and which now rested on her. There was some satisfaction in his mind as Tamar moved closer to her judgment; even though Er and Onan could not be brought back, Shelah would not suffer the same fate. He would be released from his obligation to continue his brothers' line through her.

As the procession moved through the silent crowd and closer to where Judah was standing, he could see that she was carrying something. Amulets, thought Judah. Lucky charms. Something to appease her heathen gods. They wouldn't do her any good now, he laughed to himself. She was being judged by the True God, and His righteousness would prevail. This would be a lesson to all those women out there who would play the part of the harlot. And this penalty would expiate the sin which had taken his two sons. Then Tamar said something to one of her executioners and handed him the things she was carrying. The man came to Judah and handed him a seal attached to a small cord, and a staff. He spoke. "Tamar told me to tell you that she is pregnant by the man who owns these."

Judah blanched. His legs turned to rubber. The seal and the staff may as well have been the blacksmith's hammer and his head the anvil. He remembered. The shrine prostitute. Several months ago, on the road to Timnah when he was on his way to shear the sheep. Tamar was the woman he thought was the shrine prostitute. He had slept with her, and she had taken his seal and staff as a guarantee of his payment to her. And he knew. His heart flooded with shame and regret. Tamar was not the sinner, he was. She had been waiting for Shelah, faithful to her vows. He had turned a deaf ear to her pleas. He had refused to honor his sacred word and the law of the levirate marriage by withholding Shelah from her. She had to do what she did or else remain a childless widow, a shame in Israel.

Judah turned to the crowd. "There will be no execution today!" he exclaimed. "Tamar is more righteous than I!"

The crowd dispersed. Judah went to his home and cried bitter tears of remorse and repentance. And God heard and forgave. For Perez, one

A View of Genesis

of the twins born to Tamar, was in the line through which the Messiah Jesus came.

"Where sin increased, grace increased all the more..." (Romans 5:20).

"If we confess our sins, He is faithful and just and will forgive us our sins, and purify us from all unrighteousness" (1 John 1:9).

It's amazing what Jesus can and will do with the life of a sinful person, when sin is recognized, confessed, and forsaken.

Genesis 39:1-23

"Joseph had been taken down to Egypt. ... The Lord was with Joseph and he prospered." (vs. 1-2)

Little Joey was in the big city. No longer a shepherd, out in the fields where his communion with God was as sweet and fresh as the dew of the morning; but a slave, a despised Israelite, under the hand of Potiphar, the captain of Pharaoh's guard. He could have been angry and bitter, especially with his brothers and maybe with the Lord, too. Why me, Lord? I haven't done anything! I was bringing goodies from home to those guys, spent all that time hunting for them, and here I am in Egypt! Why did You allow this to happen?

Well, Joey hadn't seen nothin' yet. He was about to get framed and thrown into prison. And it wasn't any Club Leavenworth. David describes it in Psalm 105:17-18: "... Joseph, sold as a slave. They bruised his feet with shackles, his neck was put in irons." Even though he ended up in charge of all the "guests," his accommodations wouldn't have made the latest issue of Southern Living.

But the Scripture tells us three times in this chapter that the Lord was with Joseph, "and he prospered" (vs. 2); "showed him kindness and granted him favor" (vs. 21); and "gave him success in whatever he did" (vs. 23). You'd think that if God was doing all this good stuff for Joey, He'd have kept him out of the clutches of Potiphar's wife and at least got him a hearing before the parole board. It makes one wonder, if this is success and prosperity, who needs it? Give me a little non-success and keep me out of the slammer.

God's dictionary has a different definition for "success" than what we find in Webster's. Joseph did prosper. He did have success. But his prosperity was not in his circumstances, living or otherwise. His prosperity was that "The Lord was with Joseph." He spent the rest of his life in Egypt, and a lot of time in jail. But God was with him. At the end, Joseph was on top. It's like the old movies I used to see as a kid where the good guys always won and everybody cheered and bought more popcorn. David gives the rest of the story in Psalm 105:20-22, "The king ... made him ... ruler over all he possessed." Stephen said in Acts 7:9-10 that, "God was with (Joseph) and rescued him from all his troubles."

But you know, the good guys don't always end up running with the top dog. Life is sometimes hard and gets even harder, seemingly without relief. And the rest of the story may not be a seat next to Pharaoh. But God is still there. Doing His thing. Bringing joy, peace and satisfaction, just in the knowledge of His presence. If we, like Joseph, allow His presence to fill our hearts.

If being an item in "Lifestyles of the Rich and Famous" is success and prosperity, why are they all so unhappy? As the songwriter said, "Take the world, and give me Jesus." Real prosperity is being in His presence forever.

Genesis 39:1-23

"How then could I do such a wicked thing and sin against God?" (vs. 9)

When I was teaching college, the only way I could find out if the students were getting the material was to give them a test. Sometimes I thought a particular student really understood what was going on, but the results of the test proved otherwise. In other cases the opposite was true. Or maybe someone really had the stuff down pat, but the lights went out when the questions started.

In this chapter, Joseph got tested more than a candidate for an advanced degree in front of a scholarship committee. And he graduated summa cum laude. Test #1 was the murderous actions by his brothers. His answer was to keep on loving them. Test #2 was his position as a slave in Egypt, after being his father's favorite in his own home. His answer was to depend on Jehovah to help him as he went about his duties, doing his job to the max. Test #3 was his handling of success. "No one is greater in this house than I am," he said to Potiphar's wife (vs. 9), referring to his position and reputation among the servants. His answer was to refrain from taking advantage of his position, feathering his own nest and lining his own pockets. He would have made a terrible politician.

But perhaps his greatest test was Test #4. Potiphar's wife saw that he was a real hunk (vs. 6-7). So she decided that he was going to be her playmate of the month. This was astonishing, because the Hebrews were despised by the Egyptians. Day after day she tried to put the make on him, but he told her to keep her hands off the merchandise (vs. 10). It would have been so easy. Potiphar was the Henry Kissinger of his day, cameling off to various parts of the kingdom to kibitz with the local bigwigs. He was never around. So Joey could have had a continuous romp in the bedroom and kept Mrs. P. happy as part of his "official duties." Who would have known?

Well, God would have. David in Psalm 139:2-4 says, "You (God) perceive my thoughts from afar .... Before a word is on my tongue, You know it completely." And Joey knew it. Perhaps he might have said, "I know this really isn't kosher, Lord, but I really don't have a choice here. If I don't keep the lady happy, I'm a piece of dead meat." This test was a Situation Ethics Graduate Course final exam. And Joseph passed with flying colors. The only trouble was, the colors turned out to be black and white stripes, and the flying was off to the slammer. That wasn't a particularly desirable reward for making an A+.

We all have various kinds of tests in our day-to-day activities. Everything from too much change at the 7-11 store to handling success to anger and jealousy to blowing off time at work to X-rated material on the Internet. It's all out there, and we're all vulnerable. But, like Joseph, we can make it if we depend on God.

And He's the One who awards the diplomas.

"Judah said, 'Bring her out and have her burned to death!'" (vs. 24)

Did you ever notice how sometimes people and their dogs start to look and act alike? Or at least, how it seems to appear that way? Here comes Ms. Hotsy-Totsy, tripping down the street in her 5-inch spikes, nose in the air, perfectly dressed and coiffed with her dog on a jewel spangled leash. And what breed is the dog? It has to be a poodle, prancing along perfectly trimmed and combed, nose in the air, and if a mongrel happens on the scene, ten to one both Ms. and dog faint dead away or at least run for the nearest upscale hotel.

Some of the younger guys look like their greyhounds, sleek and trim, gliding along on the soccer field or basketball court and showing a burst of speed when needed. Then the old guys in the stands start to resemble their old bulldogs or basset hounds, with droopy jowls and sagging eye lids and maybe drooling a little here and there. And how about the cheerleaders? They have little fluff ball bichons that jump up and down and run around and make a lot of noise and want to play all day. At least it used to be that way before the guys became cheerleaders and the girls wanted to be line backers or kick extra points.

But if the whole world were like one doggie breed, it would have to be the pointer. Something makes a noise, and the dog points right at it. Someone does something out of order, and everybody around points. "He did it!" "She's the guilty party!" "They're to blame!" Always ready to point the finger at whomever is handy. A pointer points out the game, we pointers point out the blame. Trouble is, a lot of the time there's a lot more blame that could be pinned on the pointers.

Judah would have won the blue ribbon at the pointer dog show competition. "Tamar is guilty! Get out the matches! She's a sinner of the worst sort!" Oops. There's another side to this story. It took two to tango, and Judah was the hot dog sniffing around the dance floor. When Judah pointed his finger at Tamar, he soon found that three of his other fingers were pointing back at himself.

Jesus had something to say about this kind of person. "Why do you look at the speck of sawdust in your brother's eye and pay no attention to the plank in your own eye? ... You hypocrite, first take the plank out of your own eye, and then you will see clearly to remove the speck from your brother's eye" (Matthew 7:3-5). This is the problem with many Christians today. So consumed with finding fault with others, the way they do things, the way they say things, the way they act or don't act, that they have lost the ability to clean up their own act or even to see what needs cleaning in the first place in order to be an effective witness for Jesus.

Better we should be a mangy old mongrel that rescues people from the fire, than a pedigreed pointer that stands around pointing out how the fireman isn't holding the hose correctly. Guess which dog gets the T-bone at the rewards ceremony?

Genesis 39:1-20

"But (Joseph) refused ...'How then could I do such a wicked thing and sin against God?'" (vs. 8-9)

The heat was on. Mrs. Potiphar was throwing every trick in the book at Joey the Hunk. And even a few tricks that no woman from Eve on down had thought of. She may even have offered him a kosher peanut butter and jelly sandwich. Or a Swiss Army penknife. Or a brand new four-speed camel. She left nothing to the imagination. Even the women on Bourbon Street in New Orleans at Mardi Gras would have been aghast.

But Joey hung tough. He was not about to be devoured by the she-wolf. "Not by the hair of my chinny-chin-chin!" he shouted from his spiritual Perma-Shield enclosure. And she huffed and she puffed, but she was the one who ultimately got blown away. Although Joey ended up in the slammer, if Potiphar had really believed his wife's story about the attempted rape (vs. 16-18), Joey's head and his body would have had separate addresses before the light of the next dawn.

So how was Joseph able to resist? Believe me, it wasn't because of his Israeli Boy Scout training. Nor was it because he liked boys instead of girls. And he hadn't heard his mother say lately, "Joey, look out for those Egyptian women! They're big time bad news!" And for all we know, he hadn't learned about STD's in the Egyptian High School. But there was a reason. In fact, it was the only reason that men (or women) are consistently able to turn away from sin. It was because Joseph knew that his sin would not be primarily against Potiphar, or society, or his parents, or himself, or Mrs. P., but against God (vs. 8).

This has always been true of the great men of Scripture, as it is true of the great spiritual men of today. They have been and are convinced that little white lies are big black whoppers in God's sight. That "the little foxes that ruin the vineyards" (Song of Solomon 2:15), the little sins that we think don't harm anybody, are great big elephants that trample down the jungle as far as God is concerned. That even the sinful thoughts conceived in the dark are out there in the blinding spot-light of God's gaze (1 Corinthians 4:5). And that all sin is in reality an offense against Him. Consider what David says in Psalm 51:4 after his murder of Uriah and adultery with Bathsheba: "Against You, You only,

232   *A View of Genesis*

have I sinned and done what is evil in Your sight." Check out Daniel in his prayer and confession to God in Daniel 9:4-19. Similarly Nehemiah in his prayer of confession in Nehemiah 1:5.

Joseph resisted incredible temptation. We can also to a great extent, when we consider that every sin which we commit is an offense against God Himself, and that he has given us His Spirit to help us stand against Satan's devices.

And especially when we remember that each of our sins is another nail that held Jesus to the cross.

"(Joseph) refused to ... even be with her.... (He) ran out of the house." (vs. 10-12)

Genesis 39:6-15

"(Joseph) refused to ... even be with her.... (He) ran out of the house." (vs. 10-12)

There is reputed to be a cliff out in the western part of the United States which has a gradual slope before its sheer drop. A person can venture out so far on this precipice without incident, but there is an undesignated place beyond which a return to safety is impossible. The proverbial point of no return. There are signs and warnings that speak out about the danger. But the curious, the ignorant, the daredevil all end up in the same predicament. Over the edge. On to oblivion.

Well, Joseph found himself in a real cliffhanger. Here was Mrs. Potiphar, who, being the wife of a very high Egyptian diplomat, probably wouldn't have been nominated for the dog-of-the-month. She may not have been a Claudia Schiffer, but she surely wasn't a Flossie Flapsaddle, either. And she was pushing Joseph to the edge. Day after day (vs. 10). Trying to get him to the bedroom. Or the couch. Or the back seat of a two-hump camel. Whatever was handy.

But Joey would have none of it. You wonder what he thought in the morning. "Man, how am I going to avoid this chickadee today? What new gimmick will she come up with? How can I out-maneuver Mrs. Hot-to-trot until quitting time?" It was a constant battle of wills. And Joey knew he wouldn't win by just telling her that what she was proposing wasn't nice. Or that he had a headache.

So he devised a simple but effective solution. He just steered clear of her as much as he could. He stayed out of her way. He avoided her like the plague. He told her to hit the bricks. Instead of flirting with fascination or fooling with fantasy, Joseph remembered the rules and opted out of the opportunity. But you better believe he didn't approach the challenge casually. This was a situation which required mental determination, moral toughness and spiritual stability. And a good dose of recognizing that there was a cliff out there to be avoided.

Most of the time it's better to avoid trouble than to try to stand up to it. If you know there's an ill-tempered bull in the field, it's best to go around the fence rather than try to outrun the animal. If you must go through the field, don't wear red just to see if he's color blind. Or to test your speed against his. Sin is like the bull. It's faster, bigger, and meaner than we are, and will destroy us in an instant. Temptation is nothing to toy with. To dabble in. Paul tells us in 1 Thessalonians 5:22 to "avoid every kind of evil." Good advice. Because evil is like the cliff. Like the fire. "Can a man scoop fire into his lap without his clothes being burned? Can a man walk on hot coals without his feet being scorched?" (Proverbs 6:27-28).

So Joseph avoided the precipice. We need to do the same thing. Because one may never know when he's on his way down. Like the guy who thought everything was still OK as he was whizzing down past the 44th floor on his way to the bottom. The bottom never moves. Splat.

Genesis 39:20 - 40:1-23

"... So the warden put Joseph in charge of all those held in the prison, and he was made responsible for all that was done there. ... The captain of the guard assigned (the cupbearer and the baker) to Joseph, and he attended them." (vs. 39:22, 40:4)

The chameleon is an animal that changes with its environment. It adapts to and blends in with the surroundings. It produces a camouflage by which it is almost indistinguishable from its habitat. It survives quite nicely because of this ability.

Most people are like chameleons. "When in Rome, do as the Romans" is the key phrase in the operations manual. Keep in tune. Blend in. Don't rock the boat. Keep cool with the brothers. Say what the boss wants to hear. If he wears blue shirts and wide ties all the time, get yourself and your VISA down to the clothing store. When you're in Pittsburgh, say "Yunz guys." If in Alabama, say "Y'all." Be one of the good ol' boys talking and acting like the locals. And be sure you only mention God when you're in church, but not very aggressively there, either. Like the chameleons, both public and office politicians survive nicely in this manner.

Joseph was no chameleon. With his brothers, he worked hard himself as a shepherd and reported them for blowing off their duties (37:2). With his father, he related his dreams exactly as they were given him (37:10). With Potiphar, he did his thing in God's way, and not in accordance with the Egyptian manual (39:3). With Mrs. Potiphar, he refused the easy score and maintained his moral character (39:10). And now in prison, he didn't just adapt to survive, he went about life in his usual way, and God prospered him.

So regardless of his environment, regardless of his circumstances, regardless of the unfair, fraudulent, vicious treatment he had received from most of the people in his life, Joseph was God's Energizer Bunny — he just kept on going, and going, and going .... And never changed his colors, never lowered his standards, never compromised his position, never lost his confidence in God. A pretty unusual guy. A lesser man would have gotten the chameleon costume out long before.

236

A View of Genesis

It's interesting to note that through all Joseph's experiences, God was working, putting all His ducks in a row and molding and forming Joseph for the events which were to come, resulting ultimately in Joseph's elevation and the salvation of His people. Joseph suffered a lot before his vindication; but then so did Jesus, God Himself "found in fashion as a man," before His vindication and exaltation, while He was accomplishing our salvation.

Maybe it's easier in the short run to be a chameleon. But sooner or later, one of its natural enemies will catch it changing colors, and it's history. We should remember that no human chameleon escapes God's gaze. And it's much more important, like Joseph, to blend in with Him than with our human surroundings.

from the Rumble Seat of a Two-Humped Camel

Genesis 40:1-23

"Do not interpretations belong to God? Tell me your dreams." (vs. 8)

A lot of people are experts in a lot of things. At least they think they are. A good part of the time these "X-spurts" are just exactly that — "X" is the unknown quantity and the "spurt" is a drip under pressure. A drip thinking he has to spout off on something he doesn't have a clue about.

This is especially true with respect to spiritual things. Ten people discuss a spiritual topic and come away with twelve ideas — by the time all ten have expressed their different opinions, two have already changed their minds. How can this be? Doesn't God say the same thing to everybody? He always does, but everyone ain't hearing it the same. There are more denominations and cults and groups and factions than there are Irishmen at a wake where free beer is being served. And every one of them claims to have the straight skinny.

So how can anyone tell who is right? Is it the guy who is "successful" (translate: big crowds in big churches with big productions and big offerings)? Or is it the little church at the end of the street with just a few "faithful" attending Sunday after Sunday (translate: not much joy or vision, but a strict adherence to perceived "Biblical standards," i.e., "We don't smoke and we don't chew, and we don't run with the girls that do"). Or is it somewhere in between?

In Old Testament days, it was pretty easy to tell who had the pipeline to God. If a prophecy was given and it didn't come to pass, the prophet was a fake and shortly thereafter got stoned, and we're not talking about marijuana or booze (Deuteronomy 18:20-22). Two out of three wasn't good enough. Or nine out of ten. Or 99 out of 100. In the prison, Joseph, however, scored 100% on his prophecies regarding the baker and the butler. They had dreams, Joseph was given the interpretation by God, and it all came to pass. It was a perfect team — God was the Source, and Joseph was the servant. Pharaoh hit the nail on the head in 41:38: "Can we find anyone like this man, one in whom is the Spirit of God?"

This is how one can generally tell who is on the right track today. The person in whom the Spirit of God dwells is going to be a servant, not a showman. And he will personally have a Godly character, like Joseph exhibited throughout his life. He will speak out from the Word of God, and not his own opinions. He will also tell what God is really saying, and not worry about being "politically correct." Joseph didn't have very good news for the baker, but he gave him the straight scoop anyhow. It should be that way today. Preachers need to let people know about God's holiness as well as God's love. Jesus spoke more of hell than He did of heaven. Sin is still sin, and the man of God will call it just that.

God still needs faithful men like Joseph through whom He can interpret Himself. If He runs out of those, He can still use the stones (Luke 19:40).

Genesis 40:1-23

"The captain of the guard assigned (the chief cupbearer and chief baker) to Joseph, and he attended them." (vs. 4)

God's plots have more twists and turns to them than a John Grisham best seller. Only they aren't novels. How will God get Joey out of the slammer? How will He get him in front of Pharaoh? Will Joey ever see his father again? How is He going to preserve Israel through the famine? Tune in tomorrow ...

Of course, God could have just thrown up His hands and sent the butler, the baker, Pharaoh, Potiphar's wife, the whole kit and kaboodle of them out into outer space somewhere, in a solid, liquid or gaseous state. But for some reason, He doesn't work that way. He lets people do their own thing to a certain extent, even though all the time He's in total control. And regardless of what people are doing or not doing, it is all being woven into a tapestry according to God's exact design. That's why it's so great to be walking with God rather than struggling against Him. Even in a crowd, one person with God is majority rule. And although Joseph was in prison, God was calling all the shots through him.

Well, how was God going to make something out of this? Easy. The chief cupbearer and the chief baker were probably the people most trusted by Pharaoh. They had to be. The common method of getting rid of a monarch at that time was by poison. So the cupbearer tasted the vino before the king drank it, and the baker was in charge of the goodies. Thus the head honcho avoided the hemlock cocktail and the cyanide cookies. But apparently these two guys had ticked Pharaoh off, and they went directly to jail without passing Go. Maybe someone had heard that one of them picked up a package from the strychnine store on the way home from the Food Lion. But these guys were so important that Potiphar himself (the same guy with the wife who had been panting in Joseph's ear [vs. 4, 39:1]) assigned Joseph to personally take care of them. So God gives them a dream, clues Joey in as to what it all means, makes everything happen just like He said, and in a couple of years Joseph is Potiphar's boss. Piece of cake. Do we have a great God, or what?

The lesson here is not to get all bent out of shape when you have a flat tire in the middle of the night in outback Wyoming and it's snowing with four tired kids in the car and a wife who reminds you that she told you to get that tire fixed and you find the spare is flat after you unload the trunk and your membership in AAA expired last week. God is still working. Something good is going to happen. There is a reason for all this occurring, and it's not because you're a genetic numbskull regardless of what your wife says. So cool it. Quit thinking those terrible thoughts, and watch for a baker and/or a butler coming down the road.

God is knitting one, purling two in his tapestry. Even though you may feel the needle a little more than you would prefer.

Genesis 40:1-23

"... 'When all goes well with you, remember me .... mention me to Pharaoh and get me out of this prison.' ... The chief cupbearer, however, did not remember Joseph, he forgot him." (vs. 14, 23)

Joseph had to be frustrated. Hijacked out of home for doing good (vs. 15). In the klink for staying pure (vs. 15). Put in charge for working hard (39:22). And now forgotten. Hated by his brothers, despised by his accuser, forgotten by his beneficiary. It's enough to make a man lose his patience. Or call Anne Landers. Or the Better Business Bureau. Or Helpline Cairo. If he only had a telephone ....

"Hello. You have reached the cupbearer's residence. If you are calling from a touchtone phone, press 1 (long pause) now." Beep.

"Thank you. If you wish to review the wine list, press 1 (longer pause) now. If you wish to speak to the cupbearer's wife, press 2 (pause, pause) now. If you wish to speak to his children, press 3 (keep pausing) now. If you are applying for a server's position, press 4 (one more time) now. If you wish to speak to the cupbearer, so do a lot of other people." BEeep.

"You have dialed an unauthorized number. Please wait for a recorded message." "This is a recorded message. You have pressed the number with a finger force exceeding 100 psi. Please count to ten, and press 5 for further instructions." One, two, three ... ten. BEEeep.

"You have reached the court psychologist. You have pressed 5 with a finger force exceeding 175 psi. This means you have a problem. Please consult your conflict resolution counselor. Thank you and have a good day." BEEEEPP!

"Thank you for pressing 4, 6 and 8 simultaneously. You have reached the Publisher's Clearing House Sweepstakes registry. If you wish to order a magazine, press 1 ... now...."

Joseph had a right to be frustrated, and none of it was his fault. But he had to learn to be patient, even though it may have looked like even God had forgotten to remember. He certainly wasn't getting any phone calls from heaven, and the postman never rang twice. Or even once. Not even any junk mail.

Just like we all have to learn the same. Patience. If it were a commodity, we could bottle it and sell it and make a fortune. Unfortunately, it is a learned quality. And very few of us learn it very well. Most of us are still in Patience Sandbox 101 in kindergarten.

"Hello. You have called the Patience Emporium. Call back in six weeks for a free sample. Whoops! You have pulled the telephone from the wall. Make that ten weeks. And have a nice day."

Genesis 41:1-14

"In the morning (Pharaoh's) mind was troubled .... So Pharaoh sent for Joseph." (vs. 8, 1 4)

Two of the busiest professional occupations in the United States today are psychiatrists and divorce lawyers. It used to be that the evidence of success was being a banker or a lawyer. Then it was having a Cadillac. Then it advanced to a Mercedes. Now the evidence of status is the credentials of your therapist, or whether one has achieved UMM (upward marital mobility). (For the woman, that means acquiring successively richer and/or more visible husbands, and for the man, successively younger and blonder women with bigger busts. Or whether he has been one of Elizabeth Taylor's husbands.) The real measure of success in all of this is the size of the psychiatrist's and lawyer's bank accounts.

Somehow, all that status, wealth, visibility and whatever else goes along with the worlds of psychoanalysis and lawyers and UMM and silicone implants doesn't amount to a hill of beans when it involves how a person sleeps at night. Whether a person is king of the hill as far as the world goes doesn't matter when he puts on his pajamas. Nightmares are just as vivid in the castle as they are in the cottage. That's what Pharaoh found out. Whereas, the guy in the cottage may have dreamed about having a nice juicy steak and woke up with a smile, Pharaoh dreamed about a batch of ugly cows scarfing up his herd of prime Black Angus and woke up in a cold sweat.

So what did he do? The same thing that the rich and famous do today. He called on his psychic network. The dream analysts. The horoscope readers. And just like today, they didn't have a clue. They looked at their tea leaves, but their cups came up empty. Then the cupbearer finally remembered Joseph. And before the parole board could be called into session, Joseph was taken to the barber shop, given a new set of BVDs, and hustled to the boss's office (vs. 9-14). And the rest is history. God and the good guys win again.

Pharaoh may have been at the top of the food chain, but God saw to it that he got eaten alive by worry and fear. And his earth bound counselors had no ability to understand his problem, much less make it go away. Pharaoh had to turn to God's servant in order to avoid disaster for himself and his nation. Fortunately, he recognized that fact and acted upon it. The sad thing is, if Pharaoh were in the White House today, he wouldn't call Joseph. The media and the ACLU would have his head. God is not welcome in the Oval Office.

But God hasn't changed. He still has his "prisoners" like Joseph. Time will prove that it is better to be a prisoner with God's power, than a prince with men's problems. And forget the psychics with their tea leaves and the lawyers with their pleadings. They produce little more than Constant Comment.

Genesis 41:1-32

"...but God will give Pharaoh the answer he desires." (vs. 16)

There used to be a radio program when I was a kid called "The Answer Man." On this program all sorts of questions came up. Everything from "Why does the giraffe have a long neck?" to "What would happen if the earth was revolving two miles per hour more slowly?" He had an answer for everything. I used to be pretty impressed. Of course, I had no idea whether any of the answers were correct. For all I know, he could have said that the giraffe needed to be able to eat the leaves at the top of the trees, and if the earth were revolving more slowly it would take us longer to get to McDonald's. Sounded cool to me.

Time after time we hear the phrase, "This raises more questions than it answers." The whole world wants answers. But people want answers that are in line with their agendas, with their philosophies, with their desires. If it's not the answer we're looking for, we don't want to hear it. Don't give me information if it's not going to be confirmation. And if I don't get it the first time, I'll get a second opinion. And a third. Or more.

Pharaoh wanted some answers here, too. He knew that his dreams weren't just the result of eating too many Twinkies before bedtime. Although he certainly had dreamed many dreams in his lifetime, these were different. And they were playing with his head, big time. So he called in all his advisers, and they came up empty. In fact, they shrugged their shoulders and admitted they didn't have a clue. Forget the second opinion, he would have been happy with a first opinion. But it wasn't forthcoming.

All this time, God was priming Joseph for the big event. Now it was showtime. Joseph was standing before the head man. The Big Kahuna. "You want to know the answer, Pharaoh? Not to worry, God will give you the straight skinny." And through Joseph, He did just that.

God is still in the answer business. Only He's more dependable than the Answer Man. His answers are always right on the money; and He's ready to answer before we even come up with the questions. And He's pretty innovative with His answer methodologies. Sometimes we have

A View of Genesis

a "Joseph" through whom He speaks. Other times circumstances reveal the solutions. Once in a long while it may be through a dream. But most of the time it's in His letter to us, the Bible. It's not called His Word because no one could think of another name. It tells us, "The unfolding of Your words gives light; it gives understanding to the simple" (Psalm 119:130). Simple answers for simple people. Works every time.

Pharaoh got his answer right away. If we don't get ours that soon, it will come when God thinks the time is right. And we won't need a second opinion.

Genesis 41:1-16

"Now a young Hebrew was there with us, a servant of the captain of the guard." (vs. 1 2)

Finding good employees today is pretty difficult to do. Many prospective employees (with the help of government mandates) have the attitude that the company owes them a living, which includes minimum wages, vacations, health care, retirement benefits, child care, and a workplace environment which is tailored to their "needs" and won't infringe on their "rights." And that's even before they start. An interviewer is not permitted to ask certain questions which may reflect unfavorably on their character, work habits or tendencies. And once they are hired, it's next to impossible to release them. It makes one want to exercise great caution in the personnel (oops! Excuse me! Human Resources) department, even if the potential hire is his mother.

Well, here was Joey in prison. Potiphar (the captain of the guard — see 39:1) had assigned him to take care of the chief baker and chief cupbearer. He did his job so well that the cupbearer, when he was recounting his experience in prison to Pharaoh, described Joseph as "the servant" of the captain of the guard. Not "the prisoner," but "the servant," The Hebrew word used here has the meaning of one who is in authority, but also subject to higher authority. Sort of a middle manager. Even in prison, Joseph had the respect and confidence of the one whose wife he had been accused of trying to rape. And even more interesting, Joseph performed the duties given him at his usual standard of integrity and excellence. And it's not likely that he ever suggested to Potiphar that his "workplace environment" should be adjusted to more affirmatively accommodate his "needs" or his "rights."

The difference with Joey is that he knew who the Real Boss was. Paul also knew. "Whatever you do, work at it with all your heart, as working for the Lord, not for men, since you know you will receive an inheritance from the Lord as your reward. It is the Lord Christ you are serving" (Colossians 3:23-24). And Joseph never knew any other Boss. Maybe someone else was telling him what to do, but nobody else was his Master. The Master Who saw his every move, knew his every thought and planned his every step.

That's the way it is supposed to be with us. The Human Resource Department in which our files are located is in heaven, even though our employment location is on the earth. And when we are working with our heart's best efforts, the Lord will bless the activities of our head and our hands. And do you know what? The human boss will notice. He may die of shock that someone would work like this, but rest assured, he will notice.

And we shouldn't worry about overtime pay. We'll have an eternity to enjoy the benefits provided through Jesus.

"'I cannot (interpret your dream),' Joseph replied to Pharaoh, 'but God will give Pharaoh the answer he desires.'" (vs. 16)

Joseph had Pharaoh right where he wanted him. Sitting on a throne, but the bags under his eyes, disheveled hair, and more than likely a wrinkled king's robe betrayed him. Worried sick over the ugly cow and skinny grain-head dreams. Scared out of his wits. Couldn't even give a second thought to his harem. And Joseph was the key to the puzzle, the answer to the problem. He could interpret the dreams and set the big man's mind at ease. Was this a negotiator's dream, or what? A shrewd little Jewish boy could have come away with the keys to the kingdom. Taken home the entire kibbutz.

But Joey didn't even ask for the keys to his prison cell. What was wrong with this kid? First he turns his back on a regular romp in the rumpus room with Mrs. Potiphar, which lands him in the hoosegow for all his virtue. Now he lets Pharaoh off the hook. He could have gotten back home to his father on the first high speed camel caravan if he'd have asked. The chief cupbearer had the skids greased. "Things turned out just like the young Hebrew said, after we had told him our dreams!" But no, he had to let it all get away. He would never make the cover of Entrepreneur acting like this.

Well, Joey was a humble and honest young man. Humanly speaking, it would have made sense for him to at least negotiate his release from the slammer. After all, he had been there for several years, and God didn't seem to be very interested in his plight. Hey! Ya gotta do what ya gotta do! But that's not what Joey had to do. He wasn't into his own glory, wealth or advantage. His goal was the glory of God. He wouldn't take credit for an ability that he had already demonstrated — neither would he acknowledge the introduction the cupbearer had given to Pharaoh. "It is God, not me! He is everything, I am nothing!"

Not like most of us today, is it? Humility is not much in evidence any where, and you can't find it for sale at WalMart. Not only do we want credit for anything which is done, we get all bent out of shape if it's given to someone else. And forget God. His job is to make it work, and let me have the glory.

But the more we get to know God, the more we realize that Joseph did the right thing. God isn't about to share His glory with anyone, and if Joseph had tried to cut a deal for himself, maybe God would have left him hanging when it was time to give the interpretation. But even if God hadn't, it was still the right thing to do. James tells us, "God opposes the proud, but gives grace to the humble" (James 4:6).

And as Joseph soon found out, He gives a lot of other things besides grace, too.

Genesis 41:1-24

"I told this to the magicians, but none could explain it to me." (vs. 24)

I remember in high school there was this kid who everybody thought was the greatest thing since sliced bread. He was the best looking, most athletic, most popular and (in the opinion of us lesser lights) the most conceited kid in the history of man. The girls gathered around his locker like someone was giving away lottery tickets, and when His Eminence appeared, there were more eyelashes flapping than there are wings beating when a flock of pigeons discovers a fresh supply of bread crumbs in the park next to the statues. If the high school had named a king, he would have been second only to Elvis.

But one day, the unthinkable happened. There was an event which brought the king to his knees. He ran into a situation he couldn't handle, and none of his cronies could help, either. It ended up that one of the nerds bailed him out, and after that he was regarded by most as more like the ape than he was like Tarzan.

Well, Pharaoh found himself in something like this situation, in the morning after his dream. In those times in Egypt, the Pharaoh (which was a title like "king," "president," etc.) was considered by the people, including Himself, as a god. A good illustration of this attitude is found in Exodus 5:2, when Moses was asking the then Pharaoh to let the Israelites go into the desert to worship. "Who is the Lord, that I should obey Him?" was Pharaoh's comment. He really believed his press clippings, and the other Pharaohs were no different. So the Pharaoh in this passage woke up after his dream, and when neither he nor the magicians nor the wise men, nobody, not even the palace talk show hosts could come up with an answer, he was really bummed out. It was up to Joseph, a jailbird and a despised Hebrew, to burn off the fog around Pharaoh's cabeza. So much for the god thing in his case.

It seems like our God, the God of eternity, the only true God, takes it personal when a mere man tries to claim some of His turf. Or gets too high an opinion of himself. Throughout the Scripture, as well as throughout the history of man, when someone has established himself as the chief hotshot, God has, in His own time, whacked him up alongside the head in one way or another. In fact, in Psalm 2:4-5, it says that God gets a good chuckle out of these impostors before He lets them have it:

"The One enthroned in heaven laughs; the Lord scoffs at them; then He rebukes them in his anger and terrifies them in His wrath."

So let us be careful about getting too confident of our abilities, assets or position, or too big for our britches in any other way. We may get up in the morning and find out that God is letting us know that He's still the Boss.

It's much better to be a little chimpanzee in God's zoo, than to try to be an eight hundred pound gorilla in our own jungle.

Genesis 41:25-45

"The plan seemed good to Pharaoh and to all his officials. So Pharaoh asked them, 'Can we find anyone like this man, one in whom is the spirit of God?'" (vs. 37-38)

Joseph had finished giving God's message to Pharaoh. The king now knew what his nightmare was all about. But interestingly enough, God not only told him the problem, He also outlined the solution. Pharaoh had consulted all his brain trust just to get some clue as to what all the skinny cows and ugly grain heads meant. Had God stopped the message after the interpretation, Pharaoh would have had a few more sleepless nights. Or a whole lot of them. But God was in the process of getting Joey into the position He had determined, so He gave Pharaoh the full course dinner instead of leaving him sucking on a lemon.

That's just like God, isn't it? When we go to Him with a nasty situation, He just doesn't explain the problem to us, He lets us know how to deal with it. And not only that, He leads us along through the instructions step by step, doing a lot of the work Himself. David got all excited about this when he said, "Praise be to the Lord, to God our Saviour, Who daily bears our burdens. Our God is a God Who saves; from the Sovereign Lord comes escape from death" (Psalm 68:19-20).

There is a *sine qua non* here, however. In order for God to act, there usually must be a clear channel for His Spirit. He certainly can and oftentimes does decide to just move in and straighten out a situation on His own. But that was not to be the case in Pharaoh's dilemma, and it usually isn't the case with us. Joseph was the vessel through whom God's solution was given. And as Pharaoh noted, the Spirit of God was in him.

The Scriptures tell us that when we accept Jesus, God comes in with the whole package. The Spirit of God comes to dwell in us. So we have the same capacity to understand and deal with problems as Joseph did. But remember, Joseph was in tune with God. He didn't do his own thing all day or all week or all month or all year, and then run to God with a help wanted sign when he got into trouble. He kept his hands clean and his accounts short with God. And as it is said a few times, "the Lord was with Joseph and gave him success in whatever he did"

A View of Genesis

(39:2, 3, 23). In God's plan for Joseph, there were a lot of bumps along the way, but he got to the desired destination in one piece and no worse for the wear. And along the path, everyone else within earshot of Joseph got blessed as well.

So to be a channel of blessing for ourselves and others, we need to keep clear channels and open lines with God. We can be sure that any obstruction will never come from His end.

Genesis 41:1-38

"Can we find anyone like this man, one in whom is the Spirit of God?" (vs. 38)

I used to teach a college class which involved both oral and written reports. The students had to get up in front of the class and give reports orally on any business topic. Then came the hard part. They had to defend their reports. Their buddies were like a school of piranha. In less than two minutes, most were reduced to a stuttering mass of protoplasm. It generally wasn't a pretty sight.

Joseph was asked to give an oral report. Only he didn't even have any time to prepare. There he was, standing in front of Pharaoh and all his supposedly savvy seers, having to come up with a dream interpretation which, if it didn't ring true, would have been his ticket to the chopping block. I'll bet most of Pharaoh's Mickey Mouse Magicians were laughing up their sleeves and licking their chops at the sight of this young pup of a Hebrew, coming from the cell to the castle to speak the words of wisdom which had eluded their finite minds.

Well, Joey had an advantage. The cupbearer knew it, and pretty soon Pharaoh and the whole castle contingent did as well. The Spirit of God was with him. It was so evident that Pharaoh moved Joey to the head of the class, the Associate Professor, if you will. And he didn't wait until the dreams unfolded the way that Joseph had predicted to test their mettle. He moved Joey right then and there.

What was there about Joseph that convinced Pharaoh that the Spirit was in him?

Well, to begin with, he showed humility (vs. 16). "It's all God, Pharaoh. Not me." Then he spoke in simplicity and clarity (25-36). There was a notable lack of the "gas of human eloquence," and he didn't have a message with seven points, all of which began with the letter "P." He said it all in 300 words or less. (Are you listening, preachers?) His presentation was confident, but not theatrical. There was also an obvious lack of self-interest in Joey's presentation. When he got to the solution part of the speech, he didn't close with, "And I, Joseph, am Your Man!" Further, the content was full of discernment and wisdom. And it had the character of truth and reality. In short, the Spirit was written all over

Joseph and his presentation. And perhaps most important, we can be sure that Joseph had prayed a ton before he stood before the Big Kahuna. God had prepared Pharaoh to hear, understand, agree and act.

That's how we need to be when we're telling people the message of God. Clear. Humble. Truthful. Straight-forward. Quietly confident. Earnest. Brief and to the point. But more than anything, bathed in prayer and purity. God will do the rest.

Like Paul said in 1 Corinthians 2:1-4, "... I did not come with eloquence or superior wisdom ... but with a demonstration of the Spirit's power." Pharaoh realized this with Joseph, and it remains true to this day. It's what's inside that counts.

"Joseph was thirty years old when he entered the service of Pharaoh king of Egypt." (vs. 46)

Can you imagine the President of the United States going to Sing Sing Prison, taking one of the young inmates, a foreigner at that, and making him the most powerful person in the nation besides himself? A kid who had never been to college, whose only job (and that as a slave) had been as the manager of a household in the nation's capital, and who was in the pokey for abuse of his authority and attempted rape? Even the Washington Post would be speechless. At first. Then there would be a howl like you never heard since Richard Nixon's impeachment. Or Jackie Kennedy's marriage to Ari Onassis. Or some Republican winning an election.

That's what Pharaoh did. Here was Joseph the Hebrew, sitting low in Pharaoh's prison one minute, and standing tall in Pharaoh's chariot the next. Uneducated, unknown, unappreciated. However low his previous place in society had been, his present position was that much higher. It wasn't just rags to riches, it was Death Valley to Mt. Everest. Joe's Bar and Grille Sandlot Team to the New York Yankees. The McKees Rocks Ugly Sisters Squad to the Dallas Cheerleaders.

Well, what would Joey think about all this? He had been in Egypt for thirteen years, in prison for a lot of that time. He had a few scores to settle. Mrs. Potiphar might be high on the list. Socking it to a few of his brothers may have been on the agenda. Maybe even the cupbearer was worthy of a few shots. It was payback time. But it never entered his mind. He was on a mission ordained by God, and he couldn't be bothered with such trivial matters. Trivial, you say? Yes, trivial. His sense of the presence of God and his commitment to God's purposes reduced what most of us might consider to be the first order of business to something not worthy of consideration. Even the years of his lost youth, which may have engendered bitterness with God in some of us, never was an issue. Or even a thought.

Some of us who have had unfortunate reverses in life, perhaps due to the actions of others or what we perceive to be the inaction of God, are unhappy people. Why me, Lord? What did I do to deserve this? Why am I in the state I'm in? When are You going to do something to get me out of this? If anyone had a right to howl, it was Joseph. Or Paul. In fact, when the Lord was talking to Ananias about Paul, He said, "I will show him how much he must suffer for My Name" (Acts 9:16). Not an encouraging introduction to one's life's work.

So maybe we shouldn't scream about being a day late and a dollar short. If we're in God's program, things will work themselves out in His time. We may get the chariot like Joseph, or the business end of an ax like Paul. Whatever happens, 200 years from now we'll be with Jesus. For now, it's mind over matter. We shouldn't mind, because it doesn't matter.

"Joseph named his firstborn Manasseh and said, 'It is because God has made me forget all my trouble and all my father's household.' The second son he named Ephraim and said, 'It is because God has made me fruitful in the land of my suffering.'" (vs. 51-52)

Joseph was on top of the Egyptian heap. His office would have been in the Pyramid Penthouse, had they been in existence. Right next to Pharaoh, with a key to the executive washroom. It was a new gig for the Hebrew young man; formerly a captive, a slave, a prisoner; now a prime minister with the authority to sign Pharaoh's name in the royal checkbook. And married off to a woman with the highest Egyptian aristocratic and spiritual credentials. (This would come back to haunt Joseph's line in the future, but for now, it was the recognition that Joseph had made the royal register.)

Soon Joseph found himself in the expectant father's waiting room. Since he didn't have a book with Bible names to consult, he had to come up with names for his kids on his own. In that time, people named children according to events (either present or prophetic), circumstances or attitudes. No one ever would have named his son Chauncey, or Elvis, or Engelbert, or some other name where the kid would have to duke it out every day in the school yard. So Joseph came up with Manasseh, and for #2 son it was Ephraim. Manasseh means, "causing forgetfulness." In Joseph's case, this wasn't because he felt Alzheimer's coming on; he was thankful to God for putting all his past troubles behind him, and keeping him from being homesick (vs. 51). With Ephraim, which means "doubly fruitful," it wasn't because he now had two sons instead of one, but because God had taken him, a despised Hebrew, and put him at the top of a Gentile nation in order to bring blessing to the Egyptians, as well as for his own people.

In a way, these names taken together illustrate a great spiritual and practical truth. People are not going to be fruitful in the present if they are bitter about the past. And Joseph had every reason to be sucking a perpetual lemon. But with God's help, he was able to put all the hurt, all the wrongs, all the anger, all the mistreatment behind him, and go on to be one of the greatest men in the history of Egypt. He was fruitful in the present because he forgot the past.

We can't do much about the past, but we can do a lot about the present and the future. With Joseph, God brought good out of evil, privilege out of pain, triumph out of tragedy, freedom out of captivity, honor out of dishonor. All this would not have happened if Joseph had spent his time in the prison library boning up on methods to achieve maximum revenge. He knew that God was doing a little present pruning, so that his future life would yield bushels and bushels of fruit. And God does the same thing in our lives. Check out John 15:1-2.

One of the best things to remember is that it's often good to forget.

Genesis 41:53-57

"The seven years of abundance in Egypt came to an end, and the seven years of famine began, just as Joseph had said." (vs. 53)

Joseph had been for seven years zipping around the countryside in one of Pharaoh's souped-up chariots, collecting a fifth of the annual bumper crops and storing the grain in government granaries (vs. 34, 46-49). The whole program was such a big government operation that we might come to the conclusion that God is a Democrat. Or a Socialist. He certainly wouldn't have won the Libertarian vote. Then the famine began, and everybody decided that it was a good thing they had listened to God's instructions through Joseph, Democrat or no.

A lot of times we may wonder why God does things or allows events to occur. Why some things drop on us like a piano from the fifth floor, while other things become apparent a long time before they arrive, and we get time to prepare for the eventuality. Take this passage, for instance. What did God have in mind when He thought up the idea to have seven good years and seven bad years at this time in Egypt? Was He bored with the routine and wanted to mix things up a tad? And why did he let the Egyptian brain trust know the details in advance?

Usually in Scripture, a famine meant that God was ticked off with a nation and was lowering the boom. This wasn't the case here, however, since He told Egypt through Joseph how to prepare for it. So there must have been another reason. Maybe it was His way of getting the nation of Israel down to Egypt. Or a forum to showcase Joseph, with all the lessons about Godly living we get through him. Or just to let Pharaoh know that he, Pharaoh, fell way short of making it as a god. Whatever it was, we also know that there is some instruction in there for us, too.

One of the things we can learn from this passage is that we shouldn't expect good times to last forever. So we should prepare for the lean years, like the ant prepares for winter (Proverbs 6:6-8). In fact, Solomon, in Ecclesiastes 12, applies this principle to the whole of man's spiritual life. "Remember your Creator in the days of your youth, before the days of trouble come..." (12:1), he says; and then he goes on to describe the aging of the body, mind and spirit until death arrives. This is good advice. To most of us in our youth, old age and death are the last things we think about. And few of us think about God and the fact that someday our lives will be gone, and we will have to give our account to Him Who judges righteously. For all the years we were here, not just the last fifteen minutes.

Solomon knew that it's tough to get old. We get stiff in the body, soft in the head, slow in the feet and set in our ways. And the older we get, the less likely we are to get with it for God. Unless that has been a life long pursuit. The enthusiastic commitment of youth will prepare us for the declining spiritual energy of old age.

If we're gassed up on the racetrack, we probably won't conk out in the junkyard.

Genesis 42:1-5

"... Jacob ... said to his sons, 'Why do you just keep looking at each other? ... Go down (to Egypt) and buy some grain for us. ...'" (vs. 1-2)

When I was in the Marines, we used to have mock battles in our combat training exercises. The officers being trained would be evaluated on their performances, often even while the faux battle was in progress. And sometimes the evaluation was very vocal, with accompanying gratuitous comments concerning our manhood, intelligence and intestinal fortitude. Not something you would brag about to your girlfriend. I recall that on one particular occasion a young officer hesitated to make a decision, and the instructor was immediately all over him like a cold sweat. "Don't just stand there! Do something! Die if you have to, but at least do something!" We were told that if we made a decision, we had a fifty percent chance of being right and surviving. If we did nothing, we didn't have a prayer.

Well, here was Jacob tearing his hair out over the indecision and inactivity of his sons. The world was starving, and they were sitting around picking lint out of their belly buttons. Or maybe they were planning the world's first Amway meeting. Whatever they were doing, Jacob wasn't impressed. It wasn't making things happen or putting food on the table in Canaan. So he told them to get their collective rears in gear and hit the trail for Egypt. Off they went, with Jacob muttering in his beard that he must have raised a batch of space cadets.

Joseph's brothers were an awful lot like many of us are today, aren't they? There's spiritual food to be had, but much of the time we just sit around looking at each other and slowly starve. An additional problem is that when we look at each other, our minds get off the fact that there is great food out there, and instead we concentrate on the other person's faults. So it adds up to a double whammy against any meaningful progress we might make toward spiritual maturity. Not to mention what it does to the unity of the church, and its testimony to unbelievers.

God never intended that we sit around doing nothing and starve. He has set the rich food of the Scripture before us, and as we feed on His Word, our souls are enlarged, our hearts encouraged, our minds enlightened, and our lives enriched. As the prophet Jeremiah said, "When your words came, I ate them; they were my joy and my heart's delight"

(Jeremiah 15:16). But He will not force feed us. We have to come to His dining room, pull ourselves up to the spiritual table and make use of the utensils at our disposal.

And God's dining room is always first class. He doesn't serve junk food at a drive through window.

Genesis 42:6-17

"Now Joseph was the governor of the land, the one who sold grain to all its people." (vs. 6)

You'd almost think that this should be the favorite Scripture passage of the U.S. Government. In chapter 41 and verse 34, Pharaoh's government takes twenty percent of all the grain that is harvested for seven years. What do they pay for it? Zilch. It's nothing less than a gross receipts tax. Now, in this verse (42:6), the government is selling the same grain back to the people! If the bureaucrats ever read the Bible, Joseph would be their patron saint.

Regardless of the implications, the whole process saved the lives of the people. And to be perfectly honest, the whole thing was God's idea, so we can't really blame Joseph or the government. God knew in advance what was going to be needed. And as it always does when God gets a hand in things, it worked out for the very best. Joseph was the hero, Pharaoh didn't have to face a starving nation with no solutions, Jacob and his family got to Goshen, and the people all ended up with something to eat, even though they paid for it, and their lives were saved.

But God has something for us which will save our lives, and it's free. No strings attached. In fact, it's not for sale. It can't be bought or earned. It's called eternal life. Yes, that's right, eternal life. This life isn't lived in Milwaukee or Memphis or London or Lhasa, it's lived in heaven. In God's presence. Forever, just like His life. Adam used to have a life like God's, but he blew it in the Garden of Eden. And not only for himself, he blew it for all of us. He gave us a sinful nature, and because of that nature, we all sin. And because of that sin, we all die. We died spiritually through Adam, and we will all die physically as a result. But God says, "I will give you eternal spiritual life. Even though you will still die physically, you will be born again spiritually, and never experience spiritual death again. But you have to accept this gift. I won't force it upon you."

Most people think they must do something to get on God's good side. Do good works. Give to the poor. Go to church. Keep your nose clean. Be religious. Don't sin too much. Read the Bible. All these things are good, but that's not what results in eternal life. It's a gift. It's a result of God's grace and mercy. He tells us through Paul in Ephesians 2:8-9 that, "For it is by grace you are saved, through faith, and this is not from yourselves, it is the gift of God, not by works, so that no one can boast." He just sets it out there for us to take, by trusting in Jesus. By realizing that because we have sinned we can't help ourselves, and believing that Jesus' death on Calvary's cross paid the price for this gift God is offering us.

Sound too easy? God intended it to be that way, so that a small child can understand it and receive the gift from His hand. Let the little child in you reach out and take a gift that can never break, die, hurt, disappoint or disappear.

Genesis 42:6-24

"'Surely we are being punished because of our brother' ... Reuben replied, 'Didn't I tell you not to sin against the boy? ... Now we must give an accounting for his blood.'" (vs. 21-22)

Things had not gone well for The Gang of Ten in Egypt. They had presented themselves and their money to Joseph (without having a clue that the man before them was their long-lost brother), thinking that they would get some grain to take back to their families in Canaan. But much to their surprise and chagrin, they ended up as accused spies in the same "hotel" in which Joseph had been an involuntary guest for several years (vs. 14-17). And the situation was not promising. The penalty for spying was not just a rap on the knuckles with a ruler. It was a one way escorted tour to the gallows. And there was no local Amnesty International office to protest the death penalty or hold a candle light vigil.

And they had another problem. Joseph had demanded that they bring Benjamin down to Egypt in order to prove their innocence (vs. 15-20). Jacob had already refused to let Benji go to Egypt (vs. 4). So there the brothers sat in the slammer, probably wishing they had stayed in Canaan and starved.

While they contemplated their future, they also remembered the past. The cries of Joseph in the pit 20 years before echoed in their ears. His tears, his terrified look, his pleas for mercy paraded before their eyes. The years had dulled their senses; they had kept their ugly secret perfectly, and their crime had faded into the recesses of their minds. But conscience and circumstances had finally caught up to them. The whole scene played out before them again, in 3-D technicolor and SurroundSound. The chickens had come home to roost. And they were sure that their circumstances of the present were the consequences of the past (vs. 21-22).

The Scriptures tell us, "... you can be sure your sin will find you out" (Numbers 32:23). It was true with Joseph's brothers, and it is also true with us. All sin has its consequences. It may appear that people get away with murder, figuratively and literally. But there is a price. It may come due immediately, or it may take years. Or decades. And the price tag varies. It may cost the sinner his freedom, his reputation, his money,

268   *A View of Genesis*

his sanity, or his life. The offense may be pushed deeply into his mind, but conscience continues to probe the depths to restore it to his memory. And even if there appears to be little or no retribution in this life, there is a higher court where an answer must be given. God's Court. The supreme court of the universe, where the facts are all known and there are no lawyers or appeals.

Even though God gives spiritual forgiveness when confession and repentance occur, the natural effects of sin may mark a person for life. But obedience to God, His Word and His way will let a person avoid getting painted with the devil's magic marker, and we will find out there's very little to get found out about.

Genesis 42:24-38

"Joseph gave orders to fill their bags with grain, to put each man's silver back in his sack, and to give them provisions for their journey." (vs. 25)

"I don't get mad, I just get even!" If this had been Joseph's credo, the Gang of Ten would have been in deep trouble. Here they were after twenty years in front of the very person they had popped into the pit and then shucked off as a slave, pleading to purchase a few sacks of grain. If I had been Joseph, I'd have gone home to my wife and gloated. "Sweetie, you should have been at the office today! All ten of the brothers had their faces in the dust, and did I ever rub their noses in it! Whooooeee! I've been waiting for this day for a long time! I've got their heinies in the hoosegow for three days, and then I'll have a little more fun before I decide if I'll give them anything other than a hard time! You should have heard the turkeys gobbling!" It was truly payback time.

But the thought never entered Joseph's mind. He was so in tune with God that you couldn't tell by looking at him or listening to him where God ended and Joseph began. It was payback time all right, but with Joseph, the pay window put out a different currency. Instead of anger, there was acceptance. Instead of cruelty, there was compassion. Instead of loathing, there was love. So when they headed back to Canaan (all except Simeon, who Joseph kept in Egypt as a test of the brothers' change in character), they had not only their grain, but also a refund of their cash and lunch for the trip. They never even had to stop at McDonald's.

Jesus has told us that we should show the same character as Joseph did. He tells us in The Sermon on the Mount to "love your enemies and pray for those who persecute you" (Matthew 5:44). He says further, "Do good to those who hate you, bless those who curse you, pray for those who mistreat you ... Do to others as you would have them do to you" (Luke 6:27,31). The Golden Rule. The one which has degenerated in our society to, "Do to others as they're going to do to you, only you do it first." Something has been lost in translation here. And society is supposed to be getting better and better. Unfortunately, principled conduct has been replaced by personal convenience and political correctness.

But you know, Joseph-type actions can be contagious. We can infect

A View of Genesis

others with kindness when it comes from our hearts. Oh, there probably will never be an epidemic, but if each of us can keep ourselves and help someone else out of the hate hospital, it may heal our environment just a little bit. And that kind of global warming would be beneficial to everybody.

When we get even with someone, we never get even. We just sink to their level.

Genesis 42:27-43:18

"Their hearts sank and they turned to each other trembling and said, 'What is this that God has done to us?'" (42:28)

When I was ten years old we moved from a well-settled suburban neighborhood to a very rural area. I think our home was three-fourths of a mile from civilization. From the main road, we had to go back this farm road about a mile and then up a long hill through the woods to our house, another half mile. There weren't very many houses along the farm road, and only one house going up the hill. And there was this big ill-tempered dog at one of the farm road houses, which, if he heard anybody coming in front of his property, would charge out to the road barking and snarling like his place was the bank and the intruder was John Dillinger.

It was, of course, several years before I was permitted to drive, so when I was down at the local hangout with the guys and came home after dark, I had to walk. And it was usually dark. I mean real dark. I think the moon knew when I was walking home and intentionally went to the other side of the earth. So I was scared. Scared of the dark. Scared of the trees. And real scared of that dog.

Well, the Gang of Ten in this passage was afraid a lot of the time, as well, only they had something to be frightened about. In 42:21, they were scared out of their wits when they were sitting in the slammer as accused spies. In 42:28, they got the willies when they found the money with which they had purchased grain back in their sacks. In 43:18, they shook in their sandals when they were ushered into Joseph's house on their second trip for grain. And in 44:13, they like to died of fright when Joseph's cup was found in Benji's sack.

Sometimes God allows us to be conditioned with a healthy dose of fear. Like it did to the brothers, fear probes our character, warns us of danger, softens our self-confidence, and keeps us from doing things we might otherwise do. And teaches us to pray. I learned a lot about prayer on those dark nights. And I'll bet the Gang of Ten rediscovered prayer through their experiences, too.

We're also told that, "The fear of the Lord is the beginning of wisdom" (Proverbs 1:7). This is not exactly similar to the fear the brothers felt in their circumstances, but a reverence for God which causes us to submit to His will. But Jesus also told us, "...do not be afraid of those who kill the body and after that can do no more. But ... fear Him Who, after killing the body, has the power to throw you into hell" (Luke 12:4-5). Isaiah almost had cardiac arrest when He saw the Lord (Isaiah 6:4-5). John flipped out under the same circumstances (Revelation 1:17). And we should remember that even though God loves us all, He is still the Sustainer of our lives and times, and even our very existence is subject to His will.

A daily dose of the fear of God is good medicine for us to take in order to maintain spiritual health and vitality, and it works great as a sin-blocker, too.

Genesis 42:21-34

"They said to one another, 'Surely we are being punished because of our brother.'" (42:21)

Conscience. The thing which brings stuff to mind we'd just as soon forget. Jiminy Cricket sitting on our shoulder, messing with our head and giving us a pain in the neck. Causes more sleep loss than Jay Leno and David Letterman combined. Aspirin doesn't touch it, running away won't help, and if we try to drown it in alcohol, it's still there the next morning to help the headache hurt even more.

Well, it was morning in Egypt, and most of the tourists were looking forward to cutting up in Cairo. Not the Gang of Ten, however. Their hotel had not been first class, the breakfast would not be gourmet, and the reception they were going to attend with Joseph was not the kind reserved for foreign dignitaries. In fact, the place of interest they would most likely be visiting was the gallows. This had not been in their AAA TravelPak. To make it worse, they had a visitor. It wasn't their lawyer or their pastor. Mr. Conscience had come to see them. Hadn't heard much from him for a long time. He took them on a travelogue back to Dothan, 20 years before. It wasn't a pleasant trip. They heard their own voices. "Here comes that dreamer! ... Let's kill him and throw him in one of these cisterns!" (37:19-20). They remembered their father's grief when they lied to him about Joseph's fate. And now, said Mr. Conscience, it's time to pay the piper. Payoff time had come.

Conscience is one of God's best weapons. He uses it all the time. When it works, like it did with the brothers in this passage, it brings about repentance. And when people repent, their direction changes, their actions change, and their attitude changes. We can see that with the brothers in a number of ways. They gave a true report to Jacob (vs. 29-34). They were humble before Joseph (42:6, 43:19-28). They were not envious of Benjamin (even though they knew that like Joseph had been, Benjamin was now their father's favorite son) when he got more provisions than the others (43:34). And Judah offered himself as a slave in Benjamin's place (44:18-34).

But all consciences don't work real well. The Bible says that some people have "weak" (underdeveloped), "defiled" (1 Corinthians 8:7), all messed up consciences; unable to sort things out correctly. Others have "seared"

A View of Genesis

consciences (1 Timothy 4:2), the kind which we think would normally be found in Hollywood, incapable of sorting things out correctly. (Interestingly enough, the 1 Timothy text refers to religious leaders). Then there are "evil" consciences (Hebrews 10:22), those unwilling to sort things out correctly. But God can give us a "clean" conscience, cleansed by the blood of Jesus shed on Calvary's cross (Hebrews 9:14). This is what Paul had (1 Timothy 1:3), and what enabled him to be so effective in the service of God.

If what we see in the mirror is a guilty conscience, it can be exchanged for a clean conscience in God's Service Center. It's found on the Repentance Rack.

"They said to one another, 'Surely we are being punished because of our brother.'" (42:21)

Genesis 42:29-43:14

"Their father Jacob said to them, ... 'Everything is against me!'" (42:36)

"Nobody likes me, everybody hates me, I'm going to go eat worms!" That's the song Jacob sang when the Gang of Ten Minus One came back from Egypt. And it was all the brothers' fault. They had "deprived (Jacob) of (his) children. Joseph is no more, and now Simeon is no more" (vs. 36). And now they wanted to take Benjamin back to Egypt. They would have had better luck asking Popeye to give up his spinach.

It seems that Jake had forgotten God's words so often repeated to him. "All peoples will be blessed through you and your offspring. I am with you and will watch over you wherever you go ... " (28:15). "A nation and community of nations will come from you, and kings will come from your body. The land I gave to Abraham and Isaac I also give to you ..." (35:11-12). He had forgotten Bethel and Peniel and all the other places where God had pulled his chestnuts out of the fire. When God heard Jacob singing this sour tune, it's a wonder He didn't call up His talent agency and ask for another soloist.

When his back was really to the wall, however, Jacob relented and let Benji go to Egypt. It was either that or starve. Finally, he put the matter where it belonged, back in the hands of God (43:11-14). He changed his tune to, "Que sera, sera, whatever will be, will be. If I am bereaved, I am bereaved." Of course, it was in God's hands all the time. God was just doing a little of this and a little of that to change a few attitudes and outlooks before He made everything cool again.

God has a habit of doing things like that. He did it again with Esther the Queen when His people were up against one of the many Hitler-types they have faced through their existence. Mordecai told her that if she didn't work her magic on the king, they all were going to get it in the neck. Including her. So she shrugged her pretty shoulders and said, "I'll give it a go! If I perish, I perish." Read all about it in Esther 4:1-16.

Most of us don't sing real pretty, either. Something goes wrong or doesn't go according to our plan or schedule, and we can't get a sweet note out because our mouth is too puckered up. If we have a nice boat or a nice house or a nice job and Charlie down the street has a bigger boat or a larger house or a better job, it's time for the Lem'n-Blends to crank it up. And God should hunt for His earplugs. We really need to turn to that page in God's songbook where the ditty goes, "And we know that in all things God works for the good of those who love Him, who have been called according to His purpose" (Romans 8:28). It's a happier tune, makes us better singers, and God is more pleased with the performance.

And maybe we can add a refrain for God's benefit: "if it works for You, it's A-OK with me!"

Genesis 44:1-34

"Now, then, please let your servant remain here as my lord's slave in place of the boy." (vs. 33)

After the palace soiree in chapter 43, the Gang of Ten Plus One was feeling pretty good about things. The Prime Minister of Egypt had obviously taken a liking to them, and the nights in Pharaoh's tank were a memory long gone. But unbeknownst to them, the dark clouds were gathering. The real storm was about to break. What they had passed before were just a few daily quizzes. The final exam was ready to be administered. And it would be a dilly.

Even though Joseph had always given God the credit and glory for his ability to interpret dreams and foretell events, he had a silver cup which was referred to as his "divination cup" (vs. 5). It is unlikely that he ever used it in this manner, but he had to appear thoroughly Egyptian to his brothers and not blow his cover before he was ready to spill the beans. So he told his steward to slip it in Benjamin's sack, and then chase the guys down and "find" the allegedly stolen item where it had been placed. Nasty trick. But it would test the brothers to the core, to see whether they would throw Benji to the wolves like they had done before to Joey.

So the steward's eight-cylinder camels quickly caught the brothers' one-cylinder donkeys, and the accusation was made. You'd have thought that Snow White had been accused of running a brothel, with all the howls of denial. But surprise! surprise! surprise! There the cup was in Benji's sack, big as life and twice as real. MacBeth's witches couldn't have stirred up a bigger pot of trouble.

But Judah rose to the occasion. He was a changed man. In chapter 37, he had been the author of Joseph's sale into Egypt. In chapter 38, he had impregnated his daughter-in-law. Later in the same chapter, he had mercilessly ordered her executed, after he had broken his vow to her. But God had been working, and Judah now demonstrated that his heart was sacrificial rather than self-centered. He had sold his brother into slavery. Now he was to become a slave himself for that brother's younger brother. The gracious heart of God had produced a heart of grace in Judah.

That's what God's grace can do in our hearts and lives. And He will work in us, whether we like it or not, changing us to be like Jesus (Romans 8:29); as Paul says, "it is God Who works in you to do and to act according to His good purpose" (Philippians 2:13). Just like in Judah. From greed to giving. From mayhem to mercy. From selfishness to sacrifice. And it wasn't all in one easy lesson. Neither will it be for us.

If God were making violins, a Stradivarius in comparison would sell at K-Mart. We can be the quality instruments of grace He puts in His showcase.

Genesis 45:1-15

"Joseph said to his brothers, 'I am Joseph.'" (vs. 3)

Wow! Can you imagine what went through the brothers' heads when Joseph made this announcement? Without a doubt, they all, except Benjamin perhaps, thought that they were a piece of dead meat. The freight train had come, and they found themselves smack in the middle of the crossing. Knocked clean into the middle of next week. Reduced to a collective stammering blob of protoplasm. They were so astonished that Joseph had to expand on his re-introduction. "I am your brother Joseph, the one you sold into Egypt!" (vs. 5). Maybe they were trying to remember if there was a Joseph who sold figs door to door back in Canaan. No such luck. This Joseph was the real thing.

Well, what to do now? There was no place to run and no place to hide. They were entirely at Joseph's mercy. The object of their scorn, hatred and anger was standing before them, and he was holding all the cards. Their lives were in his hands, and there was nothing they could do about it. They couldn't lie their way out, work their way out, buy their way out, bargain their way out, plead their way out. The clock had struck twelve, and they were all pumpkins.

But Joseph wasn't in a pumpkin-carving mode. He was so delighted to see his brothers, especially Benjamin, and to hear about his father, that he cried up a river (vs. 14-15). And not only did he not sock it to his brothers, he insisted that they should all come to Goshen to live, and he would see to their prosperity (vs. 9-11). Is this grace, or what? The brothers probably couldn't believe their ears.

Saul (a.k.a. Paul) had a similar experience to Joseph's brothers on his way to Damascus. He was bopping on down from Jerusalem, hunting for any Christians he might find, and he didn't have a nice quiet dinner for them in mind. Except maybe dinner for the lions. All of a sudden he found himself in the spotlight, flat on the ground, and a strange voice speaking. "Who are you, Lord?" he asked. There was a simple reply, just as astonishing and terrifying to Saul as Joseph's announcement to his brothers. "I am Jesus!" (Acts 9:1-5). He also, like Joseph, had to expand on His introduction. " ... Whom you are persecuting" (9:5). Saul was in the same boat as Joseph's brothers. Saul was eloquent in his silence.

Sometime in the future, and many believe very soon, Jesus will make that same announcement to the whole world. "I am Jesus!" The angels said to His disciples, "This same Jesus, Who has been taken from you into heaven, will come back ... "(Acts 1:11). The apostle John says, "... every eye will see Him, even those who pierced Him..." (Revelation 1:7). Those who have scorned Him, those who have ignored Him, those who have hated Him. But here the similarity with Joseph ends. Jesus will come in judgment, not in grace. And there will be no way out.

But Jesus offers us the way in now, so we don't have to look for a way out then.

Genesis 45:1-15

"...God sent me ahead of you to preserve for you a remnant ... and to save your lives by a great deliverance." (vs. 7; see also vs. 5 and vs. 8)

One night in Pensacola, Florida, when I was in Marine flight training, I went out for a walk. I ended up sitting down in the middle of a golf course. Sat there for half the night. It was one of those nights you remember forever. I can see it as clearly right now as I can see the bulges I now have which weren't there when I was a Marine. I think that God had called out all the stars He ever made and stationed them right over that golf course in Pensacola. I felt like Abraham, when God took him outside and told him to count the stars, if indeed he could, and told him that his offspring would reach that number (Genesis 15:5). It was a balmy night with a gentle wind which cavorted from tree to tree, each branch in turn waving good-bye as the breeze left one tree for another. The scene was a testimony to the immensity of God and the puniness of man — this writer, to be specific.

And I thought to myself, why am I on this earth? And why am I in Pensacola? I hated flight training, and soon ended up back in Quantico running up and down hills with a pack on my back and a rifle over my shoulder. (That was a bummer, too.) But on that night in Pensacola, I was impressed that God, so immense, so magnificent and Who created all that beauty, had something in His plan specifically for me to do. Not only in the future, but right then and there as well.

In this passage, Joseph had figured out why God had taken him on the road he had traveled. (He told his brothers three times.) It hadn't been a super highway, but a pretty bumpy trail with a high toll charge. It was to save the lives of his brethren and their posterity — the offspring that God had promised Abraham and the line to Jesus, the prophesied Saviour of mankind. That was pretty heavy duty, and Joseph had paid the price. But it was now time to rejoice and give God the glory for His great plan of salvation. Joseph had no doubt wondered what God was doing along the way, but now the plan was clear and he had no regrets.

I guess we all wonder sometimes (if not most of the time) why things happen to us, why we are where we are and where we are headed in

God's plan. Perhaps God will reveal these mysteries to us before we get to heaven, perhaps not. But we can be sure that God has a specific plan in mind for each of us, and not just on Thursdays. Every detail is planned out. And He doesn't have to improvise. He knows when we are going to jump on a horse and ride off in six different directions, and He already has His cowboys ready to bring us back to His corral.

It may not be our duty to save a nation and its posterity like Joseph did, but even if our life is used to bring one person to the Lord Jesus, we can say the same as he did: "God has sent me ... to save your (spiritual) life by a great deliverance." It's the immensity of God acting through puny man to put another star in His sky of salvation. Like in Pensacola. Big sky. Mucho stars. Always room for one more.

A View of Genesis

Genesis 45:16:28

"Pharaoh said to Joseph, 'Tell your brothers, ... bring your father and your families back to me. I will give you the best of the land of Egypt and you can enjoy the fat of the land. ... Never mind about your belongings, because the best of all Egypt will be yours.'" (vs. 17-20)

Pharaoh was delighted that Joseph had been reunited with his brothers. (Maybe if he had known what the guys had done to young Joey, he'd have wanted to run them up the flagpole and leave them flapping in the breeze.) And Joseph was such a favorite in the palace that Pharaoh not only opened his checkbook to the family, but gave them his Visa Platinum card, too. Here was the Head Honcho of the Hemisphere unwittingly being God's source of supply for the hated Hebrews. Gives one the idea that God is really running the show, doesn't it?

Pharaoh also told them to have a garage sale before they came. Leave the antiques and other assorted junque in Canaan. Bring the missus and shop till you drop in Egypt. (And he didn't mean in K-Mart. He was talking Macy's and Bloomingdale's.) The best, and send me the bill. Just get your fannies down here and we can handle the rest.

In a way, what Pharaoh told Joseph's brothers to do is what God wants us to do. God doesn't want the baggage we bring when we come to Him. He has "the fat of His land" for us. Instead of the "filthy rags of our own righteous acts" (Isaiah 64:6), He will clothe us in the fine linen of the righteousness of Christ (Revelation 19:8). Instead of the "weak and miserable principles of this world" (Galatians 4:3,9), He will outfit us with "the prize of the high calling of God in Christ Jesus" (Philippians 3:14). Instead of the "burden of sin" which we carry, of which John Bunyan in *The Pilgrim's Progress* spoke so eloquently, Jesus says, "Take My yoke upon you and learn from Me ... and you will find rest for your souls. For My yoke is easy, and My burden is light" (Matthew 11:29-30). He just wants us to come as we are. Poor? That's great. Paul says, "My God will meet all your needs according to His glorious riches in Christ Jesus" (Philippians 4:19). Spiritually blind? Just what God is looking for. He has "salve to put on your eyes, so you can see" (Revelation 3:18). How about spiritually naked? Come into His haberdashery. "I counsel you to buy from Me ... white clothes to wear, so you can cover your shameful nakedness" (Revelation 3:18).

God has invited us into His mega-mall for all our needs, and it's all been charged to Jesus.

Genesis 45:21-28

"Then (Joseph) sent his brothers away, and as they were leaving he said to them, 'Don't quarrel on the way.'" (vs. 24)

Before the renowned atheist Madalyn Murray O'Hair disappeared without a trace, she had a few debates with Bob Harrington, a.k.a. "The Chaplain of Bourbon Street." In one of the debates, Harrington is reputed to have said, "Madalyn, why don't you join the Christian Army?" O'Hair shot back, "I'd be afraid to. It's the only army I know that kills its own wounded." Unfortunately, for once in her life Madalyn was pretty accurate. Only it just doesn't kill its own wounded. It may be more accurate to say that it shoots at anything that's moving.

Joseph knew his brothers well. He had watched them fight with each other before he was shipped off to Egypt. He had listened to them argue among themselves before they knew who he was and that he understood their language. He knew their natures, their personalities, their tendencies. And with all the goodies he was sending back with them, Joseph figured that there may be some wheeling and dealing before the brothers got past the first mile marker.

Well, as O'Hair observed, we Christians are plagued with the same humanness as were the brothers. Only we squabble over the silliest things. Did you ever notice how people tend to sit in the same place in church week after week (especially in smaller churches where there are few visitors)? If someone sits in another's seat (or even worse, parks in his parking place) some week, what happens? It's a more grievous act than if John 3:16 were redacted from the Bible. And how about when drums and guitars and drama are used on Sunday morning? You'd have thought that the devil himself had organized the service. Better the kids should be on drugs or out getting pregnant than bring their modern music into the sanctuary. And when I was a kid, if we played football on Sunday or did anything more active than a half-hearted snore, we were on our way to hell in a hand basket. And dancing or movies? Dante's Inferno, 63rd circle without a doubt.

To be sure, there are some things to die for. Like the basics — salvation by faith, the deity of Christ, the infallibility of Scripture, etc. When some folks want to "Re-image Jesus," it must be strongly pointed out that Jesus is the image (the "exact representation") of God's being (Hebrews 1:3), and even Zsa Zsa Gabor's hairdresser couldn't improve on that. But the other things are best smothered by the love of Jesus, not accentuated by the smell of battle. Paul got after a couple of women for whacking at each other in the Philippian Church (Philippians 4:2). Many times over in his epistles he addresses this problem of disunity in the churches. It's the devil's work, and we should all do our best to see that he spends the maximum amount of time at the unemployment office.

Then maybe people like Madalyn will head for the Lord's Army Recruiting Depot.

"...When (Jacob) saw the carts Joseph had sent to carry him back, ... Israel said, 'I'm convinced! My son Joseph is still alive. I will go see him before I die.'" (vs. 27-28)

The Gang of Ten Plus One had come back from Egypt with the incredible tale that Joseph, MIA and presumed dead for twenty-plus years, was really alive and in the driver's seat in Egypt. Jacob thought that his sons must have found Hallucination Heaven somewhere between Egypt and Canaan. They had fed him so much baloney over the years that they may as well have been deli clerks rather than shepherds. It is understandable that he didn't immediately kill the fatted calf and throw a party like the prodigal son's father did in Luke 15.

But then there was the hard evidence. The guys had said all these wonderful words, these revelations about Jacob's long lost, beloved son. But words with the Gang of Ten were like letters from the Publishers Clearinghouse Sweepstakes; promising everything, with a one-in-kazillion chance that it could ever be. However, there were the wagons, loaded down with the best of Egypt, before his very eyes. Wagons were virtually unknown in Canaan, and it was most unusual that they were permitted to be taken outside of Egypt. Some high-falutin' honcho in Egypt had to have given permission, and it all started to make sense. Joseph must really be alive! And surely, his sons would not admit their actions of twenty years ago, while perpetrating what would now be the cruelest hoax imaginable.

Most of us get the same kind of reaction as did the Gang of Ten when they told Jacob all these wonderful things. Our actions over the years have spoken so loudly that people can't hear what we say. Although we may not be like the "malicious man ... whose speech is charming ... (but) seven abominations fill his heart" (Proverbs 26:25), our lives are consistently inconsistent with what we profess. And people judge the truth of our message by how we act, not by what we say. Can a believer speak about the riches of Jesus to his landlord, when he's six months behind in the rent? Can an employee speak to his boss about serving the Lord, when he spends most of his time at the coffee machine? Can a young man testify about the moral glories of Christ, when his girl friend has to be a tenth degree black belt to fend him off?

Well, it's time to bring on the wagons. Let people see for themselves that there is substance to our speech. Reality to our profession. Walk to our talk. And let them see that the wagons are filled with the joy that Jesus brings, the love that Jesus gives, the peace that Jesus offers, and the life that Jesus provides.

They'll want to climb on the wagon train that's heading for heaven.

Genesis 46:1-27

"I will go down to Egypt with you, and I will surely bring you back again." (vs. 4)

The story is told about a guy who was driving in New England and became hopelessly lost on one of the back roads. He finally spotted a farmhouse and went to the door to get directions. A grizzled old farmer appeared, and the traveler asked him how to get to a certain city. The old man thought a bit, then shook his head and said, "You can't get there from here."

That's what Jacob must have thought when he was told by his sons that he should go to Egypt. God had told him that he was to have the land of Canaan for his and his posterity's possession. He was there. Why should he go to Egypt? Egypt was not the promised land. It was where Abraham had gone with disastrous results, and where Isaac had been specifically told by God not to go, that the promise and the inheritance was in Canaan (26:2-7). Jacob couldn't get to the fullness of God's promises and presence in Egypt. This didn't make any sense at all. But then, Joseph was in Egypt. And the famine was in Canaan. There was a real conflict here. His heart was with his long lost son, his stomach was with the wagons filled with Egypt's provisions, but his soul was with his God, Who had guided him faithfully and flawlessly these many years.

Well, Jacob decided to start out toward Egypt, but he would make a stop before he got too far. Beersheba. Here was where God had appeared to Abraham, when He told Abraham to offer Isaac as a burnt offering (21:33-22:2). Isaac had also met the Lord here for instruction and blessing (26:23-25). Jacob would do the same thing, offering sacrifices and waiting on God to give him direction. And God did not disappoint him. "Do not be afraid to go down to Egypt, for I will make you into a great nation there. I will go down to Egypt with you, and I will surely bring you back again" (vs. 3-4). That was it. God had spoken. Off to Egypt it was. He could get to God's blessings from there after all.

Sometimes it seems in our lives that we're in such a fog, we can't get to God from here. And the direction we're headed seems to be taking us further away. Our desire is to please Him, to follow Him, but He is in

Boston where it's snowing, and we're headed south on I-95 toward Miami where the sun always shines. Well, maybe it would be good for us to pull off at a rest area, do a little worshipping and listen for His instructions. This direction won't come over the CB radio, but if we focus on His person, His character, His promises, and listen to what He's telling us in His Word, the fog will lift and the path will become clear. Maybe He wants us in Miami for the winter. Or He might tell us to put on the snow tires and come back to Boston. Or stay at the rest stop for a while.

But one thing is sure. When we belong to God, we can always get to where He is from where we are. He's never more than a prayer away.

Genesis 46:8-27

"...the members of Jacob's family, which went to Egypt, were seventy in all." (vs. 27)

Sometimes I wonder whether the Spirit of God, when He was giving the Scriptures through the "designated writers," just wanted to see if we could read goofy names. Or throw in a few zingers for those who like to give their children Biblical names to fret over. Look at the roster of names in this passage, and it's easy to come to that conclusion. But then, there could also be the name of the first Jewish law firm here — Muppim, Huppim and Ard (vs. 21). Probably specialized in property rights and camel accidents.

But there's always a reason for these passages; God doesn't have any filler material for His Word. And we often skip over portions like this and miss out on some good stuff. Maybe that's the case with this one.

Whereas God doesn't give a hoot for political correctness, He is very exact when it comes to historical matters. This passage is important because it gives the basis for the independent family units which ultimately made up the entire Hebrew nation, the people of God. Check out the census in Numbers 26, taken after the nation was depleted by a plague caused by idol worship. For the most part, the same names that appear here appear there. And the various tribes of the Hebrew nation are very important as its history is traced, right through to the line of Jesus the Messiah. And whether or not one wants to admit it, Jesus was and is the central figure of all history. The Bible states that, and its historical accuracy is central to that fact.

The passage also gives a glimpse into the eternal nature of God. If we study the content, we find that it would have been impossible for some of these people to have been born at the time Jacob went to Egypt. Take for instance verse 21, the ten sons of Benjamin. When Jacob left Canaan, Benjamin was only twenty-three or twenty-four years old. It's even questionable whether he was married at the time. And as we remember with Tamar, illegitimate pregnancy was not just shrugged off. Not to mention somebody being so sexually active that he would have ten sons by the time he was twenty-four. They'd have locked him up in a monastery and fed him green olives, if they could have found one. But these sons (actually Naaman and Ard were Benjamin's grandsons) already existed in God's world, and they were "in the loins of their father," something we frequently encounter in the Old Testament. God is eternal, His viewpoint is eternal, and we get hopelessly lost when we try to put Him in the same "time box" in which we exist. What happened two thousand years ago and what will happen two thousand years from now is "in the present time" with God. This should be an immeasurable help to us when we start to think that the whole world is out of control and God is still in ancient Rome, trying to catch up with civilization. He knows what's going on, and it's all front and center on His radar screen.

This passage also tells us something about the dependability and truth of the Bible. What other book could give the names of actual persons a couple of generations down the line? With absolute accuracy? It is just a microcosm of the prophetic genius of the Scripture. If one wants to question the truth of the Word of God, let him start with prophecy. Let him look at the progress of the Jewish people down through the years, as it is prophesied by the Scripture. Let him look at the many prophesies of the Messiah Jesus, all fulfilled exactly as they were given. Let him look at the prophesies of the nations and kingdoms of the earth, each and every one coming to pass with specificity. The vitality of the Christian faith is based on the truth and dependability of the Word of God. It is passages such as this that vouch for its credibility and assure us of its reality.

So we can go through the Scripture and be absolutely confident of all that it has to tell us. The way to heaven is through Jesus. No other way. He says in John 14:1-3 that we can believe Him when He tells us that He is preparing a dwelling place for us in heaven, and that He's going to come back to personally escort us there.

And do you know what? We won't need Muppim, Huppim and Ard to represent us at the closing.

"Then you will be allowed to settle in the region of Goshen, for all shepherds are detestable to the Egyptians." (46:34)

One of the mysteries of life is the fact that there is so much racial, ethnic, class and religious hatred in the world. As Rodney King (an African-American man who had an altercation with the Los Angeles police) said, "Why can't we all just get along?" Why should anyone react to whether a person is a Catholic or a Protestant or a Hindu or white or black or a German or an Italian or a Serb or a banker, butcher, garage door salesman or a garbage man?

But people do react to these things, so much so that ethnic wars are fought, racial violence is rampant, class segregation is practiced, and in the name of religion unspeakable atrocities are committed. And I guess we shouldn't be too surprised, since such prejudices are as old as mankind. Maybe that's why people are taller now than they were in the past; everybody has strained harder and harder to be able to look down on someone else.

It seems that the Egyptians were experts in the prejudice thing. Not only did they despise the Hebrews for being Hebrews (43:32), if the Hebrews were shepherds, they were counted worthy of a second shot of scorn (46:34). So Joseph's family was not only low on the totem pole, they would not have even been welcome on the reservation had it not been for Joseph's position with Pharaoh. And it's very strange that Joseph would tell them to advertise the fact that their occupation was raising cattle and sheep (46:33). But he had a reason, and God did, too.

Joseph's reason was that Goshen, near the Nile delta, was the lushest area in the land. Pharaoh's own flocks and herds were located there. It would be the best location for his family's prosperity through the remainder of the famine. But God had a reason, too. Jacob's family was becoming more and more intertwined with the Canaanites through intermarriage and other interrelationships. And the Hebrew nation, which God had selected as His own people, was in danger of losing its identity before it ever got established. Goshen was away from the general populace of Egypt, so it served God's purposes well to take the family to a place where they could become the mighty nation He had intended. And that's exactly what happened, as Exodus 1:7-10 relates. The Egyptian prejudice in God's hands became a vehicle of blessing, prosperity and enlargement.

We can control our attitudes toward people of another race, class, religion, or heritage. But we can't do very much about someone else's prejudice toward us. Except a few things. First, we can love them like Jesus does, regardless of how they feel about us. Next, we can reflect God's Person so much, like Joseph did, so that they will forget what it is about us that they don't like. And third, we can trust that God will use any prejudice against us to bring blessing to our lives.

People might look down on us, but we can look up past them and see God.

Genesis 47:7-10

"And Jacob said to Pharaoh, 'The years of my pilgrimage are a hundred and thirty. My years have been few and difficult. ...'" (vs. 9)

I saw a sign on an apartment complex the other day that said, "if you lived here, you'd be home now." I guess that statement is generally true. But with a lot of people, it's not. Home is somewhere else, regardless of where they might be living at the moment. Home is where the heart is. Where the roots are. Where Scruffy the mongrel sits patiently, looking down the road for the familiar Chevy to come around the corner. One of my sons who lives in another city said it all one Thanksgiving. When we were going around the table saying what we were thankful for, he said, "I'm thankful that I now live close enough so I could drive home for Thanksgiving." Thrilled his mother out of her apron. I was happy, too, until she gave him a bigger piece of pumpkin pie than she gave me.

Pharaoh asked Jacob, "How old are you?" (vs. 8). We don't know what prompted the question. Maybe Jacob looked so shopworn that Pharaoh figured he would find out Jake's age and break out the hemlock before he got to the same place. Or maybe it was his way of welcoming Jacob to Egypt, wondering why Jake had spent so much time away from Joseph in some place other than in Pharaoh's homeland. Or maybe he was just nebby. You can bet your boots that he wouldn't have asked the same question if it had been Joseph's mother. Anyhow, Pharaoh must have figured that Jacob was going to stick around a while in his new home.

But Jacob let Pharaoh know that he had a different home. He was on a journey. A pilgrimage. And if Pharaoh's next question was going to be, "Are we having fun yet?" he got the answer in advance. Not very much. Tramping through the world on the way to the promises had been difficult. A hassle. Sorrow and conflict and disappointment and struggle. Pharaoh should maybe expect him to sing, "It's a Wonderful Life"? It would be more like a verse or so of, "It's Not an Easy Road."

Well, we're also on a pilgrimage. Like the song says, "This world is not my home, I'm just a-passin' through." Most of the time it's not easy.

Jacob had created a lot of his own problems, and sometimes we do, too. But often our trials are because we're living in enemy territory. The world. And the world doesn't look very kindly on Christians. The Religious Right. Dangerous, sinister, mean-spirited zealots. But as Jesus said, "If the world hates you, keep in mind that it hated Me first" (John 15:18). So we shouldn't be surprised. Or discouraged.

But Paul says that our home, our citizenship, is in heaven (2 Corinthians 5:8, Philippians 3:20). And since it is, we ought to be focused on those things which will matter in our eternal home, and our efforts centered around preparing for our final trip there.

It won't matter what the world says then. Its voice will be drowned out by the Hallelujah Chorus.

Genesis 47:13-26

"Joseph said to the people, 'I have bought you and your land for Pharaoh.'" (vs.23)

The famine was running full tilt in Egypt, and the people used up all their savings accounts and cashed in their IRA's to get food. That still wasn't enough, however, so they asked Joseph to give them a handout (vs. 15). But Joseph had an IQ over twenty-five, and it didn't take him long to figure out that if he just gave the people the food, he'd have a welfare roll longer than a thirty-six-foot hoagie. And just about as manageable. So Joseph exchanged Pharaoh's grain for the people's livestock, and, at the end of the next year of famine, he ended up with title to all the people's land and then even the people themselves. Must have made a lot of work for property lawyers, at least until there wasn't anything left to transfer.

Since Joseph had never read a lot of Karl Marx, he decided that a little capitalism was still good for the soul. So he instituted the first Small Business Administration incubator program. The government provided the seed grain and the land in exchange for twenty percent of the proceeds (vs. 23-24). The people could keep the rest and do with it whatever they wanted. The hardest part must have been retraining all the government bean counters into grain counters.

But the people had lost all their property, their individual freedom, and had what was really a twenty percent sharecropping arrangement. One might think that they would soon be staging the Boston Tea Party of the future. But they were actually grateful (vs. 25). They figured that Joseph had saved their lives. Fortunately the U.S. Government has never figured out how to get all our assets and have us become indentured servants to boot, in exchange for some surplus food (although with one more Taxpayers' Relief Act they may come close). If they ever do, we're all in trouble.

When you think about it, all of us, like the Egyptians, have gone through a famine and have sold ourselves to something or someone, too. Regardless of our position in life, at one time or another we all have experienced a famine in our souls. The Preacher in Ecclesiastes 3:11 tells us that, "(God) has set eternity in the hearts of men"; that is, man is never satisfied with the purely temporal, but has a consciousness of and longing for the eternal. Some have sold themselves to work, to pleasure, to money, to booze, or to the devil himself in order to try to fill this void. But many have realized that Jesus has already paid the price for our souls. Paul tells us that, "You are not your own; you were bought with a price" (1 Corinthians 6:20). Peter tells us how much, "... the precious blood of Christ" (1 Peter 1:19). And when we "sell" our souls and lives to Jesus, we get a fabulous bundle of goodies in return: eternal life, present peace, Divine love, the comfort and joy of the Holy Spirit, so much we could never write it all down.

If we belong to Jesus, we'll never be an item in the devil's fire sale.

A View of Genesis

"Do not bury me in Egypt, but … carry me out of Egypt and bury me where (my fathers) are buried." (vs. 29)

In the Korean War, Marine Corps General "Chesty" Puller and his troops were camped in the Chosin Reservoir. There was a high ridge which extended entirely around their position. One morning, one of his aides burst into his tent and exclaimed, "General Puller! The enemy has us completely surrounded!" Puller went outside and surveyed the scene. Sure enough, there were North Koreans the entire way around the perimeter. He thought a moment and replied, "Those poor (censored)." Then he rallied his marines and fought his way out, taking all his dead and wounded with him.

Jacob had been in Egypt for seventeen years (vs. 28). He was aware that his life was about over. He didn't want to be left in Egypt, dead or alive. So he made Joseph swear that he would bury his body in Canaan. As a matter of fact, when Jacob died, there were more chariots in the procession than there would have been black limos if he had been a major mob figure (50:7-14). Even Al Capone would have been jealous.

When Chesty Puller came out of the Chosin Reservoir, he brought his dead with him not only out of respect, but also to provide closure for their kin. He simply refused to leave their bodies on foreign soil. But in Jacob's case, he had a completely different reason to insist that he be buried in Canaan and not in Egypt. No, Canaan wasn't "holy ground." Nor was there any better scenery or climate there. And the Hebrew nation didn't have a national cemetery in Canaan, although Abraham, Isaac, Rebecca and Rachel were buried there. But even that wasn't the basis for his request. Unlike the closure which was provided when the bodies of Puller's dead marines were delivered to their loved ones, Jacob's final excursion was the expression of the dawning of his eternity. Canaan was where God's promise would be fulfilled! Egypt and Goshen or any place in between was just a water stop for Jacob's Hallelujah Train. He was looking for the resurrection, and even though his earthly life would end without experiencing the realization of the promised land, he was convinced that it was already in the bag.

Sometimes Christians' lives are a lot like Jacob's life. The years are "few and difficult" (vs. 9), and at the end of this life what we think the promises of God should have been (generally peace, happiness and prosperity) have not been fulfilled. So we blame Him on our way to the graveyard. Instead, we ought to be like Jacob and look for God's promises from an eternal perspective. Then we won't ever be figuring that God had better hurry up and get us the biggie blessing, before the last long ride in the big black limousine occurs.

We may be looking for God's all-day lollipop here, but His all-eternity lollipop lasts a lot longer and tastes a lot better, even though it may arrive a little later.

Genesis 48:1-11

"Israel said to Joseph, 'I never expected to see your face again, and now God has allowed me to see your children, too.'" (vs. 11)

Jacob was on his last legs, and Joseph, along with his two sons, had come to be with him during the last hours. He reviewed the promises of God to himself and his posterity (vs. 3-4), and then declared to Joseph that the two young men, Ephraim and Manasseh, would become as his own sons in the sharing of the Lord's inheritance through Joseph (vs. 5). And historically, all that Jacob said came to pass.

Then Joseph presented his sons to Jacob, who was overcome with happiness when he saw them (vs. 10). In an emotional statement, he expressed gratitude to God for allowing him this moment (vs. 11). For more than twenty years, he had thought Joseph was dead. Now he had not only enjoyed the fellowship of his beloved son, he had also been enabled by God to see Joseph's children. It was almost too good to be true.

But true it was, and God had brought it all about. As Jacob reviewed his own life and Joseph's life, there were so many circumstances and situations and happenings which were so improbable, even impossible, that God's signature was all over the place. He had blessed Jacob already beyond his wildest imagination. Oh, yes, getting there may not have been half the fun, but God had been in control all the way, even though He permitted the natural consequences of both Jacob's and other people's sin to garbage up the trail.

Sooner or later in our lives, we will respond the same as did Jacob. God is good! He is the God of wonders. In Moses' and the nation's song of deliverance from Egypt, they sang, "Who among the gods is like You, O Lord? Who is like You — majestic in holiness, awesome in glory, working wonders" (Exodus 15:11). Paul tells us that God "is able to do immeasurably more than all we ask or imagine" (Ephesians 3:20). There are things we desire, things we hope for, things we pray for, and our God Who responds is able to bring anything into being according to His will. And so many times, our requests and our desires are too small. Not too small for Him to grant, but too small for His greatness, too small for His mercy, and too small for His grace. Then God acts and brings blessings into our lives which, like Jacob's blessings, are far beyond our dreams and expectations.

So let's go to the heavenly library and check out God's version of "Great Expectations." And for best results, don't let it sit on the shelf. Open it up and do a little speed reading.

Genesis 48:1-22

"May (Ephraim and Manasseh) be called by my name and the names of my fathers Abraham and Isaac, and may they increase greatly upon the earth." (vs. 16)

Here was Grandpa Jake meeting his grandsons for the first time. And the first thing he did was to give them a blessing. In fact, he went further than that. He adopted them as his own sons. He told their Dad that they would be great nations (vs. 19). That they would take a portion of their uncles' inheritance.

I wonder what Ephraim and Manasseh thought? "Man, this old guy who never saw us before and who can hardly see us now is saying all these weird things! And he can't even keep us straight. Why should we want to be part of this family of Hebrew shepherds anyhow? Boy, the Egyptian girls sure won't be impressed! Let's get Dad out of here before we all end up in Weirdsville!"

That's what I'd have thought, anyhow. Here were two guys about twenty years old, who had the world by the tail. They rode around on Pharaoh's stretch-camel limo with their family; their Dad was the #2 man in the government, so they hobnobbed with the elite; their other grandfather was the major religious figure around, so no one messed with them there, either; they had the finest education available in both the knowledge and customs of the culture; and they lived in a palace in Egypt, not in a tent in Goshen. Why on earth would anyone want to switch?

Well, Joseph was a wise and spiritual man, a man in tune with God, and doubtless he explained the whole scenario to the boys. Egypt is in man's world, but Canaan is of God's world. The promises of Egypt are temporal, but God's promises are eternal. The posterity of Egypt will perish, but God's posterity in Abraham, Isaac and Jacob will live on forever. The God of Israel is the True God, but the gods of Egypt are fraudulent. That may not be the way it appears, guys, but that's the way it is.

We need to remember that our God is the same as Joseph's God. That we are in the world, but not of the world. That the promises of this world are fleeting, but God's promises in Jesus can never be compromised or diminished (2 Corinthians 1:20). That the world and everything in it will disappear (2 Peter 3:10), but we will stand firm in Christ (2 Corinthians 1:21-22). That the god of this world is doomed (Revelation 20:10), but Jesus has been exalted and will reign forever (Philippians 2:9-10).

Ephraim and Manasseh chose to follow their father's footsteps. Men of greatness came from their tribes — Joshua, Gideon, Samuel. If we follow our Father's footsteps, our children and our children's children will also beat a path to heaven's door.

Genesis 48:1-22

"But Israel reached out his right hand and put it on Ephraim's head, though he was the younger; ... Joseph ... was displeased. ..." (vs. 14, 17)

Protocol and tradition and political correctness are very important these days. If a person doesn't do something according to Hoyle or Emily Post or Miss Manners or someone else's sensibilities, then it's like everybody from the guy's mother-in-law to the local paper to Jesse Jackson to Larry King Live to Rush Limbaugh gets involved and has to make a federal case out of it. Janet Reno seems to be the only person in town ignoring things any more.

I guess that it was the same in Joseph's time. Jacob was in the process of blessing the two boys, and this was a big deal. It was even more important than the guys getting their camel driver's licenses. It had to do with the rights and privileges of being the first born. He got a double portion of all the family goodies, and numerous other advantages to boot. Of course, if the first born was a girl, that was a bummer, and all the hoopla was put on hold until a son came along. That says a lot about tradition, but not much for gender neutrality. NOW wasn't very active in those days. Anyhow, Jacob was almost blind, and as he went to bless the boys, it appeared that he got messed up with the birth order. Joseph had his sons in the proper position in front of Jacob, but the old man crossed his arms and put his right hand on the younger son's head (vs. 14). This violated protocol and tradition and political correctness. Joseph tried to change the position of Jacob's hands, but Jacob told him in so many words to butt out, that he knew what he was doing (vs. 17-20). So Ephraim got the blessing instead of Manasseh and, as it turned out, that's what God intended.

God doesn't pay very much attention to men's traditions, and He could care less about being politically correct or following Miss Manners' imperatives. In fact, He has His own agenda, which He follows to a "T." Joseph brought the boys to Jacob for the patriarchal blessing, figuring that the standard procedure would be followed. When it wasn't, he got all bummed out, thinking maybe that Jacob's elevator wasn't quite making it to the top floor. But if Joseph had known his history, he would have remembered that the younger son had been preferred over the older son many times before: for example, Seth over Cain; Shem over Japheth; Isaac over Ishmael; and his own father over Esau. So he shouldn't have gotten uptight when Ephraim got the nod from Jacob.

God doesn't act according to the way that our society thinks He should, either. Whether a person is the firstborn or sixth in a family of seven; a bank president or a guy who just got fired as a used-car salesman; a national hero or an ordinary Joe, it doesn't cut any ice with Him. He blesses whomever He pleases.

So we shouldn't lose any sleep if someone else appears to have God baking his cakes. If we are faithful, His daily bread wagon will bring us a few cookies, too.

Genesis 48:15-16

"Then (Jacob) blessed Joseph and said, 'May the God before Whom my fathers Abraham and Isaac walked, the God Who has been my Shepherd all my life to this day, the Angel Who has delivered me from all harm — may He bless these boys ... and may they increase greatly upon the earth.'" (vs. 15-16)

I have a Hebrew friend who has at various stages of his life claimed to be an atheist, an agnostic, and an animist, and I wouldn't be surprised if sometime soon he makes something religious out of algorithms. I think he's a charter member of the god-of-the-month club. His latest spiritual adventure took him to the Midwest, where he got involved in one of the Native-American religions. If there were an instant deity mix, he would have had it on his shopping list long ago. The only One he won't try is his Messiah Jesus.

There have been a kazillion so-called gods around since Adam and Eve got their exit cards punched at Eden-gate. Natural, theoretical, hypothetical, mythological, and for the most part, illogical gods. God speaks about these imitation deities in Isaiah 44:6-20. He says, "I am the first and I am the last; apart from Me there is no God   ... All who make idols are nothing, and the things they treasure are worthless ..." (vs. 6, 9).

But Jacob had a real thing going with the real God. He knew the God Who presides ("the God before Whom my fathers ... walked" — vs. 15); the God Who provides ("Who has been my Shepherd" — vs. 15); the God Who persists ("my Shepherd all my life to this day" — vs. 15), the God Who protects ("the Angel Who has delivered me from all harm" — vs. 16); and the God Who performs ("may they increase greatly upon the earth" — vs. 16). For Jacob, it was a no-brainer. His was the God Who was an eternity ahead of any substitute.

People have a lot of different gods today, too. Paul speaks about those whose "god is their stomach" (Philippians 3:19 — and from the looks of some, they must have been worshipping for a long time). This refers to the hedonists of our society. Then there are those who worship money. And others of whom it may be said, "He is a self-made man, and he worships his creator." Paul talks about people who, "... became fools and exchanged the glory of the immortal God for images made to look like mortal man and birds and animals and reptiles" (Romans 1:23).

Actually, anything which comes between man and God is an idol, a god, even legitimate things, when it is exalted to a place of pre-eminence in a person's life. And most of us, if we really examine ourselves, can point to something which we must confess takes preference to the worship of Jacob's God, the Eternal Deity.

So let's make sure we turn over our lives to Jesus, turn on our hearts to His worship, and turn up our noses at anything less.

Genesis 48:1-22

"Israel said to Joseph, 'I am about to die, but God will be with you and take you back to the land of your fathers.'" (vs. 21)

I know a lot of old people, and I'm getting to that stage in life myself. When the biggest event in the month is the arrival of the social security check. When the letters AARP are more important than RSVP. When the most significant triumph of today is remembering what happened yesterday. And some of the old people I know are pretty mellow, but an awful lot of them are downright crotchety. Their pains in the back become a pain in the neck to everyone around them. In their thinking, there are only two kinds of kids — hoodlums and their grandchildren. And their view from the passing lane is that all the cars on the road moving faster than 25 MPH are driven by lunatics, a fact that they loudly proclaim. One might get the idea from Jacob's answer to Pharaoh in Genesis 47:9 ("My years have been few and difficult") that he was becoming a real sourpuss. But was that the case? Let's see in this chapter what was really going on in Jake's cranium, as he reviewed his past, contemplated his present and anticipated his future.

In verses 3-4, we see Jacob looking <u>upward in faith</u>. God had promised him a home and a people, and he had not a shred of doubt that this was in the bag. In verse 10, we find him looking <u>outward in love.</u> His beloved son and grandsons were with him, and he was filled with an inexpressible love for those who were most precious to his heart. In verse 11 we see him looking <u>inward with joy,</u> as he almost bursts with delight in telling Joseph how God has allowed him this moment. Then in verses 15-16 Jacob looks <u>backward with thanksgiving</u>. God had been more to him than he could ever have expected or deserved. And in verse 21, Jacob looks <u>onward with hope</u>. God would take Jacob's posterity and his body back to Canaan, back to the Promised Land, and there fulfill all the promise of the future.

You know, this faith, hope (which really means "a certain expectation"), joy and love business isn't just for the old folks. We're told a lot about these things for our present consumption. Paul tells us of the permanence and universal importance of faith, hope and love in 1 Corinthians 13:13. He also points out in Romans 5:2-5 that we have peace with God through faith, we have joy in the hope of the glory of God, and we have God's love in our hearts through the presence of the Holy Spirit. In Ephesians 4:2-5, we're instructed to love each other, because we have been called to one hope as a result of one faith. And there are many other Scriptures which point us to the same things.

Just imagine if everyone, young and old, had the same attitude as Jacob did in this chapter. It doesn't take a genius to figure out that CNN's evening news would take on a different character.

And we might even smile at that old fogey slowpoke driver in the passing lane.

Genesis 48:21 - 49:1

"Then Israel said to Joseph, 'I am about to die. ...'"(vs. 21)

My friend, Joe, had an experience with death. He was only in his late forties, but he had health problems big time. One evening he had a heart attack so severe that he couldn't be moved to the hospital. His family gathered at his bedside to say their good-byes. His took his ring off his finger and gave it to his wife. It was all over. Except for one thing. God had decided that it was not his time. So my friend recovered, miraculously, and lived another thirty-five years.

Later on I asked him, "Joe, what's it like to die?" "Nothing to it," he told me. "It's a piece of cake. I was totally at peace with God, and I was looking forward to an eternity with Jesus! The only regret I had was for my family, but I knew the Lord would take care of them, too."

Jacob was in that same condition. He was about to pass through the check out counter, and he knew it. But he wasn't hassled about it. He would gather his sons around him and have the final family huddle (49:1). Then he would pull the covers over his head and pass on (49:33). Simple. Like getting on the camel caravan with a one-way ticket, headed for the ultimate five-star oasis. Forever.

It's safe to say that we all will come to eternity's launching pad sooner or later. Unless Jesus returns in our lifetime, none of us will get out of this world alive. Scripture tells us that, "... man is destined to die once, and after that to face judgment ... " (Hebrews 9:27). So it makes sense to get ready for the occasion. Like Israel was told in Amos 4:12, "Prepare to meet your God." Like Jacob did. Like my friend, Joe, had done.

Well, how did they do it? What is the process? Different people seem to have different answers. Do enough good works so that when the balances are checked, they will outweigh the bad. Go to this church or follow that creed. Whatever you do, be sincere. Walk around with a long face and a big Bible with large print and red letters, and lots of notes. Don't shove ducks into a pond or howl at the moon. Keep the 11th commandment ("Thou shalt not get caught").

But Jacob and my friend, Joe, weren't into those things. They believed God. They trusted in Jesus — Jacob by faith in God's promise of the Redeemer and Joe by faith in the Person and sacrifice of the historical and Biblical Jesus. In reading about Jacob's life, it's obvious he wasn't saved by his good works or his golden personality. Joe would have told us the same thing. It was entirely "by grace ... through faith, ... the gift of God, not by works, so that no one can boast" (Ephesians 2:8-9). That's why when these men saw death, they didn't see a cloaked spectre with a scythe, but a Savior ready to welcome them into His presence.

Real Christianity certainly is good to live by, but it's the only thing to die by.

Genesis 49:1-33

"Assemble and listen, sons of Jacob; listen to your father Israel." (vs. 2)

What would you think of a father's immediate pre-mortem estate plan which consisted of calling all the kids together (males only, please), telling them what his predictions of their futures were, and saying nary a word about any financial matters? If you were a lawyer, you would be happy, since a substantial amount of work would be a phone call away. Women's rights groups would be unhappy, and probably organize a boycott of the funeral. Well, none of that would have mattered in the Hebrew nation, because that's how things were done in those days. And nobody seemed to lose any sleep over it. I guess it was better than hearing the patriarch say with a wicked grin, "Being of sound mind and sound body, I got nothing to say to you turkeys, and I spent the last shekel yesterday!"

In Jacob's estate plan, he called his sons together to "tell you what will happen to you in days to come" (vs. 1), and "what (he) said to them when he blessed them, giving each the blessing appropriate to them" (vs. 28). In saying, "in days to come," Jacob referred to both the post-Egypt future of the nation Israel during its time in Canaan, as well as to its position and condition at the time of the coming of the Messiah. If we analyze this text, referring to other Scriptures, we find that it sets out the entire future of God's plan for the ages, from the time of Jacob's death through the time of the future fulfillment of the eternal Kingdom of God.

We might also note (vs. 2) that the aged patriarch made reference to both his earthly name ("sons of Jacob") and the name given him by God ("your father Israel" — see 32:28) as he was about to preach his final homily. And he considered the human characteristics and human acts of many of his sons in revealing both the historical and spiritual futures of themselves and their tribes. It is an all-encompassing prophecy that combines both the experience of the natural man, Jacob, and the wisdom of the spiritual man, Israel. It shows how much in the nation's future history that his sons' natural and spiritual lives would be intertwined. How those tribes which followed God prospered, and those which didn't marched down the path to oblivion.

Sometimes we try to separate our natural lives from our spiritual lives. We may be one person on Sundays and another person on Thursdays. Ronnie Righteous in the pew, and Sammy Shortchange at the desk. Talking about the Golden Rule in church, but saying, "He who has the gold, rules" in life. A certifiable case of spiritual schizophrenia. This is certainly not what God intends for us, and through many Biblical examples such as this one concerning Jacob's sons and their future history, He shows us why it is so important to live our everyday lives consistent with the spiritual principles which He sets forth in His Word.

Like some of Jacob's sons, we'll never get it together in life, unless we get our spiritual life and natural life operating together.

"Reuben, you are my firstborn, ... turbulent as the waters, you will no longer excel." (vs. 3,4)

My wife and I love to go to Hilton Head. To walk along the South Carolina beach, seeing the vast expanse of the ocean, enjoying the gentle surf lapping at our bare feet and the cool ooze of wet sand as it squeezes between our toes. But we would never go there in the middle of a hurricane, with wild winds whipping angry waves into a frenzy, threatening to destroy anything and anybody which happens to be in its path. That's what water is like; when it is calm and peaceful, it can provide beauty and pleasure, sustenance and power. When it is turbulent and uncontrolled, it will overwhelm and destroy.

As Jacob launched into his final monologue, Reuben was first on the program. I doubt if he was very enthusiastic over his father's prognostication. According to Jacob, Reuben was "turbulent as the waters" (vs. 4, literally, "a boiling over of waters"). Undisciplined, uncontrolled, unstable. Not even suitable for calling the clan in for lunch. So although he was once the lead dog, he would have the rear view from that time on. Even though he was the firstborn, he was unworthy of the rights and privileges of that position and lost them to his brothers. He was unworthy of the priesthood, because he was unstable and self-willed. That went to Levi. He was unworthy of kingship, because he lacked courage and strength of conviction. That went to Judah. He was unworthy of the birthright, because of his sin with Bilhah (Genesis 35:22). That went to Joseph. It would be accurate to say that all this did not pretty up his resume.

And it all came to pass as Jacob said. Reuben's tribe never excelled in anything, never produced a judge, prophet, or national hero. Several of his descendants teamed up with the troublemaker Korah, who got God so ticked off that He opened up the ground, creating the world's first mass live burial (Numbers 16:1-35). Reuben's tribe also refused to fight against the Canaanite oppressor, Sisera (Judges 5:15-16). His posterity was permanently impoverished. They probably never even won at gin rummy, Scrabble, or the Pennsylvania lottery.

I guess today the shrinks would blame all of this on some kind of "rage." Rage at his parents. Rage at having to shovel too much camel dung. Rage at his brother, Joseph (probably the most likely, since Joseph would be the equivalent of today's "religious right"). But Jacob called a spade, a spade. Reuben's self-will, his self-centeredness, and his sin caused his downfall. Simple. End of story.

Hopefully, this kind of thing will not be the end of our story. Reuben could have changed everything by admitting his guilt, repenting of his sin, and walking in God's way. If we're like Reuben, we can change our futures in the same way.

If we're going to be like water, let's generate power instead of doing destruction.

Genesis 49:5-7

"Simeon and Levi are brothers;... I will scatter them ... and disperse them in Israel." (vs. 5,7)

After Jacob had gotten done with Reuben's "blessing," Simeon and Levi probably wanted to head out for a kosher pizza rather than listen to what they figured was coming. Jacob's three eldest sons were peas out of the same pod; they all acted with the pride and violence of the natural man, with or without a reason. But it wouldn't have mattered if the two boys had split before their "reading"; they would have gotten the news by express-camel mail anyhow.

If we reverse the VCR to fifty years or so before Jacob's deathbed declarations, the Saga of the Slaughter of the Shechemites would appear on the big screen (Genesis 34:1-31). Dinah, the sister of Jacob's sons, had been seduced by the Tom Cruise of the Shechemites. He went ga-ga over the girl and wanted to marry her. But in their anger, Simeon and Levi came up with a plan to send the whole Shechem male population on to their final reward, using the Jewish religious rite of circumcision as an entree for their revenge. Jacob had gone ballistic, but the damage had been done. CNN-Canaan had reported the dastardly affair to the whole countryside. The coming Crusades were a love-in compared to this event.

God wasn't too keen on the whole thing, either, especially because His covenant had been used by the boys as a means to an end. So He decided to pass on both Simeon and Levi for future benefits. He did relent in Levi's case to some degree, but that was because Levi's tribe stood up against the rest of the nation when the golden calf was rolled out (Exodus 32:26-29). They became a tribe of priests, but they had no possessions; they lived in the cities of other tribes, with a few exceptions, and the levitical tithe became the source of their income. Simeon got lost in the shuffle, ultimately being assimilated into the tribe of Judah.

Anger and revenge have no place in God's business. Yes, Jesus was angry when he threw the money changers out of the temple, but He was angry because they were using spiritual activity to make a bundle for themselves. And even though He was angry with the act, He still loved the perpetrators; it's good to remember that He died for them, too, rather than vaporizing them on the spot, which He could have done. And Jesus never took revenge, either. Peter tells us that when Jesus was insulted or attacked, He just committed whatever it was to His Father, the Righteous Judge, and let Him handle it (1 Peter 2:23).

So we need to remember that God can fight His own battles. If He wants us to help Him, He'll let us know. Until that time, He would much rather that we be on active duty in His peacemaking force.

That's where love and prayer are the most effective weapons.

A View of Genesis

Genesis 49:8-13

"Judah, your brothers will praise you; ... your father's sons will bow down to you." (vs. 8)

After Jacob had finished with the eldest three boys, it appeared that this death bed scene was going to be a long day for everybody, in more ways than one. The brothers to this point were 0 for 3. Reuben had been sent to the back of the bus by Jacob, and it didn't appear that Simeon and Levi were even going to make it on board. If I had been Judah, who was next in line, I would have asked for a recess in the proceedings.

One can imagine what was going through Judah's mind. "The old man hasn't forgotten much. He remembered Reuben's tete-a-tete with Bilhah, and Simeon and Levi wrapping the Shechemites around the axle. I guess that means he'll bring up my idea to sell Joseph to the Midianites. And maybe Tamar. And the time when ..." Judah must have thought he was a piece of dead meat.

But instead of dead meat, Judah came on like a slab of prime steak. Corn fed and USDA inspected. "You're like a lion, Judah. King of the jungle. The whole world is going to give you a heap of respect" (vs. 8-9). Judah must have been in a state of catatonic shock. How could something like this have come about?

Well, there was something that Judah did that his older brothers hadn't done. Even though they were all guilty of a whole catalog of sins, Judah was the only one who had scrapped the catalog. He had repented. No, the Scripture doesn't say that he dressed in sackcloth and ashes and crawled on his hands and knees to Peniel or Beersheba or Bethel. His actions were solid evidence that he had experienced a real change of heart. He had confessed his guilt in the Tamar affair (38:26). He put his neck on the line in order for Benjamin to make the trip to Egypt (43:8-10), and then offered himself to Joseph as a slave in Benjamin's place (44:33-34), knowing that Jacob would go completely bonkers if Benji didn't return. There must have been other evidence of Judah's turn-around, too, since Jacob had trusted him to go ahead of the family to get directions to Goshen (vs. 28). The end result was that Judah had gone to the head of the class.

All of us have a history of sin. And sin always has the same color, smell, feel, taste and sound to God. But while sin is always the same to God, there's a difference in sinners to Him. No, it doesn't have anything to do with who we are or how we sin, whether we're down-and-outers or up-and-outers. The difference, like in Judah and his brothers, lies in whether we have confessed our sin and repented of it. God says that when we confess our sin, He will forgive us, and the blood of Jesus will purify us and we will walk in His light (1 John 1:5-10).

Some give God fits with their sin. But we can give Him amnesia if we confess our sin and change our direction. It works every time (Isaiah 43:25, Psalm 103:1-18).

A View of Genesis

Genesis 49:10-12

"The scepter will not depart from Judah, nor the ruler's staff from between his feet, until He comes to Whom it belongs and the obedience of the nations is His." (vs. 10)

In my business life, I have been around a few professional football players. Some of them are so big that I pull myself up to my full height and look them square in the belly button. I remember my first meeting with one offensive lineman, which took place in a restaurant. When he walked in, the place went silent. There were two things about him that caught everyone's attention, including my own. The first was the size of his rear end. It must have covered three acres. The second was the fact that he was carrying a purse. Now I had been a Marine, and we didn't carry purses. But it was OK with me if this guy wanted to carry one. Or two or three. I surely didn't make any snide remarks about either the purse or his south end going north, and no one else did either. There was another thing about him that I discovered later. He was a Jesus-freak. He wore T-shirts and ball caps that said things like, "Jesus is alive!" or maybe one of Jesus' titles. I never heard anyone giving him grief about that, either.

One of Jesus' titles is "The Lion of the tribe of Judah, the Root of David." We find this in Revelation 5:5, where it also says that He has triumphed. Jacob in this "blessing" to Judah prophesies this whole scene. David and the line of rulers of Israel's southern kingdom came from Judah's tribe. Jesus will be the final King, sitting on David's throne and ruling the nations (Isaiah 11-12).

But at this present time, it seems like all this has a snowball's chance of happening. If Jesus came to sit on a throne today, the ACLU would sue everyone in sight, including Judah and David and Jacob posthumously. And the UN would call a special session of the security council. But it appears that Jesus doesn't seem to be very interested in appearing to claim His throne, or even to defend His rights or His character. So most of us Christians are chickens like Peter when he denied being one of Jesus' followers (Luke 22:54-62), or scaredy-cats like the disciples when they locked themselves in an attic after Jesus' crucifixion because they were afraid of the Jews (John 20:19).

But according to this passage, we ought to be more like my football player friend. Maybe we don't have to wear T-shirts and hats like he does, but we need to let people know Who we belong to and where we stand and what's going to happen in the future. Oh, they might call us Jesus-freaks and laugh out loud at us or snicker behind our backs, but like Jacob prophesied and John the Apostle said, Jesus is going to come out on top. It's only a matter of time. When He decides it's time.

I guess then my friend will be wearing his T-shirt which says, "I told you so!"

Genesis 49:13

"Zebulun will live by (toward) the seashore. ..." (vs. 13)

Zebulun, Issachar and Dan were the next trio to be targets in Jacob's shooting gallery. We remember that Reuben, Simeon and Levi were lumped together in their collective loss of the privileges of the birth-right, part of which fell into Judah's lap. While this next group of three did not get scorched to the extent of the first three, we can detect some of Jacob's disappointment in his assessment of their characters and forecast of their individual futures. We might also note that Jake departs from the birth order of his sons in dispensing his final thoughts, until he reaches Joseph and Benjamin. Zebulun now sits in the hot seat.

It almost seems that Jacob looked at Zeb, told him that he was going to live toward the sea and make a fortune as a trader, and then said, "Next!" He didn't waste a whole lot of words on son #10. But each of Jacob's prophesies concerning his sons had a purpose. Jake was not into prognostication just for the fun of it, to start a fortune cookie busi-ness, or to give future historians something to mull over. As a matter of fact, Z's tribe did establish a successful maritime trading business, buy-ing Phoenician merchandise and selling it to Damascus and points west. But there was a purpose both to the order in which these three sons received their "blessing," and to the message that the collective state-ments convey. Taken together, the three prophesies illustrate the de-clension which occurs when someone gets involved with the world system (Zebulun), becomes comfortable in its surroundings (Issachar), and then buys into that system's philosophy (Dan).

Everything seemed to go pretty well with Zebulun. In Deuteronomy 33:18-19, Zeb, together with Issachar, is characterized in Moses' bless-ing as wealthy, content and blessed. The tribe was a brave tribe, and joined in fighting Sisera (Judges 5:14-18). But they "lived" (literally, "laid themselves down") for commerce, and in their later years were not prominent within the Hebrew nation.

There is nothing wrong with being involved in commercial activities, running a tight ship and making a bundle doing it. In fact, the Proverbs tell us, "Do you see a man skilled in his work? He will serve before kings" (Proverbs 22:29). And the Bible never tells us that we should turn down a financial or commercial opportunity just because it may lead to big bucks. If Bill Gates would appear at my door with a few stock options, I wouldn't decline on the grounds I might become a kazillionaire. But the problem appears when these activities become prominent; because soon they will become pre-eminent. We become careless spiritually, and declension starts. That's the story of Zebulun.

And we need to remember that when God passes out the keys to the mansions in heaven, the schmaltziest one won't be going to the guy who spent the most time and effort wheeling and dealing on earth.

A View of Genesis

Genesis 49:14-15

"Issachar is a raw-boned donkey, lying down between two saddlebags." (vs. 14)

Whoa! What is this? Here is Jacob, calling his son a donkey. A lazy loafer. Someone who couldn't even be tempted to get out of bed for a cup of Maxwell House or Taster's Choice. Whose most appropriate action word is "Mañana." Well, that's what happened. Issachar must have been in Dreamsville when Jacob gave him a to-do list that never happened, in order to get treated like this.

But Jacob knew what he was talking about. Issachar's tribe became prosperous materially, but for the most part lay down politically and spiritually. They did have a few bright moments, notably in the fight against Sisera (Judges 5:15), but it was basically a tribe which lived in relative luxury, became complacent and greeted any spiritual challenge with a yawn and a "Who needs it?" It was the second phase of declension after Zebulun; "Z" became familiar with and involved in the world system, and Issachar found a real comfort zone in it. That's what Jake meant when he said, "lying down between two saddlebags." Becoming saddled with the burdens of the system and being lazy even with that. But this comfort zone ended up, as it inevitably does, as a channel to becoming a slave to that system (vs. 15).

Sometimes that's what happens to us, isn't it? We get a few bucks in the 401(k) plan, a few pounds under the belt from a little too much beef and potatoes (or maybe beer and potato chips) and a loaded Chevy Blazer in the garage, and we start thinking "it doesn't get any better than this." This is probably true, because it usually doesn't get any better. It gets worse. God decides it's time to get our attention, and He has a few grabbers in his knapsack. Like the guy in Luke 12:16-21 who said to himself, "Hey, Buddy, I'm cool for the duration, so let's boogie!" (12:19). Somebody asked at his funeral a few days later, "What did he leave?" The answer? He left it all.

God takes a dim view of all this. In Zephaniah 1:11-13, He gets a full head of steam up against Judah, which had become like Issachar in its involvement in commercial activities and complacency about spiritual things. Some of the words found there are, "wiped out" (vs. 11); "ruined" (vs. 11); "punish" (vs. 12); "plundered" (vs. 13); "demolished" (vs. 13). Not a pretty picture.

Well, it can get better than this. That happens when we are rising up instead of lying down. When we flower in God's system rather than flounder in the world's system. When the instruction of the Bible is more important than the inducement of Madison Avenue. When we become servants of the Almighty instead of serfs of the world, "submitting to forced labor" (vs. 15) like Issachar did.

I saw a bumper sticker the other day that said, "The one with the most toys at the end, wins." He does, all right. He wins the booby prize.

Genesis 49:16-17

"Dan will be a serpent by the roadside, a viper along the path." (vs. 17)

God had given Adam the job of naming the animals (Genesis 2:19-20). No, this isn't where we first hear of Spot, as in, "Run, Spot, run!" Or Leo the lion. Or Mickey Mouse. Or Garfield. For all we know, Adam may have spoken in Latin and was the first to name Wile E. Coyote by his generic name, "Eatibus Anythingibus."

But here we have Jacob calling his sons by animals' names. Judah was a lion, Issachar a donkey, Naphtali a deer, Benjamin a wolf, and good grief! Dan is a snake! I've heard of girls calling guys snakes before, but your father? With his dying breath? I hope Dan never had to ask Jacob for a reference.

And that's what the tribe of Dan turned out to be. A "viper along the path." Something that zapped anything that passed by. They introduced idolatry as a formal religion into Israel (Judges 18:14-31). A Danite was the first recorded person executed for blasphemy (Leviticus 24:10-16, 23). Jeroboam, who led the split of the nation into the ten northern tribes (Israel) and the two southern tribes (Judah), set up a golden calf for worship in the land occupied by Dan (1 Kings 12:29-30). Samson was a Danite; he worshipped (and successfully pursued) women and sex, until he lost his strength, his freedom, his eyes, and finally his life. The tribe of Dan has a darker history than any of the other tribes, and it is omitted from the roster of those "sealed" from Israel in Revelation 7:5-8.

Dan was the final stop on the Zebulun-Issachar-Dan road to ruin. Mess with the world (Zeb), get comfy with it (Issy), and here (Dan) is where we can easily end up. Eating out of its garbage can. Sitting in its manure pile. Worshipping at its altars of death. And that may have been what Jacob was thinking of when he called Dan a snake. Similar to Satan himself, the serpent we first meet in Genesis 3, the introducer of sin and idolatry to the world, the author of death.

There is nothing so sorry in this world as a Christian who is living like the world. Oh, I'm not talking about a person who wears blue jeans to church or sips a brew from time to time or plays a few hands of poker with the boys (or girls). I mean the person who has bought into a philosophy and a system that is material, sensual, humanistic and hedonistic. Because that's what the world has to offer. It may be what the beautiful people do, but turn them inside out and they're not so beautiful anymore. And like snakes, they poison most everybody around them in one way or another.

You can scrub it with a Brillo pad, douse it with Brut after-shave, dress it up in a Christian Dior tuxedo, stick a white carnation in its lapel, put it behind the wheel of a Rolls Royce, and there still ain't no difference. A snake is still a snake. I'd rather be Wile E. Coyote, even with the Roadrunner on the loose.

Genesis 49:19

"Gad will be attacked by a band of raiders, but he will attack them at their heels."

I guess if Jake's daughters-in-law had been hanging around while he was giving out the "blessings," most of them by now, except Mrs. Judah and perhaps Mrs. Zebulun, would have been ready to contact the nearest domestic law practitioner to begin divorce proceedings. Or to call Egypt's Dr. Kevorkian to help Jacob out of his misery. It had not been a good day at the family compound.

Mrs. Gad, however, would have been pleased. "Gad, you are a stud!" was the essence of Jake's message to #7 son. "You will be hassled by the Gilead locals, but you will whack them in the fanny as you run them out of town!"

And so it was. Gad's tribe settled on the east side of the Jordan River, in a very good area for cattle ranching (Numbers 32). And they were tough hombres, but men who also trusted in God. Check out 1 Chronicles 5:18-22, where 44,760 men of Gad, Reuben and Manasseh (with God directing the battle) decimated four local tribes, taking 100,000 captives along with 50,000 camels, 250,000 sheep and 2,000 donkeys. Old MacDonald never had such a farm. When David was fighting against Saul for the kingdom, many Gadites joined forces with him in the desert (1 Chronicles 12:8-14). They are there described as "brave warriors, ready for battle and able to handle the sword and the spear. Their faces were the faces of lions and they were swift as gazelles ... (T)he least was a match for a hundred, and the greatest for a thousand." Hollywood would have filmed its first *Terminator* series.

We Christians should be like the men of Gad. Brave warriors, ready for battle and able to handle the sword and the spear. Not literally, of course, but in a spiritual sense. I don't know what we'd do with 100,000 captives and 250,000 sheep anyhow, except maybe feed the captives a lot of lamb chops. But Paul tells us that we are in a spiritual battle. He says in Ephesians 6:10-17 that we should "be strong in the Lord and in His mighty power. Put on the full armor of God, so that you can take your stand against the devil's schemes. For our struggle is ... against the powers of this dark world, and against the spiritual forces of evil in the heavenly realms." He then lists the weapons we have to fight this battle, one of which is "the sword of the Spirit, which is the Word of God." The trouble is, most of us are not very adept with this sword, because we don't spend enough time working with it. So we're very reticent or tentative in using the Scripture to counter the flawed logic and ungodly philosophies of this present age.

But it's never too late to start training. And with God's help, we can take a few captives ourselves. They'll be eternally grateful to us for fighting the battle.

But they can keep their sheep and their camels and their donkeys.

"Gad will be attacked by a band of raiders, but he will attack them at their heels."

"Asher's food will be rich; he will provide delicacies fit for a king."

Well, it was Asher's turn to get the word about his herd, and it may have set visions of sugar plums dancing in his head. It sounded like his future was to sit around the club, sipping Dom Perignon out of a glass slipper and puffing on Cohiba cigars. Some might consider this a great idea for a Thursday afternoon.

Even the name "Asher" means "blessed" or "happy." And it is true that Asher's tribe in the years to come realized wealth and success; they inhabited the very fertile area on the coast of the Mediterranean Sea particularly suited to the growth of olive groves, from which rich oil was derived. When Moses spoke of Asher, "Let him bathe his feet in oil" (Deuteronomy 33:24), he wasn't implying that this tribe would end up as camel mechanics; it was from this region that Solomon provided 115,000 gallons of pressed olive oil annually to Hiram in exchange for cedar and pine logs for use in the building of the temple (1 Kings 5:10).

But the tribe finally succumbed to this wealth and leisure, and we don't hear much of them in the final analysis. The only Asherite of any note mentioned later seems to be Anna the prophetess, who, along with one other person, recognized the coming of the Messiah in the baby Jesus (Luke 2:36-38). They seem to have just faded out of the picture.

With all the advantages Asher had, the tribe should have been in the forefront for generation after generation. But somewhere along the road, they took the fork with the dead end. More often than not, that's what happens when the blessings of the Lord fall into misuse or disuse. That person just seems to fade out of the picture, into the shadows, off the radar screen. A life notable for its irrelevance. A testimony without impact. A talent unfulfilled. Yes, there may be a taste of the good life for a while, but like a piece of cheap spearmint gum, it soon is like chewing on a piece of plastic. And the longer you chew on it, the worse it tastes.

But it doesn't have to be that way. Solomon tells us, "The blessing of the Lord brings wealth, and He adds no trouble to it" (Proverbs 10:22). He wasn't speaking about wealth as in Bill Gates, or Sam Walton, or even Elvis. He was speaking about the wealth of a fulfilled and satisfied life, one with God in control and the assurance of His guidance and salvation. God's blessing of real wealth, the kind that can't be followed in the Wall Street Journal or found in the ATM machine. A life that doesn't knuckle under to trouble, because the Lord is right there to "make the rough ground level, the rugged places a plain" (Isaiah 40:4). The life and heritage that Asher's tribe could have enjoyed for generations to come, if they had focused on the quality of God rather than the quantity of oil.

It doesn't make any sense to struggle for wealth and then with wealth in this life, when we can snuggle up into the wealth of God's love for eternity.

Genesis 49:21

"Naphtali is a deer set free; he utters beautiful words."

I've learned a lot from my friend Tunch. He was a professional football player, an all-Pro at his position. Although he's lost about 30 pounds or so from his playing weight, he's still big enough to make an impression. He was a Muslim, but became a Christian after he started playing pro ball. And he's an all-Pro in the spiritual ball game, too. He's even more dedicated to the Eternal Coach and His game plan than he was to any sideline coach in his career. He tells everyone about Jesus, and is totally unconcerned whether it's politically correct or practically convenient. He is a "deer set free," a buck let loose, and he "utters beautiful words," the words of light and life. Because of his example, I've learned a lot about being spiritually aggressive, letting it all hang out.

Naphtali probably wondered what Jacob was talking about when he got this message from the old patriarch. He certainly wasn't noted for his oratorical skills to this point, and he hadn't noticed any antlers in the mirror. But that was not the case with his descendants (I'm talking about the speaking part, forget the antlers). The song of Barak (a Naphtalite) and Deborah in Judges 5 is a case in point. And all the twelve apostles, except Judas, were from the area in Galilee where the tribe of Naphtali had settled. These men were "deer set free"; free from the smothering legalism of the Pharisees; free from the burden of a system which offered rules and no reality; free from a bankrupt religiosity which could never give assurance of peace with God. And their words were beautiful; read the speeches of Peter in Acts 2, 3, 4, 10 and 11; the answer of Peter and John when they were ordered not to speak in the Name of Jesus: "Judge for yourselves whether it is right in God's sight to obey you rather than God. For we cannot help speaking about what we have seen and heard" (Acts 4:19-20). And the message of Philip to the Ethiopian official (Acts 8:35). Beautiful words. Exciting words. Enlightening words. Eternal words.

If Tunch were Jewish, I'd bet he was a descendant of Naphtali. And all the rest of us Christians should be adopted children of Jacob's #6 son. Free from the intimidation of a polytheistic and multicultural society which demands toleration, if not accommodation for and acceptance of every kind of social and religious concept, except for the preaching of Jesus as the only True God and the demands of His righteousness. Free from fear of the anger and ridicule which is inevitably dumped on those who will stand for the inclusiveness, but also the exclusivity of the Gospel and its unequivocal terms. Free to speak the beautiful words of life, with clarity and conviction, without compromise or concession.

Most people are trapped inside the world's corral, living by its rules, eating its hay, and talking its language. Let's speak the beautiful words to those who need to be loosed from their captivity, and help them hop over the fence to freedom in God's country. Naphtali will be cheering us on.

A View of Genesis

Genesis 49:22-26

"Joseph is a fruitful vine, a fruitful vine near a spring, whose branches climb over a wall." (vs. 22)

When Jake got to his favorite son, he really warmed up to the task. He fell all over himself with superlatives. And Joey himself deserved all the kudos; but remember, Jake was talking about "what will happen in the days to come" (49:1). Even though this passage might seem to be a recitation of Joseph's history, it was also a prophecy for the tribes of Ephraim and Manasseh for the future. And they had some big time heavy hitters; for example, Joshua and Deborah were Ephramites, and Gideon and Jephthah were from Manasseh's tribe.

It's interesting to think about why Joseph was "a fruitful vine" and "the prince among his brothers" (vs. 26). Was his astrological sign more favorable? Not a factor. Was it a result of Rachel's midnight madness mandrake mother mixture (30:14-15)? Nah. Did his parents send him to a day care center with a better early developmental program? With all the women around the wigwam, Joey never spent a day in such an establishment.

Maybe we find the answer to this in the first Psalm. In this Psalm, David talks about the guy (or the girl — we're equal opportunity here — where the masculine appears, it will be construed to include the feminine) who "is like a tree planted by streams of water, which yields its fruit in season ... Whatever he does prospers" (vs. 3). Does this sound like Joseph, the fruitful vine? And all those passages about, "The Lord was with Joseph and he prospered" (e.g., Genesis 39:2, 23)? You betcha. Psalm 1:1-2 fits Joey like a Gucci spandex exercise outfit. "Blessed is the man who doesn't walk in the counsel of the wicked, or stand in the way of sinners, or sit in the seat of mockers. But his delight is in the law of the Lord, and on His law he meditates day and night." This doesn't mean he did the all-nighters in the library studying ecclesiastical law. It means that he made God's principles an integral part of his physical, intellectual, moral and emotional fabric. Compared to Joey, even Mother Teresa may have been a juvenile delinquent.

And that's why there aren't a whole lot of Josephs today. People who love and read and study and obey the Word of God are about as scarce as NOW members at an anti-abortion rally. Psalm 119:9 tells us, "How can a young man keep his way pure? By living according to Your Word." And 119:105 says, "Your Word is a lamp to my feet, and a light to my path." In fact, if we get a large cup of coffee or a two-liter Diet Coke, stretch out in the easy chair and read the 176 verses of Psalm 119, we will find out how the study of and obedience to God's Word will help us to become Joseph's spiritual clone. The best prescription for spiritual health and personal prosperity is a generous portion of Biblical Bread taken daily, chewed thoughtfully and thoroughly, and swallowed completely.

Genesis 49:22-26

"But his bow remained steady, his strong arms stayed limber, because of the Mighty One of Jacob. ..." (vs. 24)

There was a guy named Arminius in the Middle Ages who stood up for God's principles against the religious and philosophical intellectuals of the day. It is said that one day he was being hassled by these liberals, and they were doing a heavy duty job on him. "Arminius, the whole world is against you!" they said. "Not a problem," he retorted. "God and I are against the world." And that is a winner.

That's what Jacob said in his blessing of Joseph and his tribe to come. "Joey, you've taken the enemy's heavy artillery, the smoke has cleared, and your flag is still high on the pole." If Francis Scott Key had been around, he'd have written the first version of "The Star Spangled Banner." And do you know what? Going beyond the individual tribes of Ephraim and Manasseh to consider the Hebrew nation as a whole, it is obvious that the nation has taken shots like no other ethnic or national group, ever to rise again against almost impossible odds. The Jewish people are still God's chosen people, and His covenant with Abraham and Isaac and Jacob, in spite of the nation's repetitive and continual disobedience, is eternally in place and will be fulfilled in the latter days.

Christians today take some pretty good shots, too. Last time I checked, the Los Angeles Times and the Washington Post were not raving (in appreciation, anyhow) about Christians who publicly proclaim that the country, its leaders and its people need to practice the righteous principles of the Word of God. The religious intellectuals and social engineers have decided that "sin" is something that vanished with the five cent cigar. People lie and cheat and steal and murder because they are culturally deprived or economically disadvantaged or a product of societal oppression. And somehow, it's all the fault of that mean-spirited, judgmental, rigid and unloving Christian community. Get rid of them and their righteousness, and the world will be a kinder and gentler place. But this kind of harassment and ridicule that we might experience in America is pretty mild. Try being a visible Christian in China. Or Turkey. Or Iran. Better have your estate plan drafted. They are the modern version of their predecessors in faith spoken of in Hebrews

11:36-38 who were stoned, burned, sawed in pieces, "destitute, persecuted and mistreated" (vs. 37). Stuff you don't read in self-help books.

But like Joseph and Arminius, they were, and we are, winners with God. Paul talks about this in Romans 8:31-39. And he names a pretty impressive array of opponents. Trouble, hardship, persecution, famine, nakedness, danger and sword (vs. 35), death, life, angels, demons, present, future, height, depth, anything else in all creation can't separate us from God's love (vs. 38-39). Sounds to me like God has the whole thing wired.

And even though Paul didn't mention the ACLU, it has to fit in there somewhere.

Genesis 49:27

"Benjamin is a ravenous wolf; in the morning he devours his prey; in the evening he divides the plunder."

When my six sons were all living at home, dinner time wasn't exactly like a formal affair at some five star resort. It was more like a reenactment of the plague of locusts in Egypt. Food disappeared faster than a bargain at an after-Christmas sale. If the serving bowls had been edible, they would have been history. Benjamin, a ravenous wolf, would have fit right in.

But a dinner-time scene wasn't in Jake's mind when he "blessed" Benji. His tribe would be the most aggressive tribe of the nation. The one that needed a shot of Ritalin in its morning coffee. If they saw a fight going on somewhere, they might ask, "Is this a private affair, or can we join in?" Maybe they were really Irishmen. They were fierce like wolves and, as this verse notes, pretty successful; they had something to eat in the morning and to divide in the evening. An all day buffet.

We see evidence of this nature in Judges 19-21, when they fought against the rest of Israel. Some Benjamites had done a real no-no, and all Israel demanded that the bad guys be hung out to dry. The Benji's told the rest of the nation to stuff it. So Israel put together a strike force of 400,000 men (20:17). The Benji Bombers showed up with 26,700, including 700 southpaws who could shave a gnat's mustache with a slingshot (20:15-16). After the first two days, the score was the B-B's — 40,000, Israel — zip (vs. 19-25). If God hadn't gotten into the act on the third day, New York City might never have had a garment district. The Bombers would have cleaned Israel's clock. As it turned out, the entire Benjamite tribe was wiped out, including women, children, cats and dogs, except for 600 men (20:46-48). But they fought like wolves and gave it a good go.

Paul was a Benjamite (Philippians 3:5). And he was one tough dude. Before the Lord brought him to his knees on the road to Damascus, he terrorized the entire Christian community. After he became a Christian, if someone was indifferent or hostile to or careless with the Gospel, Paul took no prisoners. He challenged Peter eyeball to eyeball on a doctrinal matter (Galatians 2:1 1). He threatened to come to Corinth with a whip because of their arrogance (1 Corinthians 5:21). He insisted that John Mark be thrown off the team for non-performance (Acts 15:37-39).

A lot of us are pussy cats when it comes to standing up for Jesus. When the roll is called up yonder we might be there, but when the battle cry is sounded here, some of us are pretty hard to find. This doesn't mean we have to charge up the hill against the devil like John Wayne and his Hollywood marines in the movies, but it would be nice to see a lot more of us doing something other than hunkering down in our foxholes waiting for the armistice.

A wolf is always higher in the food chain than a pussycat. Don't get eaten alive.

Genesis 49:29-50:11

"Jacob ... breathed his last and was gathered to his people. ... The physicians embalmed him ... and the Egyptians mourned for him seventy days. ... They lamented loudly and bitterly." (49:33, 50:2, 10)

My Dad was the greatest man who ever lived, other than The Lord Himself. He was a great man of God, could do almost anything, and knew almost everything. He was a mechanical engineer who made things you couldn't even imagine, spoke six languages either fluently or passably, played a mandolin and a clarinet and told funny stories. The night I realized he knew almost everything was when a few of my friends and I were playing poker at our house and he appeared on the scene. In those days, if you went to movies or dances or played poker, you were on your way to the devil's domain in a chartered Concorde. Since spiritual men didn't play poker and my Dad was a spiritual man, I figured he would think we were playing a modified version of Old Maid. I found out I was wrong, when he looked over my shoulder at the hand I was holding and suggested that I draw to the inside straight.

He died when he was ninety. I saw his body before the morticians got there, when his eyes were still open. He had steel blue eyes, and as he lay there in death, I noticed that they were the brightest shade of blue I had ever seen. And there was this expression of peace on his face I will never forget. I was sad, but happy for him. He was with Jesus.

Well, Jacob died, and the funeral procession second only to Princess Di's was convened. It was a seventy-day wake (50:3). If these guys had been Irish, the country would have run out of booze. Then the whole cortege, almost enough of them to make a Cecil B. De Mille movie, moved on to Canaan. For seven more days they "lamented loudly and bitterly" (50:10). You'd have thought they were holding auditions for MTV. We don't know if or why Joseph and his brothers joined in the doleful dirge. Maybe the brothers were still smarting over Jacob's last will and testament. But Jake had made it clear he was headed for a happier home.

Paul tells us that we don't grieve for our loved ones who "have fallen asleep in (Jesus)" as do those people who have no hope of the resurrection. (1 Thessalonians 4:13-14). He also tells us that because of Jesus, "Death has been swallowed up in victory" (1 Corinthians 16:51-57). Although I've never seen a corpse that looked very victorious, and my Dad has never sent me a postcard from his mansion saying, "Having lots of fun, wish you were here," I have the absolute promise of the Word of God that death for the believer is just a passage way from here to heaven. It's the ultimate trip, and when I take it, I know I'll see my Dad again.

And he won't catch me playing any poker there.

Genesis 50:15-21

"Joseph said to them, 'Don't be afraid. Am I in the place of God? You intended to harm me, but God intended it for good. ...'" (vs. 19-20)

The brothers broke out in a cold sweat on the way back from the cemetery. Jacob was dead, and now Joseph could, and in their minds probably would, break out the heavy artillery and aim it right in their direction. With his position and power, it would be like dynamiting fish in a barrel. So they concocted a story about Jake instructing them before he died to tell Joey that he should break out the peace pipe and let the smoke in the wigwam blot out the past (vs. 17).

For good measure, they all hit the deck in front of Joseph and volunteered to be his slaves (vs. 18). I wonder if Joey's dream about the sheaves of grain (37:5-7) entered anybody's mind? If it did, nobody, including Joseph, let on. But he would have none of it. He probably had more slaves than he could use, anyhow. This would be just another bunch of mouths to feed. That wasn't his reason, however, for not measuring them up for a rope necktie. Joseph really understood what life with God was all about. He had committed himself to God, and took whatever came along as part of God's plan; enduring the suffering, enjoying the sufficiency, enriching the surroundings, and experiencing the satisfaction. His life was all of God, and nothing of himself. He knew all about little, and he knew all about lots. He lived in the prison, and he lived in the palace. He experienced the famine, and he experienced the feast. He was acquainted with trouble, and he was acquainted with triumph. He gave God His rightful place, and let the brothers know that neither their ugliness toward himself nor any motive involved was an item for discussion. Any report of it would end up on the editor's cutting room floor. God had taken their rage and turned it into their redemption.

What would happen if we were like Joseph? If instead of whacking the person who cuts in the grocery line over the noggin with a stalk of celery, we offer to help carry her groceries? Instead of plotting revenge against the guy who is stabbing us in the back at work, we get him a hot cup of coffee (resisting the urge to yank his head back and pour it up his nose) and give him a ride home? Instead of trying to get even for people's slights, we try to get enthused for their success? One thing that might happen is a lot of activity for anyone who knows CPR. They would faint dead away. But the main thing that would happen is that God would be honored, and it would be a great witness to the world around us.

So we should be like Joseph, and instead of turning the tables on an adversary, set the table for a veritable feast of peace and love. It's a great home or office entertainment idea.

Genesis 50:15-26

"Joseph said to them, '... Am I in the place of God?'" (vs. 19)

There are a lot of people today, especially some TV preachers, who act like they think that God is up in heaven waiting breathlessly to get His instructions from them for tomorrow morning. Or in many instances, tomorrow isn't soon enough. He's called upon to saddle up and do a particular job RIGHT NOW! Solve this crisis! Heal that person! Save this marriage! Move the people to fill the coffers to overflowing! (This last demand always seems to find its way into the program.)

And then there are those who always seem to know exactly what God should do. How He should handle a particular circumstance. What action He should take in a specific situation. When He should bring about a certain response or result. And if He doesn't act in concert with these expectations, God is less than faithful, or He has turned against them in their hour of need.

I guess I'm cut out of the same bolt of cloth. When I got out of graduate school, I had God's program for my life all set. An absolutely masterful plan. He would make me a very rich Christian, and I would support all the missionaries that He could recruit to go to the land of the fierce tribe of the Fuzzy-Wuzzies. And they could write me letters of gratitude for such generous support, which I would read (and pray over, of course) while floating on my big yellow rubber-duckie raft in my Olympic size swimming pool on the right side of the tracks. And, if He sent a few messengers to Hawaii, I might even visit them to encourage them in their work. Well, the Lord saw through that one, and He's seen through everything else I've tried to slip into His agenda ever since.

Joseph knew the score in this ball game. He had been blistered in the first through the fourth innings, but had come out on top somewhere around the bottom of the fifth. But he realized that God had been giving the signals and calling the pitches. Now that the game was over and the losers were begging for mercy, he let them know that all the plays, including the results, were because God decided that it would be that way. So could he claim credit for the win, or exact revenge for the whuppin' he took in the first through the fourth? Not a chance. It was God's plan, not his; and he wasn't about to mess with the proceedings.

God has a plan for each of us. Sometimes it hurts, and sometimes it feels real good. But it's usually something completely different from our blueprint. Daniel probably didn't have in his Day Timer, "7:00 PM — trip to lion's den." Or Stephen, "12:00 Tuesday — get stoned." Or Job, "See Dr. for boils next week." It wasn't easy for them, and it's not for us, either. But like Joseph and these others, it's all easier when we realize that we're not in charge, we're not in the place of God. He has it all in the Master Day Timer.

And that's one Day Timer which contains an absolutely masterful plan.

Genesis 50:22-26

"Joseph said to his brothers, 'I am about to die. But God will surely come to your aid and take you up out of this land. ...'" (50:24) "Israel said to Joseph, 'I am about to die, but God will be with you and take you back to the land of your fathers ...'" (48:21)

On a few occasions I have gotten the mistaken impression that I was pretty important in a certain position or to a particular organization. Once when I was the president of a professional firm, I felt that it would be difficult for the firm to function if I weren't around. Then I ended up in the hospital for a month and, to my chagrin, discovered that everything was going quite well; better, in fact, and don't call us, we'll call you. Fortunately I held a significant block of stock, otherwise I may have had to fill out an employment application when I went back.

But some people are very critical in leadership positions. Jacob and Joseph are good examples. Jacob was the patriarch of Israel, and he held the family together and kept it on track. Joseph was the nation's bridge to Egypt and liaison to the government, its provider through the famine and its patron in prosperity.

So as they were about to head on to their final reward, each of them would leave a set of size 36 sandals to fill. But not to worry, said they. God's purposes would be fulfilled whether or not they were around. And they were both convinced that it was all a done deal, so much so that each of them commanded that the final resting place of his remains would be in the land of promise (47:29-30, 50:25).

But each of them also left an important message to the surviving brothers about God's presence and His promise to their families. "God will be with you." "God will come to your aid" (literally, "oversee you"). And even though that in itself should have been enough, both of them added that God would get them outta there, and into the Canaan version of the mansion over the hilltop.

You know, Jesus told his disciples something similar. In the Upper Room Discourse (John 13-17), He told them (and through this passage tells us as well) that He was going away. He was going to His Father. But not to worry, He would send the Counselor, the Holy Spirit, to guide them and to teach them. And He would come back to take them to live with Himself and His Father.

Jacob and Joseph died, and their bones rest in Canaan to this day. And God led the nation out of Egypt, true to His promise. Jesus died, too, but He rose again. And also true to His promise, He has sent us the Holy Spirit, and now He is preparing a place where He will take those who belong to Him through faith.

We may find out we're not very important around here, but we were so important to Jesus that He went to the cross for each of us. And even though that's more than enough, wait till we see what happens when He takes us outta here!

A View of Genesis

Genesis 50:22-26

"So Joseph died ... and ... was placed in a coffin in Egypt." (vs. 26)

Well, we come to the end of Genesis. It is a book that begins with creation, and ends with a coffin. Starts with life, finishes in death. Opens in Eden, a paradise, and closes in Egypt, a type of the world. Commences with innocence, and concludes with corruption.

And in between, we read about the eternal existence of God, and the opening chapter of the history of man. How God created man in His own image, giving him a perfect environment for fellowship with and service for Himself. How man defiled that environment, and continued in a downward spiral to his own virtual elimination. How God saved a remnant, and then chose a nation for His own possession in the midst of renewed degeneration.

Genesis is a record of individual men and women and their interaction with God. An account of the good, the bad and the ugly. Those who loved God or defied Him, who followed after Him or rebelled against Him, who obeyed Him or ignored Him. It is an historical narrative of real people who lived in actual places at specific times. Oh, yes, there are those who say that Genesis is mainly an allegory, that Adam and Eve are "representative man," that most of these characters are a figment of an overactive imagination. But that's their problem. Those who read and study the Word of God, who see both intrinsic and extrinsic evidence as to its credibility (as if it needed any) know better. And we base our temporal present and eternal future on the factual existence and specific activity of the God to Whom we are introduced in Genesis, the book of beginnings.

Genesis also gives us an opportunity to study ourselves. To see in the people we meet in its chapters our own actions and reactions. To observe that we have similar natures, similar desires, similar strengths, similar frailties as did those we read about. And to understand that we have a similar responsibility as did they to respond to an eternal God, the One Who created us and Who, as Job stated, has "determined the days of man ... and set limits he cannot exceed" (Job 14:5).

At the end of Genesis, Joseph's body was in a coffin, having lived out the days allotted to him by God. But he had looked toward the day of deliverance, when God would bring the nation out of Egypt into the Promised Land (Hebrews 11:22). We also look toward that day when Jesus will call us to our Promised Land, where we will live for eternity in His presence, to be forever united with those who have gone on before. And do you know what? The people we read about in Genesis (and all the Bible) who trusted in God will also be there. It will be a grand reunion with everybody from Adam to Zechariah, from Anna to Zipporah.

And I, Phinehas Phigtree, will be cruising around the streets of gold on my two- humped camel, eternally grateful that there won't be any speed limit there.

A View of Genesis